EXPORTING,
IMPORTING,
AND BEYOND

Business titles from Adams Media

Accounting for the New Business, by Christopher R. Malburg
Adams Businesses You Can Start Almanac
Adams Streetwise Small Business Start-Up, by Bob Adams
Adams Streetwise Hiring Top Performers, by Bob Adams and Peter Veruki
All-In-One Business Planner, by Christopher R. Malburg
Buying Your Own Business, by Russell Robb
Entrepreneurial Growth Strategies, by Lawrence W. Tuller
How to Become Successfully Self-Employed, by Brian R. Smith
Managing People, by Darien McWhirter
Marketing Magic, by Don Debelak
The Personnel Policy Handbook for Growing Companies, by Darien McWhirter
Selling 101: A Course for Business Owners and Non-Sales People,
by Michael T. McGaulley
Service, Service, Service: A Secret Weapon for Your Growing Business,
by Steve Albrecht
The Small Business Legal Kit, by J. W. Dicks
The Small Business Valuation Book, by Lawrence W. Tuller
Winning the Entrepreneur's Game, by David E. Rye

ADAMS

EXPORTING, IMPORTING, AND BEYOND

How to "Go Global" with
Your Small Business

LAWRENCE W. TULLER

Adams Media Corporation
Holbrook, Massachusetts

Published by Adams Media Corporation
260 Center Street, Holbrook, MA 02343

ISBN: 1-55850-777-9

Printed in the United States of America.

J   I   H   G   F   E   D   C   B

Library of Congress Cataloging-in-Publication Data
Tuller, Lawrence W.
Exporting, importing, and beyond : how to "go global" with your
small business / Lawrence W. Tuller.
p.   cm.
Includes bibliographical references and index.
ISBN 1-55850-777-9 (pb.)
1. Foreign trade promotion—United States—Handbooks, manuals, etc.
2. Exports—United States—Handbooks, manuals, etc. 3. Imports—United States—
Handbooks, manuals, etc. 4. Small business—United States—Handbooks, manuals, etc.
I. Title. II. Series.
HF1455.T78   1994
658.8'4—dc20   94-36546
CIP

This publication is designed to provide accurate and authoritative information with regard to the
subject matter covered. It is sold with the understanding that the publisher is not engaged in
rendering legal, accounting, or other professional advice. If legal advice or other expert assistance is required, the services of a competent professional person should be sought.
— From a *Declaration of Principles* jointly adopted by a Committee of the American Bar
Association and a Committee of Publishers and Associations

This book is available at quantity discounts for bulk purchases.
For information, call 1-800-872-5627 (in Massachusetts, 617-767-8100).

Visit our home page at http://www.adamsmedia.com

Table of Contents

Introduction

As the world watched the wind-down and conclusion of negotiations for the Uruguay Round of the General Agreement on Tariffs and Trade (otherwise known as GATT) and debates over the North American Free Trade Agreement (NAFTA), the talks rose in stature, hitting the front pages of the *Wall Street Journal*, the *New York Times*, the *Washington Post*, and in fact every metropolitan newspaper in the country. No longer limited to the floors of Congress or the halls of academia, the concept of foreign trade struck mainstream America like a cannonball.

The increased importance and visibility of foreign trade is symptomatic of a deep trend that has emerged in the United States and throughout the world: The economies of the major powers (the United States, Western Europe, and Japan) have become more intertwined and more dependent on one another than ever before. Our food, clothing, shoes, building materials, automobiles, machine tools, electronics, appliances, money, professional services, and education—in fact, virtually every product and service we use in our daily lives—now includes some component of foreign labor, materials, or technology.

The battle for our customers' loyalty, raw materials, energy, and labor has been joined by strong foreign competitors intent on carving out a piece of the American pie. Since U.S. markets can no longer be relied upon to support economic growth, companies in all industries and of all sizes are reaching beyond our borders for new market opportunities. Scarcities of raw materials and energy, escalating costs of skilled labor, constraints on U.S. banks, and pressures to compete with new technologies have compelled U.S. industry to search out new resources throughout the world, regardless of where they may be located.

Fortunately, as if by magic, the emergence of Latin American, East Asian, and Eastern European economies has opened a vast storehouse of resources and customers heretofore unavailable to U.S. companies. The opportunities for growing our businesses are there: to benefit from them, all we need is to broaden our horizons, to open our eyes to the international marketplace.

While skeptics may question the wisdom of exploring unfamiliar shores, statistics prove that foreign trade is the prime creator of new jobs in the United States. In fact, 75 percent of U.S.-manufactured goods are now either exported or subject to foreign competition; more than 30 percent of U.S. farm acreage grows crops that are exported; and, perhaps most startling of all, U.S. exports now account for a larger portion of the U.S. economy than new-car sales or new-home sales.

The impact of foreign trade is not limited to Fortune 500 companies, or even the Fortune 1000; the impact is just as great on small businesses that manufacture, distribute, or sell products, and on many small service businesses as well. To ignore the foreign-trade revolution is tantamount to closing one's eyes to economic survival.

This book takes the mystery out of foreign trade. It explains the marketing, financial, and organizational characteristics that differ markedly from those in domestic business and that smaller companies must learn in order to compete in world markets—whether exporting, importing, or establishing a foreign presence through joint ventures or business acquisitions. Of equal importance is what this book does not include.

Don't look for samples of shipping and collection documents or instructions for preparing them; these can be be obtained free from government agencies, banks, and freight forwarders. Don't look for checklists to help you decide whether your company should enter foreign trade: I would never presume to guess your company's strategic objectives or resources. And don't expect a survey of world markets: Such analyses can be found in another of my books, *The World Markets Desk Book: A Region-by-Region Survey of Global Trade Opportunities.*

What you will find between these covers are comprehensive explanations and discussions of

- International economic, financial, and market factors that influence the profitability of foreign trade
- The impact of U.S. tax laws on your foreign-trade marketing strategies, supplemented with out-of-the-ordinary tax-saving tactics
- Tips for dealing with personal and business protocol in foreign lands
- Names and addresses of sources of information and assistance to help you develop and implement your export, import, and foreign direct investment strategies
- Suggestions to help you develop sales finance strategies and arrange financing for your overseas facilities
- Ideas for marketing, distributing, and advertising your products or technology in foreign markets
- The mechanics of sourcing foreign partners and setting up foreign joint ventures
- Alternative strategies for buying part or all of a foreign business

Getting started in foreign trade is at best a difficult undertaking. It requires significantly more strategic planning, long-term commitment, and flexible resources than opening new U.S. markets. On the other hand, the rewards from foreign trade are also significantly greater; whether measured by the capture of new markets, the sourcing of lower-cost or higher-quality materials and labor, or higher returns on investment.

Be aware, however, that the benefits from exporting, foreign sourcing, or foreign facilities must be viewed as long-term. It takes several years to develop foreign customer loyalty and supplier reliability. Initial advertising and sales promotion expenditures have to be amortized over years, not months. And the bureaucratic maze of tariffs, licenses, and customs regulations (both from Washington and from host-country governments) can be staggering.

International trade is not the place to experiment. Don't expect foreign markets to accept newly designed products. Don't try to sell products overseas that have been rejected by U.S. markets. And don't mistakenly suppose that foreign customers will settle for lower quality or less service than U.S. customers.

Neither should you enter international trade if your company is currently losing money or in financial difficulty. It has been proven time and again that success in international trade can be achieved only if your products are well established in domestic markets and your company is financially viable.

If done haphazardly, getting started in foreign trade can be costly and time-consuming. It is always advisable to learn the ropes, from an expert. Should you desire help in developing your marketing, financing, or sourcing strategies, drop me a line on your company letterhead at

Lawrence W. Tuller
ZYX-VU, Ltd.
P.O.Box 347
Southeastern, Pennsylvania 19399
Fax: (610) 408-9575

I wish you well in your foreign-trade experiences. Hopefully, the facts, ideas, and insights in this book will help smooth the way. Godspeed!

— LAWRENCE W. TULLER
Berwyn, Pennsylvania

Part I
Getting Ready for Global Trade

Chapter 1
Global Opportunities

With part or all of virtually everything we own or use—our food, cars, clothing, shoes, homes, roads, bridges, medicines, and capital—coming from foreign sources, it's easy to see that the American economy has become inextricably tied to the economies and resources of Europe, Latin America, the Middle East, Africa, and the Pacific Basin. It is equally clear that it would be foolish to ignore those factors that could cause an interruption in the continued cross-border flow of foreign money, goods, and services.

Yet many Americans remain unconvinced. The wide range of benefits to be derived from a U.S. economy integrated with world markets escapes them. Vocal special interest groups like labor unions, environmentalists, and political reactionaries continue to advocate protectionism. They dogmatically eschew the arguments of foreign-trade advocates, dismissing out of hand the inevitable increased prosperity, broadened choices, and improved living standards that foreign trade brings to American households.

NAFTA was all but killed. Japan-bashing has become a popular pastime. The cries from Eastern Europe, the erstwhile Soviet Union, Latin America, and Africa for assistance in stabilizing their economies have gone largely unanswered.

On the other hand, nearly one-fifth of the 25,000 small and midsize American companies (less than $150 million in sales or 500 employees) currently engage in exporting or foreign sourcing. Every year another thousand or so join the fray. Federal trade officials estimate that nearly 50 percent of all U.S. businesses with sales in excess of $2 million will be engaged in some form of international trade by the year 2000.

These figures suggest that there is still a lot of scope for aggressive businesses to capture a share of rapidly growing world markets and plentiful resources. For many years to come, global trade will be an integral part of successful growth strategies. This book will show you how to evaluate such opportunities, how to learn about new global resources and markets, and how to turn a seemingly complex set of market and financial conditions to your advantage.

Before beginning the journey, however, it would probably be helpful to briefly review the three types of activities—exporting, importing (or sourcing), and offshore production—that make up "international trade." Although these terms are generally self-explanatory, enough conflicting interpretations flood the media to warrant a short explanation of each.

EXPORTING

In the broadest sense, *exporting* refers to the sale of goods, services, or technology produced by a company resident in one country to customers resident in a different country. *Importing*, of course, is just the reverse: the purchase of goods, services, or technology by a company resident in one country from sellers resident in another. In the case of manufactured goods, the meaning is fairly clear. An American company manufactures goods that are shipped to customers in Germany, Argentina, or India. Or, an American company purchases goods manufactured in Malaysia, Italy, or Mexico.

In the case of services, exporting and importing are not as well defined. U.S. contractors are said to export services when they construct buildings, roads, or utilities in a foreign country. Consultants export when they perform services for foreign clients. U.S. investment banks export when they arrange financing from global sources or when they assist customers in structuring foreign business acquisitions. On the other hand, the opening of a Sheraton, Hyatt, or Marriott hotel overseas is not considered to be exporting.

The sale or purchase of technology or management know-how also gets a bit sticky. For instance, a U.S. company that licenses a French company to use its technology for the manufacture of products in France is considered to be an exporter. A U.S. company that purchases the right to use German-designed engine components is said to be an importer. When McDonald's franchises restaurants in Russia, it becomes an exporter; but when Coca Cola opens a plant in Miramar, it is not an exporter. Publishers that sell book rights to English publishing houses export those copyrights; but a television network with overseas reception does not export broadcasted news.

The term "foreign sourcing," or merely "sourcing," can also be confusing. *Sourcing* refers to the purchase of foreign-produced parts, components, materials, and energy. It also refers to the use of foreign labor to make assemblies or components that will be shipped back to a U.S. parent company for integration into finished products. Foreign sourcing may also refer to raising capital in off-shore capital markets or from foreign banks. Foreign sourcing of technology means the acquisition of patented processes or materials from foreign suppliers.

When we talk about "foreign production facilities," or merely "foreign facilities," we mean a manufacturing plant, distribution center, retail outlet, or office in a foreign location. Setting up or acquiring such foreign facilities is called *foreign direct investment*. These facilities may be used to produce goods and services for sale in local markets, for export to other foreign countries, or for export back to the United States. Foreign facilities may be used to produce finished products or parts, assemblies, and components for shipment back to the parent U.S. company, as in foreign sourcing.

A foreign direct investment may involve the acquisition of complete ownership in a business or facility, a majority or minority interest in an operating business, a majority or minority interest in an infrastructure project (such as a power utility or port authority), or an equal or unequal interest in a joint venture or other strategic alliance.

Exporting is certainly the most popular form of international trade, and the easiest for small businesses to enter. Companies without foreign sales agents can easily contract with an export trading company or export management company to handle overseas marketing. These export agents also have the ability to manage all shipping documentation. Collections can be assured through the use of letters of credit or customer bank guarantees. In fact, exporting is usually easier and more profitable, and holds less risk than selling domestically.

Once a company has started exporting, developing growth strategies that involve foreign sourcing or foreign direct investments is a natural next step in building competitive market positions. Imported materials, parts, and components are, in many cases, less costly than similar items purchased domestically. Profit margins can be increased by assembling labor-intensive products with low-cost labor in developing nations. The judicious use of free-trade zones in the United States and offshore avoids the extra costs of customs duties and taxes. Direct shipment from a foreign manufacturing location to foreign customers may reduce shipping costs below those incurred when exporting from the United States. And capital raised in Europe, Latin America, or East Asia is in many cases less costly and more available than U.S. financing.

One major difference between exporting (either from the United States or from an offshore facility to a third country) and selling goods and services in U.S. markets is that in order to close an order, exporters usually help foreign customers finance their purchases. Companies engaged solely in domestic trade are hardly ever called upon to provide financing beyond customary thirty- or sixty-day trade credit. When shipping offshore, however, buyers expect U.S. exporters to provide not only trade credit but government financing support and bank guarantees. This close interaction of marketing and financing can be confusing and a hard pill to swallow, especially for those businesses that follow the traditional American custom of separating marketing and finance activities.

A second major difference between exporting and domestic sales is that the former normally carries very little collection risk. Bad debts, which plague certain domestic markets, can be virtually eliminated when exporting through the use of irrevocable letters of credit (L/Cs) confirmed by a U.S. bank, government guarantees from the Export-Import Bank of the United States (Eximbank), and government-backed insurance from the Federal Credit Insurance Association.

Margins are also generally higher on export sales. American goods continue to be sought after in virtually every international market, enabling exporters to charge higher prices than are possible in competitive U.S. markets. The exception, of course, is generic products, where U.S. imports have no advantage over competitive products manufactured locally. To the extent that the market cannot distinguish between imported and locally produced goods, the two price structures are similar.

Perhaps the most troublesome aspect of beginning an export program is the need to develop policies that address the disparate cultures, market forces, banking systems, and legal requirements for doing business in foreign markets. More often than not, this calls for a revised assessment of marketing, financial, and administrative activities, and in some cases the complete restructuring of a company's management organization. The major export factors that require revised corporate strategies and organizations are

1. Exporting companies must help foreign customers obtain financing to pay for the goods.

2. Different languages, cultures, and market demands complicate communication with customers and the negotiation of sales contracts.

3. The management of ocean shipping and customs clearance adds complexity to and increases the cost of the transaction.

4. In the event of disputes with customers, no court system can be called upon as a last resort (other than international arbitration, which is seldom a viable alternative for small and midsize exporters).

5. In some foreign markets, political upheaval and/or the expropriation of bank accounts or products prior to delivery are risks that must be addressed (usually through insurance).

6. Exchange-rate fluctuations and translations from soft to hard currency require added expertise in financial management.

A GLOBAL MENTALITY

Although exporting is certainly a viable strategy for increasing sales, it does not, by itself, offer much of an entrance to world markets. To take advantage of global opportunities, a company must go beyond exporting. It must

- Become intimately involved in sourcing materials and supplies overseas and then importing them to the United States.

- Maximize its distribution channels by utilizing foreign warehousing centers.

- Compete in the global marketplace by establishing manufacturing facilities, service centers, and sales offices in other countries.

- Recruit competent technical and management personnel from the global reservoir.

- Source the least expensive, longest-term capital available in world markets.

- Learn to use the vagaries of currency fluctuations to its advantage.

- Be quick to seize opportunities to expand through joint ventures and partnerships with other American companies or with foreign nationals.

In other words, American producers can no longer define sources of materials, labor, and management; customer bases; or sources of capital as domestic or international. Business opportunities must be viewed through global glasses. Only by recognizing the world as one market and resource reservoir can companies survive against aggressive, forward-thinking foreign and U.S. competitors.

Such transnational practices require radical changes in the mindset of business owners and managers and how they view growth strategies. To compete globally, we must develop a *global mentality*, a mental attitude that focuses on opportunities and risks in the global marketplace, not merely in the United States. Market strategies and financial plans must be rethought. Management training, production methods, and financing options must reflect global opportunities and pressures. Definitions of markets, labor pools, technical resources, and money management must be geared to the world as a market for products and a fount of resources.

A global perspective does not come easily. Our American tradition of independence and freedom of action makes it is difficult to readjust our thinking to the interdependence of a global economy. Being accustomed to doing business in market-controlled environments, governed by elected officials, makes state-controlled pricing and product selection difficult to comprehend. Oligarchal or social welfare systems present new challenges, unmatched in the United States. Yet, to survive in the twenty-first century, we must learn to cope with these complex characteristics of international trade.

A global mentality requires changes in thinking about four areas:

- Management ability and training
- Market strategy
- Financing options
- Strategic planning

The traditional parochialism embedded in American management philosophy must be the first to go. Corporate objectives aimed at increasing company earnings and shareholder returns for the next month, quarter, or year make it impossible to develop meaningful growth strategies. The fear of reprisals for failing to meet such short-term goals leads top executives and managers down narrow, often blind alleys in search of ways to meet current high debt-service payments, dividend promises, or earnings per share expectations, all in direct contrast to the global imperative of long-term, strategically sound policies.

This preoccupation with monthly, quarterly, and annual performance breeds short-term actions to deal with immediate market demand, local market shares, and opportunities for serving current customers. Short-term actions often lead to reactive rather than proactive strategies, which in turn promote crisis management practices. Social, political, and financial pressures make it nearly impossible to structure a company for the long haul when today's needs must be met today. And managers continue to believe that "if you don't solve today's problems today, you won't be around to worry about tomorrow."

To compete in world markets, this attitude must change. Those companies that have proved successful in the international sphere have managed for the long haul, not the short term. When Bechtel recruits management personnel for a five-year overseas construction job plus continuing operating responsibility for ten years or more, the company looks for people who can manage the project for the duration. It looks for people who are adept at dealing with diverse cultures and languages. It looks for people who are dedicated to maximizing operating efficiencies over the long term, not just for the next month or the next year.

When Boeing begins the design effort for a new generation of commercial aircraft, the research and development expenses will be amortized against production planes sold in world markets ten, fifteen, or twenty years in the future. The company's strategic planning recognizes this long-term effort.

Strategic planning for global markets must recognize long-term growth opportunities in such diverse regions as Latin America, China, the erstwhile Soviet Union, and India. Plans must be laid to penetrate global markets with products manufactured in overseas locations as well as those exported from the United States. Companies must structure both domestic and foreign operations to bring in materials, personnel, and other resources from the least-cost, highest-quality suppliers, regardless of their location.

Managers must be as cognizant of competitive advantages from selective importing as they are of high-margin export opportunities. Market strategies must recognize competitive threats from global companies as well as from local or regional businesses. The impact of government-owned businesses that compete with private industry must be analyzed. Long-term demographic changes and political restructuring must be projected.

Unfamiliar financing alternatives must also be evaluated. Companies must exploit financing structures designed for specific opportunities. Short-term commercial bank loans may be satisfactory for financing the production and sale of nuts and bolts in the United States, but not for financing exports to customers in South Africa. The start-up of a new factory in Ohio might be managed with term loans, but building a plant in Brazil requires more creative capital sourcing. Bank loans and venture capital may be sufficient for making a leveraged buyout in Massachusetts; but this tack will never fly for buying a going business in France.

A financial global mentality must weigh the pros and cons of various countertrade measures, foreign stock and bond issues, and indirect assistance from multilateral and bilateral agencies. Financial managers of the future must become conversant with the techniques for managing different types of letters of credit, obtaining merchant bank assistance, financing through development banks, tapping emerging capital markets, and hedging exchange-rate fluctuations.

Exporting, importing, or making a foreign direct investment without experienced international personnel usually results in costly errors. Placing an American manager without international experience in charge of a foreign plant, distribution center, or sales office nearly always results in failure. Selling to foreign customers, arranging cross-border financing, or negotiating foreign contracts without prior exposure to the complexities and nuances of international trade nearly always leads to disaster. International expertise must be acquired prior to engaging in international trade, either by employing managers with this experience or by contracting with professional advisers.

Regardless of the benefits international trade may bring to the table, without concrete experience, it is virtually impossible to succeed. And even with expert assistance and a global mentality, certain matters must be addressed right at the beginning. Figure 1.1 lists the most common questions asked by companies that are new to international trade.

Figure 1-1
Questions Commonly Asked when Beginning International Trade

1. How can I compete with host-country companies when I have to add overseas shipping and customs costs to my prices?
2. How can I identify the best overseas markets for my specific products?
3. How do I sell to customers who speak a different language?
4. How can I prevent foreign governments from expropriating my property or products?
5. What about exchange rates? They keep fluctuating widely. How can I avoid losing money on currency differentials?
6. Many foreign markets are government-controlled. How can I sell in those markets?
7. How can I determine the creditworthiness of foreign customers?
8. How can I ensure payment of my invoices?
9. What recourse do I have if a foreign customer doesn't pay?
10. Shipping overseas is complicated. Where do I find out about shipping containers and shipping documentation?
11. Aren't customs fees pretty high?
12. What if the ship sinks before it arrives at its destination?
13. I understand that in many cases exporters have to finance customers. Since we're not a wealthy company, how can we afford to do that?
14. How do I sell to a foreign customer who doesn't have the money to pay for my products?
15. What if customers pay in currencies that cannot be converted to dollars?
16. How do I move money between countries?
17. How can I communicate with my overseas locations?
18. International travel is difficult and costly. How do I supervise my people stationed in a foreign country?
19. What about taxes? Am I taxed twice, once in the foreign country and again by the IRS?
20. If I deposit collections in a foreign bank, how do I get the money back to the United States?
21. Where do I find a lawyer that knows foreign laws?
22. What about the method of doing business in a specific country? Most are not free markets. How do I learn the local customs?

---

23. Where do I find foreign personnel to sell my products or manage my facility?
24. How do I train them?
25. What fringe benefits are required by law?
26. How do I get an audit done overseas?
27. What about passports, travel visas, and work permits? Where and how do I get them?
28. If I want to sell to Saudi Arabia, for instance, how do I locate other American companies doing business there?
29. What U.S. government agencies can I go to for assistance?
30. I hate to get involved in government bureaucracy. Are there any private organizations that offer assistance?
31. How do I become familiar with a specific country's laws, tax statutes, labor codes, and other rules of doing business?

This book provides a base of information and recommendations for answering these questions. Although such answers will certainly vary in different situations, the overall solutions are similar enough to be addressed more or less generically.

Selling products or services in foreign countries is virtually impossible without a thorough grasp of the marketing customs prevalent in that country. And such customs vary from country to country. What works in Germany won't work in Saudi Arabia. Marketing protocol in China isn't the same as that followed in Brazil. Procedures for locating customers, checking credit, setting selling prices, negotiating contracts, helping customers arrange financing, delivering the goods, and collecting receivables must be based on the customs and laws of the host country.

To more clearly define foreign market potential, it might help to briefly review four major categories of exporting:

- Technology licensing
- Franchising
- Exporting products from the United States
- Manufacturing products within the host country

Technology Licensing

For some businesses and in some countries, the nature of the product, government trade and investment barriers, or lack of management talent may preclude either exporting or direct investment. Yet, market demand for the company's products may be strong. Licensing technology to local companies may be the key to unlocking the door to future trade. Technology licensing has been used extensively for many years in the developing markets of East Asia, Eastern Europe, and the erstwhile Soviet Union.

The major advantage of licensing over either exporting or foreign direct investment is that it provides an entree to global markets without requiring financial commitments. The biggest disadvantages are

1. Making sure you receive all royalty payments due

2. Complying with local tax laws that might delay or reduce royalty payments

3. Losing control over the technology, as well as the production and marketing of proprietary products.

In many instances, however, loss of control poses less of a problem as time goes on and newer technologies are developed domestically to replace those licensed overseas. Overall, the ease of entry into local markets and the low cost of technology licensing frequently outweigh the risks entailed. (See Chapter 15 for a complete discussion of the pros and cons of technology licensing.)

Franchising

Franchising foreign companies also offers an opportunity to enter the global arena without significant cost or financing commitments. Most larger companies that have franchised overseas for years—McDonald's, Kentucky Fried Chicken, Radio Shack, and so on—do, however, assist franchisees to finance start-ups, either through leasing arrangements or with short-term working capital loans.

If a company lacks domestic franchise experience, however, overseas franchising strategies can easily backfire, costing more than a business start-up. Companies that have successfully franchised offshore have nearly always had a sound franchise base in the United States. The case of Weltight Sash and Door Company demonstrates how the lack of franchising experience can lead to horrendous decisions and ultimate failure.

Weltight, a manufacturer of aluminum doors and windows, distributed these products throughout the Midwest from a series of home remodeling centers. The company's owner heard about terrific opportunities in several large residential developments underway in Norway and Sweden. Wishing to tap this apparently enormous new market, he traveled to the Scandinavian countries to survey conditions for himself. While there, he noticed several franchises sporting American names; however, he didn't take the time to investigate how they were set up or if they were even profitable.

Returning home, the Weltight owner announced that the company would immediately begin franchising distributorships in Norway. Franchise agreements were negotiated with three Norwegian distributors, located in Bergen, Oslo, and Trondheim. Weltight transferred $300,000 to each distributor for start-up working capital loans and agreed to guarantee loans from local Norwegian banks for the purchase of installation tools and vehicles.

The franchising experiment lasted about two years, during which time all three distributorships folded. Weltight lost its initial investment of $900,000 and, as guarantor, was liable for another $315,000 to settle bank debts. That was the last time international trade or franchising was mentioned at Weltight.

Companies that are already franchising in the United States, however, should have little difficulty doing so overseas, as long as product lines, distribution policies, franchise procedures, and contracts are all adapted to the specific market being served. (Chapter 15 covers additional franchising topics.)

Exporting from the United States

Exporting products from the United States is generally the least-risk way for smaller companies to enter the global marketplace. Exporting doesn't require much additional overhead expense, credit risks are relatively low, and the peculiarities of foreign taxes, labor laws, and business licensing can be avoided by selling through export management or export trading companies. Moreover, the difficulty of managing foreign employees never arises.

This is not to say that every company can immediately jump into an export program without addressing issues that are significantly different from those encountered in domestic markets. Issues causing the most confusion seem to be

- Booking foreign orders
- Delivering products
- Financing customer purchases
- Collecting from customers
- Managing currency convertibility

Booking Foreign Orders

You will never realize high margins unless customers are willing and able to buy your products. For domestic markets, it's relatively easy to develop advertising programs and sales promotions to publicize your products' benefits. A variety of selling methods can be used, including direct mail, telemarketing, and direct sales calls. A common language, excellent communications facilities, a relatively comprehensible body of contract law, and an army of lawyers, public accountants, and consultants make contract negotiations straightforward. None of these conditions are present when exporting.

Language and cultural differences exacerbate an already complex selling process. Strange shipping and customs requirements complicate delivery logistics. Although salaried international sales departments invariably turn more sales at higher margins than commissioned sales representatives, such an option may be too costly for your company.

One solution is to contract with an export management company to handle selling activities, sales contract negotiations, and shipping documentation. Many of these highly specialized companies have networks of commissioned sales agents throughout the world. And all have the capacity to manage the complete shipping process. Some export management companies concentrate on certain regions, such as East Asia, Europe, or the Middle East. Others provide worldwide sales coverage (see Chapter 12).

Delivering Products

Transporting products from the United States to overseas customers is substantially more complex than domestic shipping. The preparation of paperwork for ocean shipping and customs clearance can be time-consuming and costly. Furthermore, ocean freight carries certain risks: The boat might sink, the products might be damaged, or piracy might occur on the high seas. Although premiums to insure against such losses run high, several private marine carriers offer adequate coverage (see Chapter 14).

In addition to marketing assistance, export management companies can be hired to handle all shipping matters: customs clearances, containerization, shipping papers, freight forwarding, and so on. Although this involves additional expense, it also relieves exporters of any worries about complying with local laws and customs, language barriers, and potentially difficult negotiations. Export management fees vary with services performed, destination of the shipment, location of the exporter, and types of products or services marketed. By and large, however, these fees are usually less than the cost of staffing and managing your own international sales force. Also, in many cases, such added costs can be passed along to the customer in higher selling prices.

Financing Customer Purchases

Helping customers finance purchases is common practice for U.S. exporters. For larger-volume sales, exporters may assume the responsibility for arranging the entire financing package, including both short- and long-term credit and bank guarantees. However, for smaller shipments, only partial funding may be required.

A variety of financing sources stand ready to help. Eximbank is generally the first stop. Transaction financing, letters of credit, and banker's acceptances are also quite common. Documentary drafts may be used for well-known, creditworthy customers. In addition, the federal government and several state governments have agencies specifically chartered to help smaller companies arrange export financing. Many of these agencies can arrange trade credit for foreign customers as well as short-term working capital loans for U.S. exporters.

For the majority of transactions, export credit and guarantees are more plentiful and far easier to arrange than domestic financing, mainly because of the continued interest by federal, state, and city agencies in promoting export business. Even with pressures to reduce federal expenditures, it seems likely that political pressures to boost the economies of Eastern Europe, the erstwhile Soviet Union, and Latin America will force the U.S. government to increase (or at least continue) its participation in both direct export funding and credit guarantees.

Collecting from Customers

Checking the credit of domestic customers through banks and credit agencies is relatively straightforward. The same cannot be said for foreign customers. Although Dun & Bradstreet, a few federal agencies, and several foreign credit bureaus provide credit reports on foreign companies, the absence of uniform accounting standards and reporting requirements make these reports marginally useful, at best.

Assistance from federal agencies such as Eximbank, the Overseas Private Investment Corporation, and the United States and Foreign Service Corporation is the best bet. These agencies have access to reams of documents and information on virtually any foreign customer (sovereign or private) that has done business with the U.S. government or with U.S. companies. But even credit information from these agencies isn't foolproof; more often than not, it is out of date.

Collecting open accounts receivable presents similar challenges. Domestic customers can be hassled by collection agencies or threatened with lawsuits. However, these procedures are ineffective in the international marketplace. Sovereign customers will never be intimidated by threats of court action or foreclosure. Private-sector customers merely scoff at offshore dunning efforts. In international trade, domestic collection tools won't work. Other methods must be used to collect from recalcitrant customers.

Foreign collection agencies provide one solution; however, in most regions of the world they seem to be inefficient and difficult for U.S. exporters to deal with. There is no international court of law with jurisdiction over collection disputes other than the International Arbitration Court—a very costly, complex, and unsatisfactory alternative.

Purchasing U.S. government-sponsored credit insurance through the Foreign Credit Insurance Association (FCIA) is the best way to protect against nonpayment of export invoices. For a relatively low premium, the FCIA insures the collectibility of any export sale. You can insure against commercial loss as well as expropriation. In addition to insurance, letters of credit confirmed by a U.S. bank and banker's acceptances backed by the customer's bank prove effective for ensuring payment.

Exporting to less-stable countries involves a degree of political risk—that is, the risk of a foreign government's expropriating your products before they get to market or freezing bank accounts before payment can be made. However, the likelihood of losing either goods or funds through foreign expropriation can be substantially diminished by using the proper financing tools, shipping procedures, and insurance.

Irrevocable letters of credit confirmed by an American bank are a sure-fire method of avoiding expropriation. So is shipping FAS port of embarkation, which means that title passes as soon as the exporter delivers products "alongside the ship." If a foreign government seizes the goods when they arrive at the port of entry, or if a customer is otherwise unable to claim them, the exporter is off the hook.

Managing Currency Convertibility

Of the thousands of world currencies, only a handful are convertible to U.S. dollars in the open market. Hard currencies, such as English pounds, German marks, Japanese yen, and French francs, are convertible to dollars by any bank in the free world. But Russian rubles, Venezuelan bolivars, Saudi riyals, and Czech korunas, along with most of the other world currencies, are not. How then can American exporters sell to these soft-currency countries if customers cannot pay in dollars? One answer is by using countertrade.

As the name implies, countertrade involves the exchange of goods or services for other goods or services (rather than currency). These exchanged goods or services can then be used by the exporter, or they can be sold to a third party in exchange for hard currency. There is nothing mystical about countertrade. It is merely one more example of the way international trade combines marketing and financing. Although large corporations are the most frequent users of countertrade, it works just as well for smaller companies. It may be that a countertrade deal will make the difference between closing an order and losing one.

Establishing an Overseas Presence

Although exporting opens the door to global markets, companies must augment their exporting programs with offshore production facilities, distribution centers, and sales offices to maximize profits from worldwide sales. Obviously, locations must be carefully selected to provide the greatest potential for market growth.

Such a local presence enables companies to carve out market niches in the same way that foreign competitors have done in the United States. It also permits more competitive pricing than exporting because a local presence eliminates extra shipping costs, reduces the time span in moving goods to market, allows more efficient after-sale service, and lets pricing policies flow with rapidly changing local market conditions. Furthermore, goods can usually be produced at lower costs than in U.S.-based facilities. In addition to being distributed in local markets, foreign-produced goods can be exported to customers in other countries or shipped back to the United States.

As previously noted, an investment in a facility or project on foreign soil is commonly referred to as a foreign direct investment. Such an investment may be made by (1) starting a foreign business from scratch, (2) acquiring a majority or minority interest in a going business, or (3) forming a foreign joint venture. Before making a foreign direct investment, however, it only makes sense to become familiar with doing business in that country. That entails

1. Performing a survey of the economic, legal, and labor requirements of the host country (see Chapters 5 and 6)

2. Learning the specific marketing techniques peculiar to the host country (see Chapters 12 and 13)

3. Evaluating alternatives for financing the foreign operation (see Chapter 11).

The Country Survey

Once a preliminary determination of local economic factors has been made, additional information about the host country must be gathered. This is called a *country survey*. During a country survey, a wide range of detailed information should be accumulated about business conditions, government restrictions, market characteristics, and infrastructures of the host country. Particular attention should focus on laws that restrict foreign investment, tax requirements, labor law peculiarities, licensing prerequisites, visa and work permit rules, organization alternatives, and trade regulations. In addition, surveys should reveal unique or restrictive banking and currency regulations, especially as they relate to repatriation of earnings to the United States.

During a country survey, be sure to make arrangements with host-country legal and accounting professionals to represent the company; establish bank accounts; and hold discussions with local labor representatives to ensure the smooth opening of a new facility or the transition of ownership in an acquired one. Relationships should also be established with local trading companies, marketing representatives, and relevant government officials. A comprehensive country survey lets you avoid a great many logistic snares and guarantees that all pertinent information is made available before funds are invested.

The best way to ensure a comprehensive survey is to make one or more personal trips to the host country and stay there long enough to get a good grasp of local business customs. Learning international norms should not be a delegated task. Whether a company's objective is to acquire an interest in a going business, to start up a new business, or to initiate a joint venture, a thorough grasp of local business practices is essential. If you can't make the trip yourself, engage a qualified international consultant to perform the survey.

Evaluating the Host Country's Marketing Customs

As part of the country survey, an evaluation should be made of local marketing customs and the impact of these practices on the company's ability to do business there. Typical questions that should be answered before going further include

- Must you maintain your own sales force, or can you use local sales representatives?
- Can specific customer groups be targeted? How?
- What advertising media and sales promotions work best?
- Can an American head up the sales organization, or would it be better to let a national lead the way?
- Are all prices negotiated, or can price sheets be used?
- How are customer complaints, quality failures, deliveries, and the stocking of spare parts handled?

Financing an Overseas Presence

Establishing an overseas operation requires at least a rudimentary understanding of local and international financing options. Seldom, if ever, can funds from traditional U.S. banking sources be used to finance either the acquisition of an interest in a foreign business or the costs involved in a business startup. Host-country banking systems, capital markets, or government subsidies will probably be desirable at one time or another. Even for those cash-rich businesses that can finance their own foreign direct investment, it doesn't make sense to ignore free or low-cost money from local sources.

Additionally, each country has its own legal requirements for the capitalization of companies. Some countries insist on minimum levels of equity. Others require partial ownership by local government agencies. In a few countries, majority ownership by foreigners is forbidden, so that U.S. companies must have local partners who act as figureheads. To comply with local requirements, U.S. companies should examine all potential financing sources, including the use of foreign banks, U.S. government guarantees, joint ventures, public issues of securities on foreign exchanges, development banks, and multilateral and bilateral aid programs.

Taking a look at financing assistance from the U.S. government might be a good starting point. For example, federal financing programs under the Caribbean Basin Initiative are extremely lucrative. Financial assistance from the Overseas Private Investment Corporation can be very beneficial for direct investments in nearly all parts of the world.

INTERNATIONAL BANKING

Whether you choose to start or expand an export program or make a foreign direct investment, it is virtually impossible to do so without using banks. For exporting from the United States, U.S. banks are usually the best choice. But for financing trade or direct investment that originates in a foreign country, it nearly always makes sense to work through a foreign bank or a foreign branch of a multinational U.S. bank, such as Citibank, Chase Manhattan, Chemical Bank, or Bank of America.

Nearly all foreign banking systems are significantly different from the U.S. banking system. For example, banks in England, Germany, Israel, Japan, France, Italy, and most other countries have used off-balance-sheet financing for years as income-producing activities. U.S. banks, on the other hand, are restricted from doing so by federal and state banking regulations and by constraining accounting requirements.

Foreign banks may be the best way to finance an international transaction or the only feasible source of expansion capital. Foreign banks can be used for depositing collections, transferring funds worldwide, issuing letters of credit, and many other functions. For export trade finance, foreign banks are often easier to deal with, cheaper, and less inclined to hassle smaller customers than their American counterparts.

Foreign banks are either clearing banks or merchant banks. The same bank might have two divisions performing the different activities, as is the case with many European universal banks. In other cases, clearing and merchant banks are distinctly separate entities. Clearing banks perform functions analogous to those of commercial banks in the United States. Merchant banks are similar to U.S. investment banks.

The largest merchant banks are located in the United Kingdom, France, and Japan. Their activities range from financing international trade, to acting as underwriters for securities issues, to investing in operating companies for their own account. They are the backbone of international finance. It usually pays to check out the services of merchant banks when you first start an exporting program or plan a foreign direct investment. Many merchant banks have offices in the United States and are easy to approach.

TAX AND REPORTING REQUIREMENTS

Tax and administrative requirements also deserve careful consideration before entering into either an export program or a foreign direct investment. Compliance with U.S. and foreign tax regulations and foreign legal, accounting, and reporting requirements are necessary in any international business activity.

From the tax perspective, U.S. companies have three concerns:

- How to minimize U.S. taxes on foreign income
- How to avoid double taxation
- How to minimize taxes on foreign acquisitions.

American tax laws specify that U.S. taxpayers must report all income received from anywhere in the world, regardless of its source. However, most countries have laws that require taxes to be paid on income earned in that country, regardless of the nationality of the taxpayer, potentially resulting in the same income being taxed twice.

The U.S. government has enacted tax treaties or bilateral tax information exchange agreements (TIEAs) with most of its major trading partners. Broadly speaking, those countries that execute TIEAs agree to exchange with the IRS pertinent income and expense information about companies doing business in the country, thereby enabling agencies from both sides to audit multinational transactions. On the plus side, U.S. tax deductions or tax credits are usually available for income taxes paid to countries that have executed tax treaties.

Be aware, however, that many smaller countries, especially developing nations in Africa, Southeast Asia, and the Middle East, have not executed tax treaties. Without careful tax planning, income earned in these countries could be taxed twice.

Foreign sales corporations (FSCs) are an excellent way to save taxes on up to 15 percent of export income. FSC rules do, however, require that a separate office be established in a qualified foreign country. Chapter 3 covers a wide range of U.S. tax matters related to international trade transactions.

Chapter 2

An International Trade Primer

We wouldn't get behind the wheel if we didn't know how to drive; we wouldn't jump off a boat if we didn't know how to swim; and we shouldn't export, import, or make foreign direct investments without knowing the basic forces that drive international trade. This is not to say that international trade is entirely different from domestic business. It isn't. But without at least a cursory grasp of national trade policies, trading blocs, and exchange rates, it's extremely difficult to make intelligent strategic decisions about foreign markets and resources and virtually impossible to carry on meaningful trade.

This chapter offers a very brief overview of the types of government trade barriers that affect trading decisions and the role of exchange rates in setting export prices. It concludes by describing the salient features of global banking and financial markets.

However, it would be wrong to assume that such a cursory examination is sufficient to prepare a company for exporting or foreign direct investments. Each country has different trade and investment regulations. Each foreign market has peculiar cultural and competitive characteristics. Each export program or direct investment project requires unique financing arrangements. The material in this chapter merely opens the door, hopefully raising enough issues to encourage you to further explore those specific conditions that may affect your company's strategic decision to enter international trade.

COMPETITION FROM MULTINATIONAL CORPORATIONS

It seems inevitable that worldwide competition from multinational corporations can only increase. They influence every phase of global trade—pricing, delivery, packaging, distribution, sales finance, and personnel recruiting. They export and maintain facilities in every region of the world. They transfer technology, capital, and labor across national boundaries.

Though multinationals can be found in every industrialized country from the Netherlands to Singapore, those that compete most directly with small and mid-size American companies are (1) those domiciled in the United States, such as General Electric, General Motors, IBM, and Dow Chemical, and (2) those headquartered elsewhere but owning major facilities in the United States, such as Toyota, Philips Electric, ICI, and Mitsubishi.

Competition from these giants severely affects the ability of many small and midsize U.S. companies to carve out a market niche within their own country. However, many overseas markets, especially smaller markets in less-developed nations, do not attract the intense competition that broader European, Japanese, or American markets do. Since the best defense is often a good offense, competitive positioning provides yet another reason to look to international trade as a way to improve your company's position in U.S. markets.

It should be noted, however, that regardless of the location of foreign markets, there will be either direct or indirect competition from multinationals. These giants have the resources, knowledge, and political clout to affect the strategies of any smaller company. On the other hand, the enormous size of their organizations, their slowness in making decisions, and the fear in many developing nations of being overrun by the IBMs, Hitachis, and Exxons of the world give smaller companies a competitive edge in niche markets.

NATIONAL TRADE POLICIES

Much as government leaders from the United States, Europe, Japan, and most of the rest of the world herald free trade, not one country actually practices it. Every nation has special industries that it believes must be protected from free-market competition. In the United States, for example, steel, textiles, leather goods, motorcycles, automobiles, sugar, citrus fruits, and so on, have at one time or another been shielded from foreign competition by zealous protectionists in Washington. The European Community (now the European Union) protects its farmers, Mexico protects its cement and oil industries, Canada guards its lumber industry, the United States shields its banking industry, and Japan prevents foreigners from competing in most local markets.

Such policies are based on hundreds, if not thousands, of side agreements, formal and informal understandings, and shifting emphases, as elected governments change. All governments purport to favor free trade between countries. Yet, all support a degree of protectionism, erecting barriers to free trade.

The trade policies of developing or emerging nations tend to reflect a dichotomy of purpose. On one hand, these countries fear being overrun by the world's trade giants. On the other hand, they encourage imports and foreign investment in an effort to obtain technology and management knowhow, and to enjoy the fruits of state-of-the-art products.

Most common forms of trade barriers are specifically designed to shield certain industries that have become noncompetitive, frequently as a result of artificially high operating costs, restrictive government regulations, or the absence of current technology. Protectionist trade policies take the form of import duties (tariffs), quantity quotas, or government subsidies.

The common element in all national trade policies, however, is that they have a major influence on the ability of foreign companies to transact profitable business within that country's borders. When surveying potential export markets, it is important to search out those markets that have as few barriers as possible to the import of your products.

Protectionist Trade Restraints

Protectionist trade restraints may be formal or informal. They take various forms and have varying degrees of effectiveness. However, they all have the same purpose: to restrict cross-border trade. Most trade restraints emanate from government policies aimed at protecting the internal economic, social, or political systems of a country.

For many decades, the majority of world trade has been conducted under a set of rules between member nations known as the General Agreement on Tariffs and Trade, or GATT for short. The whole purpose of GATT is to lower trade barriers, thereby promoting free trade among the market economies of the world. As idealistic as such a goal may be, free traders continue to foresee a network of world economies, free of trade restraints of any kind.

Pragmatically, GATT has so many loopholes that even in the best of times, its free-trade objective is merely a dream. A far better goal for the world economic system might be fair trade, as ex-President George Bush put it, not free trade.

But even fair trade—that is, bilateral agreements to maintain the same level of tariffs, quotas, and subsidies between two countries—has eluded us. Japan, for example, has for years exported thousands of products to the United States, facing only modest tariffs and quotas. U.S. companies, on the other hand, have been thwarted from entering Japanese markets by highly restrictive external and internal trade restraints, effectively barring foreign competition in most Japanese markets.

The United States also employs protectionist trade policies almost indiscriminately. Tariffs, import quotas, and federal subsidies protect American companies from foreign competition in industries ranging from steel to textiles, from leather goods to motorcycles, from citrus fruit to automobiles.

Nevertheless, consumers continue to pay the higher prices such barriers create in exchange for what they perceive as high-quality, high-fashion, or high-technology foreign goods. Regardless of the form a trade barrier may take, protectionist policies enacted by the United States, Japan, Western Europe, and Third World nations have not stemmed the tide of foreign imports. On the contrary, worldwide cross-border trade continues to show annual increases.

Restrictive tariffs seldom bring the benefits envisioned when they were enacted. Therefore, tariffs that apply universally to imported goods from all countries are increasingly being replaced by nontariff barriers. One of the most common nontariff trade barrier is the *voluntary export restraint*, or VER.

VERs restrict trade in textiles, clothing, steel, automobiles, electronic products, agriculture, and machine tools, to mention but a few of the industries affected. They represent a convenient loophole to GATT, since they are bilateral agreements, affecting trade only between two countries.

A VER is an agreement whereby the government, or an industry, in the importing country arranges with the government, or the competing industry, in an exporting country to restrict the volume (not the price) of the latter's export of one or more products. Since the agreement is voluntary, the exporting country or industry has the right to rescind or modify it at any time. However, since VERs originate from importing countries, they are really voluntary only in the sense that exporters prefer VERs to more stringent barriers from the importing country.

Theoretically, VERs serve as restrictive trade measures with the purpose of either protecting or improving a country's balance of payments or providing relief for industries adversely affected by foreign competition. As with any protectionist trade barrier, to the extent that it diminishes legitimate economic competition, the result is normally a higher price to consumers in the importing country. Given the elasticity of worldwide demand, such increased prices in one country can very often drive prices up in another country. Exporters win even though their sales volume is restricted.

When evaluating the desirability of exporting to a given country, it's necessary to identify the VERs or other protectionist trade barriers that are currently in effect. It also helps to find out how competitive exporters are managing trade restraints, in terms of both the volume of export sales and the margins realized.

Strategic Trade Policies

Regardless of protectionist barriers, strategic trade policies have a major influence on the desirability of doing business in one country versus another. Examples of such policies include

- Japan's decision to close its doors to many imports
- The self-sufficiency that Mexico, Venezuela, and Argentina (and most other Latin American countries) strove to achieve during the 1980s
- The Indian government's decision to block out most imports for nearly fifty years
- European subsidies for the design and manufacture of the Airbus.

Free traders have held up the comparative advantages realized between countries engaged in free trade as the justification for continually striving to reduce trade barriers. They argue that free markets should be allowed to determine price, quality, and availability of products in the global community.

Opponents point to the enormous economic gains of Japan and Germany, both of which have significant barriers to free trade, as a strong case for government intervention in free markets. Their argument holds that such policies yield greater national benefits to these nations than free trade, thereby justifying strategic trade policies that nurture domestic businesses at the expense of foreign competitors.

It appears that U.S. lawmakers have bought this latter position. For the last twenty years, federal trade policies have attempted to shift volume and profits from more efficiently competitive foreign automobile, steel, textile, and machine tool manufacturers to U.S. companies. Although this strategy appears to work in the short term, long-term benefits remain less certain. Detroit's continued loss of market share and the massive contraction of the steel industry probably indicate that free trade might have been the best policy after all.

Although no one would argue that one or even a group of American companies could change these strategic trade policies, knowing the extent to which they exist in the United States as well as in those countries with attractive export markets enables companies to develop strategies that will maximize export benefits.

INTERNATIONAL TRADING BLOCS

During the cold war, 101 nations counted themselves as part of the "nonaligned movement." The end of U.S.-Soviet rivalry left nothing for these nations to be nonaligned against. The failure of apartheid in South Africa removed the one unifying cry that fractious African nations could rally around. The Persian Gulf war split the Arab League asunder. The collapse of the Warsaw Pact left Eastern European countries without an identifying banner. The disintegration of the Soviet Union placed the twelve socialist republics in the position of grappling with self-definition.

Throughout the world, as political and military alliances folded, nations were left with the uncomfortable problem of defining their own identity and mission.

Since 1989, this void has been filled by the shift from ideological and military homogeneity to economic alliances as the means of shaping global events. Countries on every continent have formed new alliances and revived inoperative trade agreements. And this is having a major impact on selecting export markets. To prosper in international markets, companies must devise strategic plans to take advantage of these alliances, or *trading blocs* as they are generally referred to.

Virtually dozens of new economic blocs with a variety of labels—alliances, common markets, free-trade areas, and so on—have blossomed over the last few years. Moreover, new ones seem to be coming on line in a continuing stream. In addition to the well-known European Union and the East Asian Economic Group common markets, non-Western Hemisphere alliances include

- European Free Trade Association—Iceland, Norway, Sweden, Finland, Switzerland, Liechtenstein, and Austria
- Black Sea Economic Cooperation Accord—Turkey, Russia, and seven former Soviet republics
- Hexagonal Accord—Italy, Austria, Hungary, the Czech Republic, Slovakia, Poland, and Yugoslavia (before its break-up)
- Economic Cooperation Organization (nicknamed the Islamic Common Market)—Iran, Turkey, Pakistan, five former Soviet Asian republics, and Afghanistan
- Caspian Sea Pact—the five states bordering the world's largest inland lake
- Preferential Trade Area of Africa—an eighteen-member African alliance
- Magreb Union—Algeria, Libya, Mauritania, Morocco, and Tunisia.

Not to be out-allianced, Western Hemisphere nations have formed or revived no less than twelve intra-regional alliances, common markets, and free-trade areas, led by the U.S.-Canada Free Trade Accord, the North American Free Trade Agreement (NAFTA), the Southern Cone Common Market (MERCOSUR), the

Andean Pact, the Group of Three (G3), the Caribbean Community and Common Market (CARICOM), and the Central American Common Market (CACM).

Although economic blocs come in all sizes and shapes they tend to be grouped under one of three headings:

1. *Common markets* with tariff-free trade among members but common trade barriers for the outside world, such as the European Union

2. *Free-trade areas* with duty-free trade among members but with each member allowed to set its own barriers/incentives with the outside world, such as NAFTA

3. *Economic alliances* that encourage common projects and planning between member states on issues such as development, the environment, and information links, but with some trade barriers remaining between members, such as the Caspian Sea Pact.

In this new world that values economic power above military might, the number and size of corporations is becoming more important than the size of armies. It seems likely that eventually more government funding will be dedicated to supporting foreign trade than to building military might.

Such a shift of worldwide emphasis has as profound an effect on company strategies as on national governments. The strategic importance of positioning a company to take advantage of regional trading blocs cannot be overemphasized. Although it is becoming increasingly difficult to establish new footholds in Europe or Japan, much of the Western Hemisphere—Mexico, Central America, the Caribbean, and South America—is still wide open.

As the economic power of the Western Hemisphere grows, companies firmly positioned within the region's major trading blocs can use this power to negotiate preferential trade with suppliers and customers in European and East Asian groups.

Critics and supporters agree, however, that if Western Hemisphere companies are to assume a competitive posture in world trade, there must be economic integration of at least the region's major trading partners: the United States, Canada, Mexico, Argentina, Brazil, Venezuela, and Chile, and to a lesser extent the Caribbean Basin nations of Jamaica, Trinidad and Tobago, Barbados, the Dominican Republic, Costa Rica, and Panama.

FOREIGN EXCHANGE

Foreign exchange always affects any international trade transaction. Whenever a U.S. company exports raw materials, products, or services to another country; imports materials, parts, subassemblies, or finished products; or makes a foreign direct investment in a facility or project, it has three choices of currency to use for payment:

- U.S. dollars
- The currency of the customer's country
- The currency of a third country.

A company's decision about the best currency to use should be based on its forecast of the most likely exchange rate movements.

Since the final collapse of the Bretton Woods agreement in 1973, the foreign exchange market has experienced wide fluctuations and extreme volatility. The wildest swings occur when a major currency undergoes radical central bank intervention, such as the roller-coaster ride the U.S. dollar experienced in the early 1980s. Because the world no longer operates under the more or less fixed exchange rates sanctioned by the Bretton Woods agreement, currencies move freely up or down in relation to other currencies, driven by central bank intervention and free-market forces. In many respects, foreign exchange rates react to the same forces as major issues on the world's stock exchanges.

As with securities trading, the world is full of "experts" who believe they have the answer to predicting foreign exchange rates. Statistical trend charts, formulas, relationships to interest rates and inflation rates, a country's balance of payments, and a variety of other factors lead foreign currency players to a plethora of special techniques and theories for explaining why foreign exchange rates move in one direction or another.

The fact is, however, that no one has come up with a sure-fire method for explaining these movements or accurately predicting future currency rate relationships. When all is said and done, supply and demand probably have more influence on the movement of exchange rates than anything else.

Supply and Demand Factors

The supply of and demand for various currencies are functions of the perceived influence of current conditions and expectations of future global developments on a country's economic fortunes. In financial market parlance, currency supply and demand are derivatives of the coincident interaction of fundamental economic factors and technical conditions in the market. Table 2.1 lists typical supply and demand conditions influencing exchange-rate movement.

Table 2.1
Factors Affecting the Supply of and Demand for Foreign Currency

1. *Exchange controls.* These are the formal rules and regulations set out by the central bank that govern the flow of funds in and out of a country. They include the bank's official rules for foreign exchange transactions within the country.

2. *Quantity of outstanding currency.* This is the amount of a country's currency that is available for foreign exchange transactions as determined by the country's total currency in the interbank markets.

3. *Growth in domestic money supply.* This is the growth rate of a currency within a country, as monitored and regulated by that country's central bank.

4. *Comparative value of exchange rates.* This is determined by commercial banks and dealers who buy undervalued currency and sell overvalued currency to maximize profits. A country's currency value increases when export sales exceed import purchases of goods and services.

5. *Interest rate differentials.* These are influenced by foreign currency trading of professional dealers who buy currencies of countries with higher interest rates and sell currencies of countries with lower rates to maximize investment returns.

6. *Inflation-rate differentials.* The volatility and uncertainty of a country's economic future as reflected in inflation rates influence dealers to buy currencies of countries with low inflation rates and to sell those with higher rates.

7. *Real rates of return on government securities.* High real rates of return on government obligations increase the desirability of holding a country's currency.

8. *Central bank intervention.* Central banks buy and sell their own and other countries currencies in the open market to maintain predetermined rate relationships of their own currency.

9. *Confidence in government.* Stable political systems and those whose leaders are unlikely to enact major changes in monetary or fiscal policies give investors confidence that their investments are secure. This feeling of safety, more than any other demand factor, influences major currency buy/sell decisions.

Wars, famines, internal political actions, central bank manipulations, and a variety of other uncontrollable events have over time exerted at least as much influence on supply and demand curves as interest rates or inflation rates. Predicting currency exchange-rate relationships is as much a matter of guesswork as forecasting when the next snowstorm will occur, six months in advance. Nevertheless, the pricing, and hence the profitability, of many transactions depends to a large extent on how well a company manages its foreign exchange policies.

One misconception should be dispelled immediately: that the use of letters of credit or other trade finance instruments insulates a company from foreign exchange fluctuations. While payment may be received in U.S. dollars, the price negotiated in the sales contract will be based on both the exporter's and the customer's projections of exchange-rate movements.

For example, if Company A from the United States exports goods to Company B in Germany, payment may be made by an L/C drawn on a New York bank and denominated in U.S. dollars. Assume that when the contract is negotiated on June 1, the dollar-deutsche mark exchange differential was fifty cents. Company B forecasts that the differential will increase ten cents in favor of the dollar by the time shipment is made.

When negotiating the price for the goods, Company B will insist on a low enough price to compensate for the drop in the deutsche mark's value, even though the invoice is in U.S. dollars. Conversely, if Company A sees a drop in the dollar versus the mark by the time of shipment, it will insist on a higher price to compensate. In either case, if the forecast is correct, both companies come out whole. However, if the forecast is wrong, either B will pay too much for the goods or A will receive too little.

Foreign exchange is not as mystical as currency gurus would like outsiders to believe. Certainly foreign exchange dealers and brokers have a vocabulary all their own (just as do brokers who specialize in commodities, stocks, or bonds). When communicating across borders in several different languages, common terminology is essential. Aside from confusing semantics, however, the principles of foreign exchange necessary to manage exchange rates are relatively straightforward.

Here are brief explanations of the major terms.

Timing the Transaction—Spots and Forwards

All foreign currency transactions involve the delivery of an amount of one currency in exchange for another. This exchange must take place at the same time, either when the contract is executed or at some agreed upon time in the future. Current foreign exchange rates are called *spot* prices. Those occurring at some time in the future are referred to as *forward* prices.

The transaction date may be as far into the future as both parties desire, although forward contracts seldom extend beyond a year. Spot prices generally refer to a delivery date within the next few days, although common usage limits the time period to two working days.

Covering forward exchange rates is a form of insurance. For example, assume a U.S. exporter contracts to ship products to a customer in Great Britain in six months. The price is $1,000. Payment is to be made against an L/C denominated in U.S. dollars. The exchange rate at the date of contract is $1.00 = £0.75.

The customer believes that in six months the dollar will weaken to $1.00 = £0.50, so that the shipment of goods will cost the British company £500 rather than £750. The customer places an order for a forward cover in the exchange market to become effective in six months. If the guess was right, the British company purchased the goods for a 33 percent discount. The forward cover has no effect on the U.S. exporter, who still gets $1,000.

If the reverse situation was anticipated (that is, if the customer believed the dollar would strengthen), then purchasing dollars at the current spot price would yield a higher return.

Deciding whether to cover forward to reduce exchange risk or to go with spot prices plagues companies the world over. Government export credit agencies in some countries, such as the FCIA in the United States, sell insurance against currency risks. But insurance is costly and can easily whittle down profits to the point where the transaction isn't economical.

Although no easy answer jumps out, if a company has already purchased in one currency and has already sold in another currency, then a forward cover generally makes sense. Obviously, without the expectation of a favorable rate change, or if the transaction is very small, forward covers aren't worth the bother.

Cross Rates

When a U.S. exporter ships goods to a customer in, say, Argentina and agrees to take payment in the currency of a third country, say, British pounds, the exporter's U.S. bank will quote *cross rates*. Although it is common for dealers around the world to quote rates in U.S. dollars, so that a conversion factor is required to get the cross rate, a few will quote as desired: in other words, French francs against German marks, Greek drachmas against Swiss francs, and so on. The rate against the U.S. dollar is a cross rate to dealers in third countries.

Swaps

Swaps occur when a pair of foreign exchange deals in the same two currencies happen at different delivery dates. Swaps always involve two transactions by one party, although these deals may be with one or two other parties.

For example, assume a U.S. exporter takes C$100 from a Canadian customer and then works a swap of the C$100, spot against forward, agreeing to sell a bank the C$100 on receipt at a spot price of US$0.75. Simultaneously the exporter contracts with either the same or a different bank to purchase C$100 in three months at the forward price of US$0.70. In addition to the normal profit on the export of the goods, the company picks up an exchange gain of US$5. This entire transactions is known as a *swap*. Of course, in this example the exporting company ends up with Canadian dollars and then must either sell the currency at another gain or make another swap.

Another way of looking at it is to consider a swap as a simultaneous purchase and sale of currencies with different maturities and different delivery dates: the purchase of one-month forward 3 million deutsche marks swapped for the sale of three-month forward 0.5 million British pounds. Banks frequently use swaps in the interbank market to deal with short-term currency reserve shortages.

One of the problems arising from currency purchase or sale commitments for forward delivery occurs when a company executes a contract for the export or import of goods, or for the investment in a foreign project, and doesn't know the exact date the currency will be needed. One way to deal with the problem is with a *time option* forward contract with a bank. A time option leaves the delivery date open, to be negotiated with the customer at a later date, but irrevocably fixes the exchange rate. The bank takes all the currency risk, giving a company the flexibility to use the currency only when it is needed.

Currency Invoicing

Currency invoicing might seem like a far-fetched idea, and in many cases it is. Many firms, especially smaller ones, buy and sell against contracts denominated in their own currency. This certainly is the easiest way to go and creates the least amount of confusion within the company and in relationships with the company's bank (particularly smaller banks). Given the right circumstances, however, invoicing in a currency other than U.S. dollars can add incremental profits and in some cases provide a significant competitive edge. If forward rates are at a premium relative to the exporter's currency, invoicing in the customer's currency can provide a better rate of exchange than either the current spot price or the anticipated spot price at collection time. Naturally, the customer's currency must be traded on a reliable world exchange.

Currency invoicing is especially appropriate for the export of capital goods when the buyer demands long-term credit. It can also be beneficial when lease payments are to be received over several years or when export shipments are made in increments over an extended period. If the exporter knows the dates when payments will be received, it's a simple matter to execute a forward sale of the proceeds. The only risk is not executing the forward sale concurrently with the export contract.

Importers stand to benefit from currency invoicing even more than exporters. Receiving an invoice in one's own currency simplifies the payment process and relieves the importer of the burden of entering the foreign exchange market. Also, if the foreign currency of the exporter is selling at a premium, the importer can buy forward and make an additional exchange gain. Of course, if it sells at a discount, the reverse holds.

Exporters who watch the foreign exchange market may fear a potential devaluation of the importer's currency, especially in countries experiencing high inflation rates (such as Brazil) and/or severe balance of payment deficits (such as Ireland). In such a case, customers who want to be invoiced in their own currency are frequently asked to put up a bank guarantee against devaluation (which in most cases would be risky even if a bank was willing to go along). Another trick used by exporters when customers demand currency invoicing is to jack up the price of the export shipment to cover potential devaluations—again an unfavorable condition for the importer.

When an importer's currency is traded forward at a premium to the exporter's, being invoiced in the exporter's currency can result in significant gains. The only requirement is to buy the exporter's currency forward as soon as the order is placed.

Futures and Options

Financial futures and "options" are traded in the open market in a manner similar to the way commodities futures and options are traded.

The basic principles in buying and selling foreign exchange futures are identical to those underlying forward contracts in the interbank foreign exchange market. The idea is to insure against future currency fluctuations without paying the cost of an insurance policy.

The steps involved in the buying and selling of futures and options get very complex, however, and unless you have experienced financial personnel, it's usually wise to stay away from these markets.

Getting Help

When it comes to advice about handling foreign exchange transactions, there is no ready base of competent professionals. Foreign exchange transactions flow through commercial banks, and many banks are reluctant to give customers advice about when to swap or place a forward contract, when to use futures and options, or the advantages of currency invoicing for a specific transactions. Their argument is that a bank should follow customers' instructions, not tell customers how to run their businesses.

This, of course, leaves small and midsize exporters that do not have experienced financial personnel up in the air. The best bet is to seek bank advice; and if it is not sufficient for your needs, get help from investment banks, merchant banks, or qualified international financial consultants.

INTERNATIONAL FINANCIAL SYSTEMS

The global financial system directly influences, and in many cases controls, the purse strings and the economic vicissitudes of nations. It also affects the amount of export credit available and the requirements for getting it.

To complicate matters, the global financial system is a dynamic mechanism, constantly adding new financing methods and abandoning others. Two of the most profound changes in the American banking industry brought about by global banking are the evolution of international ownership of banks and the ability of global banks to raise capital worldwide.

Banking has truly become an international affair. Foreign financial institutions now own large pieces of American commercial and investment banks, such as Marine Midland, First Boston, and Goldman, Sachs. Several American institutions, in turn, own large chunks of foreign financial institutions. This cross-fertilization promotes the integration of global objectives and adds worldwide financial stability to otherwise erratic financial markets.

It also opens the doors of European and Japanese financial markets to small and midsize companies. A U.S. company that needs to raise capital for expansion into a foreign country no longer has to rely on U.S. banks or U.S. government agencies. Bank loans can come from British, Japanese, French, or German banks. Merchant bankers now serve American firms both domestically and overseas, as well as companies from Britain, Japan, or other countries. Global banking has, in fact, opened the financial doors to everyone with a need to finance international trade.

Although an overworked cliché, the statement that "money knows no national boundaries" adequately describes the current and projected state of the world financial system. Individuals, companies, banks, and nations instantaneously move money to investments anywhere in the world that bring the highest return and offer the greatest security. The world financial system, and especially the global banking system, is experiencing a massive reshuffling of priorities. The national financial systems of developed nations have become so intertwined that perturbations in one system reverberate throughout the world. The complexity of capital makes it impossible for any nation or group of nations to control its flow.

The interdependence of the world's exchanges, government debt obligations, exchange rates, and private and public financing foretells an even greater upheaval in the future. This will inevitably result in placing the responsibility for maintaining global financial order with an independent international body, perhaps resident in the United Nations.

The current international financial system can be viewed as a hierarchy of financial institutions and regulatory bodies. At the apex are two international monetary organizations that are very much in evidence: the World Bank and the International Monetary Fund (IMF).

United Nations Financial Organizations

Over the years, the purpose of the United Nations' World Bank has shifted, until today its primary objective is to provide funds to finance investment projects in developing nations when private capital cannot be raised. Member countries make contributions to the World Bank, which subsequently issues bonds and notes to raise its lending reserves. The bank then uses these funds to make medium- and long-term loans, mainly to governments. Recently, however, the bank has placed increasing emphasis on funding projects for private-sector companies that have the wherewithal to arrange government guarantees.

The International Finance Corporation (IFC), one of the four arms of the World Bank, maintains a very active posture in providing financial assistance to private-sector enterprises. The IFC's mission is to promote local capital markets and private industry in developing countries. It accomplishes this by funding pre-investment studies without requiring government guarantees. Both debt and equity capital are used by the IFC. Technical assistance is also available.

The role of the International Monetary Fund (IMF) has increased significantly over the years. Today it is one of the most powerful and important financial institutions in the world for financing the building of infrastructures in developing countries. Before they can receive financial assistance from development banks, all projects must be approved by the IMF.

National Central Banks

Stepping down from the multinational level, central banks are the governing institutions for national banking industries. In the United States it's the Federal Reserve Bank, in Great Britain the Bank of England, in Japan the Bank of Japan, in Germany the Bundesbank, and so on.

Central banks originate and control a nation's monetary policies. They influence the growth of money and credit and the level of interest rates on short-term securities. Central banks attempt to influence long-term economic growth through control of the aggregate demand for money. Their principal method for achieving this is to convince the private sector that they view price stability as a prominent long-range objective and that their policies reflect that objective. The Bundesbank has been eminently successful in convincing German industry. Central banks in Argentina and Brazil have failed miserably. In the United States, the Fed's scorecard is average.

Commercial Banks

Commercial or clearing banks represent the next tier down in the global banking hierarchy. Aside from semantic differences, worldwide commercial banks differ markedly from each other. The structure of national banking systems is the most visible difference.

For example, more than 12,000 separate banks operate in the United States, ranging from giant money center banks to tiny rural banks. On the other end of the spectrum, in Great Britain, Switzerland, and Canada, nearly 90 percent of bank deposits are held by four or five banks. Between these extremes, the ten largest banks in Japan account for approximately 50 percent of deposits.

Government regulations that control the type of activities a bank may engage in and the maximum size loans it can make vary significantly among countries, as do constraints on new entrants into the banking system. The levels of reserves that banks must hold at the central bank also differ markedly among countries. In effect, these controls make banking a controlled monopoly within a nation's borders.

There is a strong interrelationship among banks from different countries. They borrow from and lend to one another. They participate in syndications and joint ventures. They maintain interbank near-money deposits. They share cross-ownership. In fact, money flows so freely throughout the global banking system that it appears to be traveling to and from a single bank.

Global banks also engage in nontraditional banking activities. Through holding company structures, banks freely compete in leasing, securities brokerage, shipping, insurance, real estate management and development, health care, investment banking, and a variety of other industries (except in the United States).

Cross-border ownership creates an even greater divergence from traditional banking activities by providing access to services and products prohibited by national regulations. Within national boundaries banks may enjoy monopolistic advantages, but on a global scale, immediate access to vast hoards of money, services, and products makes the industry both intensely competitive within financial markets and a viable competitor with other commercial industries.

Cross-border bank ownership and the ability of global banks to raise capital worldwide have produced profound changes in the global economy. Such cross-fertilization promotes the integration of global objectives and adds worldwide financial stability to otherwise erratic financial markets. It opens the doors of European, East Asian, and Middle East financial markets that have heretofore been closed to all but the largest multinational corporations.

Any company can now raise capital for global trade or expansion without relying on U.S. banks or government programs. Cross-border debt and equity securities can be issued on exchanges in London, New York, Tokyo, and many other cities around the world. British, Japanese, French, German, and American banks participate in short- and long-term loans in one another's back yards. Investment banks, merchant banks, and nonbanks have all entered the credit business and together with commercial banks provide a never ending source of funds for practically any company in virtually any nation.

Commercial banks are essential for any company engaged in global trade: exporting, importing, foreign direct investment, most forms of countertrade, financial swaps, foreign exchange, or government projects. Whenever monetary payment is made or received, it goes through the commercial banking system. Major international banks maintain branch offices around the world, and most companies find it advisable to develop a working relationship with one or more prior to entering the global sphere.

Commercial banks must be used for export trade finance. Whether funds originate from government or private sources, a commercial bank remains the focal point. Export credit or guarantees from central bank agencies (e.g., Eximbank in the United States, Export Credit Guarantee Department in Britain, and so on) utilize commercial banks as supporting parties to the transaction. Money (or guarantees) flows from the central bank agency through a commercial bank to either the exporter or the foreign buyer.

Trade credit instruments always emanate from commercial banks. Collections from foreign customers flow through commercial banks. Commercial banks are involved in every aspect of trade finance and cash management, although transaction efficiency and fees vary considerably among banks.

A commercial bank's expertise in handling international transactions is the most important criterion for choosing one. Companies located near a metropolitan area have no difficulty locating a bank with an international department. In the United States all major regional banks have them. The size of the bank isn't as important as its international expertise and the status of its working relationship with domestic and overseas correspondents.

Even if you don't use a commercial bank for financing overseas transactions, you still need one to handle collections, payments, and money transfers. Collections from foreign customers and payments of foreign invoices are seldom done with bank checks. Bank notes, drafts, or bills of exchange are common international payment instruments; checks are not. However, wire transfers remain the favorite for most types of payments.

Banks throughout the world maintain loose associations with other banks (correspondents) in other countries and maintain credit balances in money center banks in every major country—the United States, Britain, France, Germany, Japan, and several others. One bank's notification to another of debits or credits against these balances is referred to as a *wire transfer*. No money actually changes hands.

Investment Banks

Investment banks provide three basic services. They underwrite public issues of debt and equity securities; they trade securities in the open market; and they arrange joint ventures, mergers, acquisitions, and divestitures.

Although investment banks are rapidly becoming the preferred source of funding for major global expansion, multinational commercial banks also compete on the world stage. Many American commercial banks now engage in such esoteric activities as foreign exchange trading and interest-rate swaps.

Investment banking services go far beyond the handling of new securities issues. These banks have made significant headway in capturing a large share of the international mergers and acquisitions market. Investment banks source global buyers and sellers, syndicate bank loans, coordinate joint venture arrangements, act as intermediaries with international development banks, assist in analyzing market trends, and provide an interface with government agencies. They play a major role in financing and coordinating international joint ventures.

Through foreign acquisitions, cross-border ownership, overlapping commercial banking services, and the opening of international branches, more than fifty investment banking houses now dominate the world scene.

Development Banks

Development banks are another group of players in global finance. They function as coordinating and intermediating organizations for raising capital, attracting investment, and providing technical assistance for economic development in nonindustrialized countries.

Four coordinating international development banks focus on large developing regions: the European Bank for Reconstruction and Development (Eastern Europe), the African Development Bank and Fund (Africa), the Asian Development Bank (Asia and the Pacific), and the Inter-American Development Bank (Latin America). These banks are owned and funded by governments within the region, government agencies from industrialized nations, the World Bank, and large international banks.

Regional development banks concentrate on specific, closely knit regions encompassing several countries, such as the Eastern Caribbean or Central America.

Local development banks may be agencies of host-country governments or partially owned and funded by local businesses and banks. All development banks direct their attention to attracting new investment in infrastructure and private sector businesses.

Nonbank Financing Organizations

In recent years a variety of financing sources have sprung up outside the traditional banking circles. This is especially true in the United States, partially in response to overly conservative American commercial banks and partially as a result of confusing and often biased federal assistance programs. These sources provide new, creative financing for global trade.

Several large corporations have formed trading companies and other subsidiaries to enter the global financing market, although most concentrate on parent company needs. A few banks, notably Security Pacific, Morgan Grenfell, and Bank of Boston, have formed subsidiaries to provide export trade finance. The biggest impact, however, is being made by subsidiaries of foreign companies.

The range of services offered by nonbank financing organizations spans the spectrum of trade finance. A few of the more popular include transaction financing independent of a company's other credit lines or balance sheet debt; documentary credits; coordination with government export-import credit and insurance agencies; forfaiting and factoring; spot, forward, and futures exchange transactions; international leasing; Mexican *maquiladora* financing; counter-trade management; trade alliances; capital and interest-rate swaps; asset-based loans; project loans; guarantees; loan packaging; foreign government-subsidized export financing; and conversion of developing country debt instruments. Many of these services involve near money—that is, instruments that have the liquidity of money but are not directly transferable as a means of payment.

These nonbank financing organizations focus on smaller and midsize customers, offering firms that are otherwise shut out by commercial banks an opportunity to compete in international trade.

Although small and midsize exporters seldom come into direct contact with most of the financial institutions and organizations described in this chapter, merely knowing that they exist helps one understand some of the strange goings-on that occur in trade finance. As will be seen in Chapter 8, trade finance, and especially sales finance, is an integral part of any export marketing plan. If you keep the hierarchy of the global financial system in perspective, you should be in a better position to negotiate terms and structure trade finance to meet your company's specific needs.

Chapter 3

Tax Considerations

The Internal Revenue Code specifies that all American taxpayers—business entities as well as individuals—will be taxed on total income, from any source, earned or generated from any location in the world, regardless of whether the country of origin taxes the same income. Obviously, this leaves plenty of room for double taxation: once by a foreign government and again by the U.S. Treasury. Some offsets and deductions are permitted, however, and properly structured transactions can, for the most part, avoid double taxation.

Although several nations are excluded, tax treaties of one form or another have been negotiated with most of America's trading partners. The primary purpose of those tax treaties, known as Tax Information Exchange Agreements (TIEAs), is to provide the taxing authorities of both signatory countries with free access to information about business transactions in one country by companies domiciled in the other country. It should be noted that IRS foreign tax deductions and tax credits are not affected by TIEAs.

U.S. companies get some benefit from TIEAs, but not much. For example, employees of U.S. companies that attend meetings or conventions in TIEA countries are permitted a deduction for travel expenses without regard to the more stringent rules generally applicable to foreign conventions.

Of greater benefit, countries with executed TIEAs qualify as locations for the establishment of U.S. foreign sales corporations, or FSCs (discussed later in this chapter). Moreover, certain federal financial assistance programs mandate that the recipient country have executed a TIEA. The Caribbean Basin Initiative, for example, stipulates that a country must execute a TIEA to be eligible for project financing under Puerto Rico's Section 936 program.

FOREIGN TAX DEDUCTIONS AND CREDITS

A U.S. taxpayer may either deduct foreign income taxes paid or accrued to a foreign government or take a credit against its federal tax liability. As long as the foreign tax paid or accrued represents an income tax or a tax imposed in lieu of an income tax, it qualifies. Neither a deduction nor a tax credit may be taken for other types of taxes imposed by a foreign country. It should be noted. however, that foreign tax credits cannot be used to reduce taxes on income from sources within the United States.

As long as IRS rates were similar to those imposed by foreign countries, this limitation made some sense. Now, however, with the maximum U.S. rate for corporations standing at 35 percent and other countries, such as Germany, imposing rates far in excess of this rate, a situation can easily occur wherein the tax credit will exceed the U.S. tax liability on foreign income. The following example illustrates the calculation:

Income from German operations	$100,000
Income from U.S. operations	200,000
Total worldwide taxable income	$300,000
U.S. tax rate	35%
Tentative U.S. taxes	$105,000

Limitation:

$$\frac{\text{Foreign income} \quad \$100,000}{\text{Worldwide income} \quad \$300,000} \times \text{U.S. tax of } \$105,000 = \$35,000$$

The tax credit is limited to $35,000, even though Germany, with a tax rate of 50 percent, imposed a tax of $50,000 on the company's German income of $100,000. The difference between $50,000 and $35,000 ($15,000) can be carried back two years and forward five years. However, carrybacks and carryforwards are still subject to the limitation test in each of the applicable years. In addition, foreign losses can be used only to offset foreign income and cannot be deducted from U.S.-source income. Other less important restrictions may also apply.

Recapture of Foreign Losses

An overall foreign loss sustained in any given tax year is subject to recapture in later years. An overall foreign loss is defined as the amount by which the sum of foreign expenses, losses, and other deductions properly allocable to foreign source income exceeds the gross income from these foreign sources. Generally, the amount of foreign loss recharacterized as income is limited to the lesser of the overall foreign loss for the year earlier or 50 percent of the foreign-source taxable income of the current year.

In other words, if an American company starts up a foreign operation, sustains operating losses for the first few years, and then deducts these losses on its U.S. return, the losses will be reclassified as income in later years and taxed accordingly. It's the same principle as the recapture of depreciation when depreciated assets are sold.

Any gain on the disposition of business property used outside the United States during the preceding three-year period will also be subject to the recapture rules, with minor exceptions. Therefore, the disposition of foreign businesses or other foreign assets may result in both a reduction of the limitation on foreign tax credits and an increase in taxable income.

Locating in Puerto Rico

Puerto Rico is not considered a U.S. possession for purposes of qualifying as a foreign location under the foreign sales corporation (FSC) rules. However, Puerto Rican-based subsidiaries do benefit from Section 936 of the tax code. Under Section 936, American subsidiaries that derive a significant portion of their income from Puerto Rican income are considered "936 companies." A percentage of 936-company income derived from Puerto Rican activities is exempt from federal income taxes. If the company repatriates this income to the United States, a "toll gate" tax of 10 percent is imposed by Puerto Rico. As long as the funds remain in Puerto Rican banks or are reinvested in the commonwealth, the exemption holds.

Clearly, for any company seriously considering international trade in the Caribbean, locating a subsidiary in Puerto Rico could make a lot of sense. Not only will it get a significant tax break, it also becomes eligible for a unique financing arrangement jointly sponsored by the United States and Puerto Rico called the Section 936 program (see Chapter 11).

Credits for Taxes of a Foreign Subsidiary

If an American company chooses not to consolidate foreign subsidiaries with domestic operations for tax purposes, but does receive repatriated earnings from the subsidiary, the IRS considers these earnings dividends. The domestic corporation may then elect to take a tax credit for the amount of foreign tax levied against the foreign subsidiary's earnings. The tax base of ownership in the subsidiary is then adjusted by both the amount of the dividend and the tax paid by the subsidiary.

Foreign tax credits may also be taken when a domestic corporation is required to include in its income the undistributed earnings of a controlled foreign corporation.

A number of other special provisions relate to the inclusion or exclusion of foreign income and losses. The applicability of the foreign tax credit, excise taxes on transfers of property to foreign entities, and recognition or nonrecognition of gains on redemption of stock in a foreign-controlled corporation further muddy the waters. These rules are far too complex to discuss here, however, and generally do not apply to smaller companies.

Competent tax advisers can readily describe the effects of special foreign tax matters, and obviously should be consulted prior to entering into in any international transaction. There is one more subject relating to foreign income that may be of interest to business managers, especially owners of smaller businesses: controlled foreign corporation provisions.

Controlled Foreign Corporations

When a foreign corporation is controlled for an uninterrupted period of thirty or more days by a U.S. parent, the parent corporation is taxed on a portion of the foreign subsidiary's undistributed earnings, as well as on earnings distributed in that year. In addition to the thirty-day test, the U.S. parent must own more than 50 percent of the foreign subsidiary's voting interest for at least one day during the taxable year.

When setting up a subsidiary in a foreign country, it is imperative to consult with competent advisers who are conversant not only with local tax regulations, but with the IRS code as well. IRS rules governing foreign holdings of U.S. taxpayers can become extremely complex. Any U.S. company going abroad for the first time should carefully weigh both U.S. and foreign tax implications to be certain of taking advantage of all tax breaks allowed by both countries.

Foreign Personal Holding Company

A foreign corporation is classified as a foreign personal holding company under the following circumstances:

1. At least 60 percent (50 percent after the first year) of its gross income consists of dividends, interest, royalties, annuities, rents (unless 50 percent or more of total gross income), gains on stock and commodity transactions, income from personal service contracts, and other specified types of income.

2. More than 50 percent of the corporation's outstanding stock is owned directly or indirectly by five or fewer U.S. citizens or residents.

A U.S. shareholder of a foreign personal holding company is subject to a tax on both the distributed and undistributed income of the foreign company. The tax is imposed on all income as if it had been actually received as dividend income.

However, dividends and interest received by the foreign personal holding company from certain related foreign corporations are exempt provided that (1) the company paying the interest or dividends is related to the recipient, (2) the company is created or organized under the laws of the recipient's country, and (3) the company has a substantial part of its assets used in its trade or business located in the same foreign country. Tiered foreign subsidiaries that meet these requirements are excludable from foreign personal holding company rules. They may, however, be subject to the foreign-controlled corporation rules.

FOREIGN SALES CORPORATIONS

Exporting companies can nearly always cut their tax bill by using foreign sales corporations (FSCs). With the proper structure, an FSC can save exporters up to 15 percent of taxes on income generated through export sales. To meet IRS criteria, FSCs must be incorporated in a qualified country outside the United States, have a legitimate office in that country, and maintain separate accounting records. The FSC prepares parent-company export invoices to foreign customers and deposits collections from these invoices in a local bank.

Countries that qualify for FSC incorporation and operation are American Samoa, Australia, Austria, Barbados, Belgium, Canada, Cyprus, Denmark, Dominica, Egypt, Finland, France, Germany, Grenada, Guam, Iceland, Ireland, Jamaica, Korea, Malta, Morocco, the Netherlands (but not the Netherlands Antilles), New Zealand, the Northern Mariana Islands, Norway, Pakistan, the Philippines, Sweden, Trinidad and Tobago, and the United States Virgin Islands. Countries in this group that are not U.S. territories must have executed TIEAs with the IRS. The United Kingdom and Italy have not been included because their national laws do not give the IRS sufficient freedom to attach records.

Pragmatically, those countries that offer the most advantages for an FSC office are (1) all the U.S. possessions (American Samoa, Guam, the Northern Mariana Islands, and the U.S. Virgin Islands) and (2) Barbados, Belgium, Ireland, Jamaica, and the Netherlands. These countries have enacted legislation to eliminate or substantially reduce local taxes on FSC income.

To Qualify as an FSC

Large FSCs are used by nearly all of the Fortune 500 companies. Small FSCs can be used by companies with annual export sales of $5 million or less. As an incentive to small businesses, Congress has simplified administrative procedures and reporting requirements for small FSCs. From a practical perspective, however, companies with less than $50,000 in export sales usually find it too expensive to set up and maintain their own FSCs. Recognizing this, several states and trade organizations have started group FSCs called *shared FSCs* for small businesses with less than $50,000 annual export sales (more on shared FSCs a little later).The following criteria must be met to qualify as a FSC:

1. The FSC must be incorporated in a qualified foreign country or in a U.S. possession (not Puerto Rico).
2. There can be no more than twenty-five shareholders.
3. Preferred stock cannot be used.
4. The FSC must maintain an office in a qualified foreign country or U.S. possession.
5. Accounting records must be maintained at the FSC office, and certain other records must be maintained at the parent's U.S. office.
6. At least one non-U.S. resident must be elected to the FSC's board of directors.
7. The FSC cannot be a member of a controlled group of corporations of which a DISC is a member.
8. FSC status must be elected by unanimous consent of the stockholders within the ninety-day period preceding the taxable year for which the election is made.

In addition to these qualifying requirements, an FSC must meet two other criteria. The first, the foreign management test, will be met under the following conditions:

1. Only income that is classified as foreign trade income qualifies for exemption from income tax. Such income is defined as the gross income of the FSC attributable to foreign trading gross receipts.
2. The management of the FSC must take place outside of the United States. In other words, the FSC must be managed by someone other than a U.S. resident.

3. All shareholders and board of directors meetings must be held outside the United States.

4. The FSC's principal bank account must be outside the United States.

5. All dividends, legal fees, accounting fees, and salaries of its officers and directors must be paid from offshore FSC bank accounts.

The second criterion specifies that the "economic process" of an FSC must take place outside the United States. The test for foreign economic process takes two forms: the sales participation test and the direct costs test. To meet the sales participation test, the contract relating to an FSC sales transaction must have been solicited, negotiated, or made outside the United States. This is fairly straightforward and merely means that an exporter (or an agent, when using an export management company) must communicate with the customer and agree to the terms of sale in a location other than the United States.

The direct costs test is a bit more complex. Either one of the following meets the direct cost test:

1. The foreign direct costs incurred by the FSC, or its agent, are at least 50 percent of the total direct costs of the transaction.

2. At least 85 percent of the direct costs incurred with respect to at least two of the following activities are foreign direct costs:

   a. Advertising and sales promotion

   b. Processing customers' orders and arranging for delivery of the product

   c. Transportation from the time of acquisition of the product by the FSC to the delivery to the customer

   d. The determination and transmittal of a final invoice or statement of account to a customer, and the receipt of payment

   e. The assumption of credit risk

Small FSCs have two major advantages over large ones. First, small FSCs can meet the direct cost test with costs incurred in the United States; large FSCs must incur these costs overseas. Second, small FSCs may pay all administrative expenses out of a U.S. bank account; large ones must use an offshore bank.

It's important to note that either the FSC itself or its duly authorized agent may satisfy the requirements of these economic process tests. This agent could be an export management company or some other company providing sales and processing assistance. It could even be the parent company itself.

The economic process tests must be met on a transaction by transaction basis. The invalidation of one transaction does not invalidate other FSC business. On the other hand, the foreign management test must be met at all times during the taxable year.

Customer collections deposited in a foreign bank may be repatriated tax-free and are treated as an exempted dividend by the parent company. Furthermore, from a practical perspective, the FSC office does not have to prepare customer invoices on site. These can be prepared in the United States as part of a company's normal accounting activity. A monthly summary of paid customer invoices is then forwarded to the FSC and held as an accounting record in its office.

Small exporters find that it is not practical to set up a foreign office, staff it, and maintain local accounting records. There are many FSC management companies in all qualified foreign countries that can handle these administrative details at a very low cost. Most large U.S. banks, law firms, and accounting firms with foreign offices provide this service. There are also independent FSC management companies located in nearly all qualifying countries, usually managed by Americans. FSC management company fees are usually quite low. They range from $1,500 to $5,000 a year, depending on the volume of transactions handled and whether the FSC is small or large.

Shared FSCs

Shared FSCs have become popular for exporters with a sales volume of less than $50,000. With a shared FSC, up to twenty-five unrelated exporting companies may form a single FSC without having to issue separate classes of stock to each shareholder. The effect is to share the costs of operating an FSC, but still reap the 15 percent tax benefit. A shared FSC must still have a foreign presence, however, and meet all the other tests previously described.

This is how shared foreign sales corporations (SFSCs) work:

1. As a shareholder of an SFSC, an exporter conducts export sales transactions in the same manner as it would if it did not belong to an SFSC.

2. Upon receiving payment on a transaction, the exporter might be required to transfer part of the collected funds to the SFSC to cover operating expenses.

3. At the end of the taxable year, the exporter pays a commission to the SFSC and, in return, receives a tax-free dividend distribution.

4. The SFSC management company files a tax return.

5. The exporter reports on its tax return those transactions on which commission was paid to the SFSC.

A wide range of public- and private-sector organizations have sponsored and developed SFSCs, including states, trade associations, port authorities, banks, and free-trade zones. A sponsor may also require that any exporter participating in the SFSC meet certain requirements, such as being a member of the trade association or being resident in the state.

SPECIAL TAX CONSIDERATIONS

Several other matters related to taxes of one form or another affect a company's strategic foreign-trade decisions. Tax considerations relating to foreign acquisitions, foreign partnerships, and joint ventures are covered later in this chapter. Chapter 15 evaluates the pros and cons of using tax-haven entities for offshore transactions. In addition to these rather broad tax-planning matters, certain exporters should be aware of such special matters as customs drawbacks, the use of free-trade zones, and foreign licensing of intellectual property.

Customs Drawbacks

Customs drawbacks are a form of tax relief for U.S. exporters that import goods and commodities to be used in the processing or assembly of products for export. Chapter 16 discusses drawbacks in detail, and the topic is mentioned here only to point out that such tax relief does exist.

In essence, a customs or "duty" drawback enables exporters that include imports in their products to exclude the additional costs of U.S. import duties when pricing finished products. In certain instances, this can make the difference between being competitive and not being competitive.

Different drawbacks apply to different manufacturing and assembly processes, so it's important to get the facts on which drawbacks might apply to your particular importing needs. Such information may be obtained directly from the U.S. Customs Service at

Entry Rulings Branch
U.S. Customs Service
1301 Constitution Avenue, N.W.
Washington, DC 20229
Telephone: (202) 566-5856

Free-Trade Zones

More than 300 free-trade zones flourish in various countries around the world. Although many variations exist, the theory behind free-trade zones is that materials, parts, or finished products imported and used in an assembly or other finishing process for goods to be exported from the zone are exempt from local taxes, license fees, and customs duties, as are goods exported from the zone. As with U.S. customs drawbacks, free trade zones may keep the total cost of products at a competitive level.

Within the United States, free trade zones are called foreign-trade zones, but the idea is the same. Approximately seventy such zones are scattered throughout forty eight of the fifty states. No duties or foreign excise taxes are charged on foreign goods moving into these zones, provided they are eventually exported. Chapter 16 details the use of American foreign trade zones. For locations of these zones in your region, contact the nearest International Trade Administration office.

Licensing of Services

When you sell technology, management know-how, or intangible property—such as proprietary books, copyrighted concepts, training seminars, or software programs—the U.S. government and most foreign governments consider such sales a "material export." As such, the income derived from the sale may be subject to foreign taxes. In the case of royalties, for instance, many countries require local companies to deduct (withhold) appropriate taxes from royalty payments.

Not only does foreign tax withholding reduce the amount of cash received for your intangible sale, it also adds to the cost of doing business in that country. There is some relief, however. As previously discussed, when you sell into countries that have executed a tax treaty with the United States, foreign taxes can be deducted from your company's worldwide taxable income or credited against U.S. tax liabilities. The following section about international acquisitions points out some quirks in applying these deductions or credits that could affect how you structure a licensing transaction.

INTERNATIONAL ACQUISITIONS

Under certain circumstances, exporting companies may find it desirable to establish an overseas branch office or production facility. Although the acquisition of a going business is the fastest way to do it, some serious tax questions arise.

The basic problem centers on two features of the Code: the classification of income baskets for purposes of utilizing the foreign tax credit and the treatment of dispositions of foreign assets.

To prevent U.S. taxpayers from moving their income offshore and from engaging in other tax-saving efforts, Section 904 of the Code requires that foreign tax credits be applied separately to certain classifications of income called *baskets*. Different baskets contain income from high-withholding-tax interest, income from financial services and shipping, certain types of dividends, certain types of foreign trade income, and certain distributions from FSCs. The two most troublesome categories, however, are the passive income basket and the general income basket.

The passive basket consists of income from interest, dividends, and gains on the sale of passive assets. The general basket consists of all income not classified in one of the other baskets. General business income is normally the largest component of the general basket. Dividends, rents, interest, and royalties paid by a controlled foreign corporation to a U.S. parent retain the same characteristics they had with the foreign company, and do not take on the character of the current distribution. This prevents a U.S. parent from reclassifying distributions into lesser-used baskets such as the passive basket and forces such income into the general basket.

Since foreign tax credit limitations are limitations per basket, not in total, any excess credit from the general basket cannot be used as an offset to the passive basket. Furthermore, it is unlikely that a U.S. corporation will ever have excess foreign tax credits from one item of income in the passive basket to offset the residual U.S. tax on another item of passive income. The high-tax kickout rule sees to that. This rule specifies that passive income that is subject to a foreign income tax rate greater than the U.S. 34 percent rate is reclassified as general basket income.

The basket rules about foreign tax credit limitations sound complex—and they are. However, they have a significant impact on the way a foreign acquisition is structured. If the seller is a U.S. company, it will obviously try to minimize the foreign income taxes imposed on the transaction and maximize the application of the foreign tax credit against the U.S. tax liability. The buyer, on the other hand, should try to minimize the foreign taxes on income generated after the deal closes by obtaining a stepped up depreciation basis for assets in countries with high tax rates.

The Implications of Section 338

Section 338 of the Code states that a corporation that purchases at least 80 percent of the stock of another company may elect to treat the acquisition as a purchase of assets. The target company is then considered to have repurchased these same assets at a price equal to the amount the buyer paid for them. This, in turn, provides a new, higher depreciation base for future years.

Although Section 338 write-ups do not apply to domestic acquisitions, when the acquired company is a foreign corporation, not engaged in a U.S. trade or business, and sold by a U.S. corporation, Section 338 write-ups are still permitted.

The gain on the sale must be recognized by the selling corporation and also may result in the inclusion of subpart F income in the seller's taxable income. This is in direct contrast to buying a U.S. corporation, where the tax liability falls on the buyer. For an international purchase from a U.S. seller, a Section 338 election passes the burden of taxation to the seller. Obviously, if the seller is another foreign corporation, such tax matters are moot.

Nontaxable Foreign Acquisitions

Although in the past several years most international acquisitions have involved a cash purchase of stock and have been taxable transactions, foreign acquisitions can also be structured as tax-free reorganizations. For example, assume that a U.S. corporation, American Corp., purchases the assets, or stock, of French Products, a French subsidiary of another U.S. corporation, United States Corp. The tax owed by United States Corp. on the gain from the sale is deferred until United States Corp. disposes of the property received in the transaction—presumably stock of American Corp. The buyer, American Corp., then obtains a carryover basis in the acquired stock of French Products.

To qualify for this treatment, international acquisitions must not only meet the requirements of tax-free reorganizations for domestic acquisitions, but also meet the provisions of Section 367 of the Code.

A complete explanation of the mechanics of these provisions is far too complex to include here. However, if you are considering the acquisition of a foreign corporation, be aware that tax-free reorganizations are possible. By all means, check it out with your tax counsel!

FOREIGN PARTNERSHIPS AND JOINT VENTURES

Many less-developed countries have laws that grant foreign companies tax exemptions in return for investments. Often a local partner, either an individual or a national company, must be involved in the ownership of the business. Sometimes local partners must also participate in the management of the joint venture.

The benefits of such arrangements to the host country are obvious. Not only does it get much needed technical advice and management know-how, but foreign investors also bring hard currency into the country—which can then be used to acquire much needed imports.

Because all local tax burdens are eliminated, such arrangements can be equally advantageous to an American company starting up a business. Of course, even if the host country does not impose a tax, a foreign subsidiary's earnings will be taxed in the United States, in proportion to U.S. ownership of the company. From a business perspective, however, such expansion can mean extra profits to an American company, even after taxes.

SEGREGATING EXPORT ACTIVITIES

One of the interesting features of export trade is how profits can be increased by using separate corporations to segregate export activities from domestic trade. Although such segregation does not affect the ability of the parent company to use its assets and other resources to arrange trade finance, it does provide an extra measure of liability protection from third-party claims.

Several other advantages can be realized simply by providing a mechanism to pass export paperwork through this separate entity, commonly referred to as *reinvoicing*. Depending on the location of the separate export corporation, the following benefits might be realized:

- Invoicing to and payments from a customer can be accomplished in host-country currency, thereby centralizing the currency risk in one location.
- Concentration of international talent should increase management efficiency in such areas as receivables, payables, and multiparty transactions (such as countertrade agreements).
- Cash flow can be shifted between subsidiaries by adept management of collections and trade payments.
- Better credit terms and cooperation can be obtained from international banks.
- Centralization of credit verification and approval activities reduces cost and increases performance.

Reinvoicing is merely a shuffling of paperwork. For example, a manufacturing company in the United States sets up a separate export company in Panama. On paper, this company is responsible for the manufacturer's sales office in Cairo, Egypt. An Egyptian customer places an order for goods on the Cairo office. This sales office places the order on the manufacturing company in the United States.

The goods are shipped from the United States either to the Cairo office for reshipment or direct to the customer. The manufacturing company then invoices the export company in Panama in Panamanian balboas, or in U.S. dollars. The export company then reinvoices Cairo in Egyptian pounds. The sales office then invoices the customer in local currency. Payment is made through the same cycle, with the Panamanian company managing the exchange risk.

Chapter 15 describes how U.S. exporters can enjoy added tax benefits by reinvoicing through a tax-haven location. Many Fortune 500 companies use tax haven subsidiaries—and do so within the constraining laws of the U.S. tax code. It's not a sure-fire way to shelter all foreign income, but, judiciously managed, tax-haven subsidiaries can be beneficial to anyone with foreign interests. And, with the proper ownership structure, they are perfectly legal.

The tax laws reviewed in this chapter reflect interpretations of the U.S. tax code and subsequent regulations and rulings through 1992. Tax laws keep changing, however, so don't base strategies on these brief outlines. Check out your plans with your tax counsel before making any commitments.

Chapter 4

Sources of Information

The hardest part about getting information on export markets, sales financing options, joint venture partners, trade barriers and incentives, distribution channels—in fact, everything having to do with international trade—is not that such information is scarce but that too much information is available from too many sources. The barrage of international trade data collected and distributed by federal and state agencies, trade associations, and private organizations rivals the deluge of junk mail that fills our mailboxes and jams our fax machines. The only way to cope with such an avalanche of data is to sort out that which can be useful and ignore the rest.

Before beginning an export program or expanding to new offshore markets, it's important to gather as much pertinent information as possible from authoritative sources. "Pertinent" and "authoritative" are the operative words. This chapter discloses the major authoritative information sources. Only you can determine whether the information you get is pertinent.

In a broad sense, six types of information can be very useful for evaluating new export markets:

- Market demographics, product demand, and competition
- Advertising and sales promotion alternatives
- Distribution channels
- Customs duties, trade regulations, and tax requirements
- Transport options
- Sales finance

Of course, one could add several other items to this list for any given country, such as current and projected political stability, advantages or barriers from trading blocs, local business climate, status of U.S. government trade policies, and so on. If you plan to export to turbulent less-developed countries, all such matters should be researched. Obviously, markets in developed regions like Western Europe or Japan require less research than those in Peru, Zimbabwe, or Pakistan.

A good bit of marketing, legal, transport, and finance data can be gathered without leaving your office. However, detailed information about specific local matters, such as potential joint venture partners, tariffs and quotas, cultural anomalies, and infrastructure hurdles, must be derived locally. This requires an on-site country survey, the details of which will be covered in Chapter 6.

Information can be obtained in the United States from federal agencies, state and local trade bureaus, trade associations, banks, and professional advisers. Moreover, one can glean a fairly comprehensive overview of specific topics and countries from international trade books and periodicals.

Figure 4.1 attempts to bring order out of chaos by classifying the kinds of information that can be obtained from each of the major sources.

Figure 4-1
Types of Information by Source

U.S. Government Agencies
- Market demographics, product demand, and competition
- Distribution channels and joint venture partners
- U.S. customs, regulatory, and tax issues
- Sales finance
- Credit and insurance

State and Local Government Bureaus
- Market demographics, product demand, and competition
- Transport peculiarities
- Sales finance

Trade Associations and Trade Groups
- Market demographics, product demand, and competition
- Advertising and sales promotion alternatives
- Distribution channels
- Customs regulations and tax issues

Professional Advisers
- Distribution channels and joint venture partners
- Host-country, legal, accounting, and tax requirements
- Sales finance

Personal Research
- Market demographics, product demand, and competition
- Advertising and sales promotion alternatives
- Distribution channels
- Sales finance
- Credit and insurance

U.S. GOVERNMENT AGENCIES

The federal government collects, collates, and distributes international trade data from a variety of foreign and domestic sources. Much of it is free, although some reports, pamphlets, and booklets carry a nominal price tag. A variety of federal agencies compile data for specific purposes. Some, like several of those within the Department of Commerce, provide rather general information that might be of universal interest to U.S. exporters. Others concentrate on specific industries, areas of the world, or types of data. The street address for all Department of Commerce offices, programs, departments, and services is

> Department of Commerce
> 14th Street and Constitution Avenue N.W.
> Washington, DC 20230

Department of Commerce

The Department of Commerce (DOC) supports U.S. business interests domestically and internationally with a wealth of services, resources, and data. Before you spend time searching through reams of reports, booklets, and pamphlets from various DOC departments, however, it's a good idea to check out three catalog-type services:

- The *Trade Promotion Coordinating Committee (TPCC)* is billed as a one-stop shop for information on government programs and activities that support U.S. exporters. This office can tell you where to go to get information on a whole range of exporting support services, such as counseling, seminars and conferences, sources of overseas buyers and sales representatives, locations and dates of overseas trade fairs and trade missions, export financing, and organizations that provide technical assistance. The TPCC also publishes an invaluable directory entitled *Export Programs—A Business Directory of U.S. Government Resources*, May 1992.

  The office can be reached at

  > Trade Information Center
  > Telephone: 1-800-872-8723
  > Fax: (202) 482-4473

- The *National Trade Data Bank (NTDB)* was established by the Omnibus Trade and Competitiveness Act of 1988 to provide "reasonable access, including electronic access" to export promotion and international economic information. The NTDB is fifteen federal agencies. It contains more than 100,000 documents in the form of books, pamphlets, bulletins, and reports, such as

  1. *The Basic Guide to Exporting*, which summarizes basic export information

  2. *The World Fact Book*, which contains country-specific statistics and other data

3. *The Industrial Outlook*, which contains industry-specific statistics and data

4. Market research reports, that relate market and economic trends from combined industry-country data

5. *Foreign Traders Index*, which identifies foreign businesses seeking to import U.S. products

The NTDB database is released monthly on CD-ROM and can be used on any IBM-compatible personal computer equipped with a CD-ROM reader. For further information, contact

> Economics and Statistics Administration
> Office of Business Analysis
> HCHB Room 4885
> Telephone: (202) 482-1986

- The *Electronic Bulletin Board (EBB)* is a personal computer-based electronic bulletin board that helps you locate and read press releases and data files. Moreover, these files can be downloaded using error-free transmission protocols. The files contain information on sales leads, exchange rates, money supplies, consumer and producer price indexes, foreign trade data, industry statistics, and many more reports compiled by the Bureau of Economic Analysis, the Bureau of the Census, the Bureau of Labor Statistics, the Federal Reserve Board, the Department of the Treasury, and other federal agencies.

  The EBB can be accessed from personal computers with a modem (300, 1,200, 2,400, or 9,600 bps) and standard communications software. For further information, call the EBB office at (202) 482-1986.

Most international trade activities are centered in the DOC's International Trade Administration (ITA), located in Room 1128 at the Department of Commerce, telephone (202) 377-3808. According to its mission statement, ITA's primary objective is to provide specialized information and counseling to U.S. businesses involved in international trade. ITA staff can assist U.S. exporters in locating, gaining access to, and developing foreign markets nearly anywhere in the world. The agency also provides detailed information—such as demographics, product demand trends, and local availability of products—about specific markets.

All exporters should be familiar with three major sections of the ITA:

- U.S. and Foreign Commercial Services (US&FCS); telephone (202) 377-5777
- Trade Development (TD); telephone: (202) 377-1461
- International Economic Policy (IEP); telephone (202) 377-3022

Each of these sections offers a variety of services. World Trader Data Reports are by far the most popular.

World Trader Data Reports. World Trader Data Reports, or WTDR, are customized reports, either hard copy or computer downloaded, that contain business information about potential foreign customers. These reports include background information on the company (which may be either public- or private-sector), its reputation in the business community, its creditworthiness, and its overall reliability and suitability as a customer for U.S. businesses. Although the reports do not include financial information, they do show the potential customer's class of organization, year established, relative size and number of employees, market reach, product lines, and trade references (including bank references in some cases).

Trade Opportunities Program. Through the Trade Opportunities Program (TOP), exporters can obtain current sales leads of foreign customers seeking to buy their products or services. TOP also keeps a current listing of foreign sales agents seeking to represent U.S. exporters. This can be an especially valuable resource for companies beginning an export program who need local sources of distribution.

Agent/Distributor Service. The Agent/Distributor Service (A/DS) offers a customized search for qualified foreign representatives. The process involves distributing your company's sales literature and then choosing six foreign prospects who express an interest in representing your lines. Quite frequently, sufficient information isn't available through the TOP and you'll be better off going this route, even though there is a small charge.

Commercial News USA. Commercial News USA is a catalog published ten times each year to promote the products and services of U.S. exporters to more than 100,000 international agents, distributors, government officials, and potential customers. The catalog comprises three sections:

- Service promotions, which advertises a broad range of services for sale
- New product promotions, which advertises new products offered, including product pictures and descriptions, along with business addresses for more information
- Special industry promotions, which push technologies and products of a single industry

For $250 and a black-and-white picture of your product, you can run an advertisement in this catalog that could bring a significant number of sales leads.

In addition to providing sales leads and contacts with potential sales representatives, the ITA sponsors a series of matchmaker events, overseas trade missions, overseas catalog and video shows, foreign buyer programs, and overseas trade fairs aimed at bringing U.S. exporters together with potential foreign buyers.

Matchmaker events. Matchmaker events are specifically designed for small-business executives. Matchmaker trade delegations are structured to introduce U.S. exporters to new overseas markets. These inexpensive short trips introduce you to prospective foreign sales representatives and/or joint venture partners who are specifically interested in handling your product line.

Overseas trade missions. Trade missions are groups of U.S. executives that travel together to one or more countries to pursue sales or joint venture leads. Participants meet with local business and government leaders who can help in developing local marketing programs. Department of Commerce staff travel with the delegation and are available to arrange a full schedule of local appointments, as desired.

Overseas catalog and video shows. Catalog and video shows are promotions prepared by ITA industry experts and then distributed to selected foreign audiences. At your request, the ITA will include sales promotion literature and videos of your product lines. This can be an excellent way to promote export products without incurring the cost or time of overseas travel.

Foreign buyer programs. Periodically, the ITA conducts trade shows in the United States that are attended by foreign buyers. This is another chance to display your wares without going overseas. The shows are promoted worldwide and usually attract a sizable audience.

Overseas trade fairs. International trade fairs are usually much larger and cover more product lines than the ITA foreign buyer programs. Not only do you meet prospective buyers in person, you also have an excellent opportunity to size up your competition. These fairs are well attended, so it is likely that most if not all of your competitors will be there.

Companies that have never been involved in exporting usually face a bewildering array of possibilities for doing market research. This confusion can and often does dissuade those who are merely considering the possibility of exporting from proceeding. In an effort to push them on, the ITA maintains a bank of market research information, resources, and programs. Here are the major ones:

- *Commercial Information Management System (CIMS).* This very large computer database is linked to ITA offices worldwide. ITA trade specialists at district and branch offices use this database to offer tailor-made information packages covering

  a. Foreign business and economic climates

  b. Foreign import restrictions

  c. Tariff and nontariff barriers

  d. Competition

  e. Distribution practices

    f. Sales promotion alternatives

    g. Product standards

    h. Customer listings

Reports are available for just about any country, either in hard copy or computer downloaded. There is a minimal charge, however, determined case by case.

- *Counseling.* If you are not sure you want to get into exporting or if you don't know where to start, it's not a bad idea to set up a counseling appointment with a trade specialist at one of the US&FCS branch or district offices or at ITA's Washington office. This is an excellent way to learn the steps involved in getting started, ITA programs that can be of the greatest assistance, and enough corollary information to make a go-no-go decision.

  These offices also have videotapes that help clarify some of the more obtuse exporting concepts and regulations, with concrete examples of small and midsize companies that are prospering in their export programs.

- *Comparison Shopping.* This is another customized service; it digs out customized information about market demand, competitors' market shares, distributors, and qualified buyers. US&FCS staff conduct interviews in the host country to obtain this data specifically for your company. Obviously, a fee is charged.

  In addition to customized interviews, comparative statistical reports are available that show trends in imported products, unit values, quantities sold, and market share percentages.

While we're on the subject of US&FCS assistance, it might help to clarify exactly what this branch of the ITA does.

U.S. and Foreign Commercial Service

The U.S. and Foreign Commercial Service (US&FCS) section of the ITA (located in Room 3012 of the DOC) was created specifically to help U.S. exporters compete in global markets. Through sixty seven offices in major U.S. cities and 126 offices in foreign locations, US&FCS staff compile a wide array of business data. Specific services offered by US&FCS offices include:

- Evaluating potential local customers
- Sourcing sales agents
- Performing market research
- Counseling
- Setting up local appointments with buyers and local government bureaucrats
- Representing companies adversely affected by the imposition of new trade barriers.

District Export Councils

In addition to direct assistance from ITA and US&FCS staff, many new-to-exporting companies find it helpful to check out the experiences of veteran U.S. exporters in a given market or in dealing with a specific agency. This can be accomplished through Department of Commerce—sponsored District Export Councils (DECs). DEC member firms represent a cross section of U.S. businesses. Employees of these companies volunteer their time to counsel and assist new-to-exporting companies. Of all the services offered by the Department, this can easily be the most beneficial for businesses that are ready to make an exporting commitment.

International Economic Policy

International Economic Policy (IEP) offices provide another source of information on trade potential in specific countries. Country specialists in Washington keep abreast of rapidly changing political and economic conditions in their assigned countries, counsel new exporters, and arrange seminars on foreign trade and direct investment.

Trade Development

As with other agencies, the Trade Development (TD) program's primary mission is to help U.S. companies compete internationally. TD staff members are organized by industry specialization to identify industrywide exporting opportunities and obstacles. They compile market research data, conduct industry seminars and trade missions, and help U.S. companies locate foreign buyers. A series of industry-sensitive reports and analyses can be obtained from Trade Development offices.

ITA Publications

The International Trade Administration also publishes a variety of periodicals, reports, and bulletins. Here is a brief description of the main ones.

- *Overseas Business Reports* give market information on specific countries. The reports include trade outlook, various statistics, trade regulations, and overall country profiles. They are available for $14 each from the Government Printing Office.

- *Market Share Reports (commodity series)* compare the competitive positions of U.S. and foreign exporters by commodity and provide statistical trends in market shares. Individual country reports are available from the National Technical Information Service at $11 for each commodity report.

- *Foreign Economic Trends* shows a variety of current economic and business data for individual countries. Annual subscriptions cost $55 and individual reports $1 from the Government Printing Office.

- *Business America*, a biweekly magazine, is probably the ITA's best-known publication. It provides a wide range of information, including trade leads, export tips, individual country marketing reports and economic analyses, and advance notice of trade fairs and exhibitions. The inclusion of actual company success stories makes it a more lively read than most government publications. Annual subscriptions cost $40 and individual copies cost $1.75, both from the Government Printing Office

The ITA publications sales branch is located in Room 1617 of the DOC and can be reached by telephone at (202) 377-5494.

Bureau of Export Administration

The Bureau of Export Administration (BXA) also falls under the Department of Commerce. It is a relatively new agency whose mission is to direct U.S. export policy. It also investigates breaches of federal export control laws and administers antiboycott laws.

The bureau's main interface with exporters involves export licensing. It facilitates the application of licenses through two services:

1. *The Export Application and Information Network (ELAIN)* is a computer-based system that can be used to file export license applications directly with the Department of Commerce. It can be accessed directly through CompuServe. When applications are approved, licenses are issued electronically through the computer system. The computer access number is (203) 377-4811.

2. *The System for Tracking Export License Applications (STELA)* enables applicants to trace the status of their export license application by dialing (203) 377-2753.

Further information can be obtained from

>Bureau of Export Administration
>Exporter Assistance Staff
>Room 1099D
>Telephone: (202) 377-1455

Center for International Research

The Center for International Research (CIR) is a section in the Bureau of the Census. It maintains a computer database of worldwide demographic, economic, and social data. This database—called, quite naturally, the International Data Base—is especially helpful for developing strategic analysis of potential markets and projected market trends. The database has the following categories:

- Population, by urban/rural, age, and sex
- Vital statistics, including infant mortality rates and life expectancy tables
- Health and nutrition data

- Fertility and child survivorship
- Migration/foreign-born and refugee data
- Provinces and cities
- Marital status and marriage/family planning statistics
- Ethnic, religious, and language groups
- Literacy and education
- Labor force, employment, income, and gross national product statistics
- Household size and housing indicators

Further information can be obtained from

> Center for International Research
> Bureau of the Census
> Scuderi Building
> Washington, DC 20233
> Telephone: (301) 763-2870

Miscellaneous Department of Commerce Agencies

Four other agencies may be helpful in answering specific questions:

- *National Oceanic and Atmospheric Administration (NOAA)* promotes exports from seafood suppliers by sourcing trade leads, conducting trade missions, researching foreign markets, and conducting seminars. Telephone: (202) 443-8910.

- *National Center for Standards and Certificates Information (NCSCI)* is the government's storage center for standards information. It provides a hotline that you can use to find out about the latest notifications that may affect standards and certification requirements for your products. The telephone number is (301) 975-4041.

- *U.S. Travel and Tourism Administration (USTTA)* promotes the export of tourism related products and services. This agency also assists U.S. companies in sourcing and negotiating foreign tourism joint ventures. Telephone: (202) 377-4904.

- *Minority Business Development Agency (MBDA)* offers special assistance to minority-owned exporters. Telephone: (202) 377-2414.

Small Business Administration

Several regional offices of the Small Business Administration (SBA) are very active in small-business counseling (through Service Corps of Retired Executives, or SCORE, chapters) and in helping small businesses raise capital. However, these activities relate almost exclusively to domestic business. Most of the SBA's regional, district, and branch offices are ill equipped to do the same for international trade.

Although the SBA's mandate includes assisting small businesses to develop and finance export trade, budgetary constraints and a lack of qualified personnel severely limit the agency's involvement. Nevertheless, a few offices do have personnel who are sufficiently familiar with international trade to be of some assistance; therefore, the SBA should not be totally ignored. Your best bet is to work directly through the SBA's Washington office, which can be reached at

Office of International Trade
Small Business Administration
1441 L Street, N.W.
Washington, DC 20416
Telephone: (202) 653-7561

Officially, the SBA offers the following types of assistance:

- Export counseling
- Export training cosponsored with other federal agencies
- Legal advice through the Export Legal Assistance Network staffed by lawyers from the International Law Council of the Federal Bar Association
- Data reports from the Export Information System (XIS), classified by Standard International Trade Classification (SITC) codes established at the United Nations
- Matchmaker events, which are trade delegations organized to meet prospective foreign sales representatives and joint venture partners, similar to the matchmaker events sponsored directly by the Department of Commerce

The SBA also has an export finance program called the Export Revolving Line of Credit program (ERLC), reviewed in Chap. 9.

A wide range of publications is probably the SBA's biggest contribution to small business exporters. These reports, guides, and booklets disclose basic information about the fundamentals of exporting. A catalog of such publications can be obtained from:

SBA Publications
Office of International Trade—Room 501A
Small Business Administration
1441 L Street, N.W.
Washington, DC 20416
Telephone: (202) 653-7794

Foreign Agricultural Service

The Foreign Agricultural Service (FAS) of the Department of Agriculture is the principal agency involved in promoting U.S. agricultural exports. Its main contribution is to arrange international trade shows and trade missions with the help of a network of counselors, attaches, trade officers, commodity analysts, and marketing specialists.

FAS has trade offices in fifteen major-market countries that function as service centers for U.S. exporters and foreign buyers. Furthermore, agricultural affairs offices are located in U.S. embassies throughout the world. Export marketing support is offered through the Targeted Export Assistance program (TEA), which helps nonprofit industry trade groups finance promotional activities for agricultural exports that may be at a disadvantage because of unfair foreign trade practices.

The various FAS marketing and commodity divisions can be reached by telephone in area code (202) as follows:

Dairy, livestock, and poultry	447-8031
Forest products	382-8138
Grain and feed	447-6219
Horticulture and tropical products	447-6590
Oilseed and oilseed products	447-7037
Tobacco, cotton, and seeds	382-9516
High-value products	447-6343

Also within the FAS, the Minority and Small Business Export Program, which can be reached at (202) 382-9498, provides a mechanism to help small and minority-owned agricultural businesses get started in international trade.

The Agricultural Information and Marketing Services (AIMS) program provides information on foreign trade contacts and buyer identification, and also advertises U.S exports.

In addition, the FAS helps finance commodity exports with export credits through the Commodity Credit Corporation and the P.L.480 Food for Peace program.

In addition to providing information and finance services to exporters, the FAS publishes reports and periodicals that can, at times, be helpful. For a current listing of publications, contact the FAS directly at

FAS Publications
Foreign Agricultural Service
Room 5020, South Building
14th Street & Independence Avenue, S.W.
Washington, DC 20250
Telephone: (202) 447-7937

Eximbank

The Export-Import Bank of the United States (Eximbank) offers comprehensive financing and insurance assistance for U.S. exporters. The full range of these programs is described in Chapter 9. In addition, Eximbank maintains a special office whose mission is to encourage small businesses to sell internationally. This office provides information on the availability and use of export credit insurance, guarantees, and direct and intermediary loans. It can be reached at

Export-Import Bank of the United States
811 Vermont Avenue, N.W.
Washington, DC 20571
Telephone: (202) 289-2703 or (800) 424-5201

Eximbank and its sister organization, the Foreign Credit Insurance Association (FCIA), also produce a series of publications that may be of use to new-to-exporting companies. Order a catalog directly from

Eximbank/FCIA Publications
Public Affairs Office
Export-Import Bank of the United States
811 Vermont Avenue, N.W.
Washington, DC 20571
Telephone: (202) 566-8990 or (800) 424-5201

Department of State

Private businesses usually don't have much contact with the Department of State except in unusual circumstances, such as expropriation of foreign shipments or other matters that involve government-to-government coordination. However, the Department of State can be very helpful in supplying certain types of commercial information.

Regional Bureau country desk officers maintain day-to-day contact with international diplomatic posts. When you plan to enter a new export market, it can't hurt to check with the appropriate desk officer to make sure that no unusual political or economic events are occurring.

In addition, for specialized assistance with unusual problems, try the Office of Commercial, Legislative, and Public Affairs at (202) 647-1942. If you need to contact the Department of State by mail or in person, its address and central telephone numbers are

U.S. Department of State
2201 C Street, N.W.
Washington, DC 20520
Telephone: (202) 647-4000

U.S. Agency for International Development

The Agency for International Development (AID) administers economic assistance programs in more than sixty developing countries. These programs are designed to encourage economic development in AID-approved countries through the purchase of U.S. goods and services, financed by AID funds. When AID finances a project, one requirement placed on recipient governments is that government, or its contracted agencies, must purchase a percentage of the products and services needed to complete the project from U.S. exporters. AID projects can therefore provide excellent buyer contacts in new foreign markets. And American exporters can be assured of getting paid in U.S. dollars!

AID has a specific agency set up to act as an advocate for small and disadvantaged exporters called the Office of Small and Disadvantaged Business Utilization/Minority Resource Center. The center can be contacted directly at

Office of Small and Disadvantaged Business Utilization/
Minority Resource Center
Room 1400-A
U.S. Agency for International Development
320 21st Street, N.W.
Washington, DC 20523
Telephone: (703) 875-1551

Specifically, this office performs four services:

1. It serves as an information clearinghouse for U.S. businesses, organizations, and institutions that are interested in participating in the procurement and contracting process for AID-financed goods and services.

2. It maintains an AID Consultant Registry Information System (ACRIS), which is a computer database of more than 2,000 companies, organizations, institutions, and individual consultants with expressed capabilities that match AID project requirements.

3. It counsels U.S. businesses, organizations, and institutions on how to do business with AID.

4. It negotiates AID procurement and contracting goals for small, disadvantaged, and women-owned firms in conjunction with the SBA.

AID publications can be ordered by calling (202) 875-1590.

Other Federal Agencies Helping Exporters

Exporters that need advice on such matters as U.S. customs, ocean shipping, overseas mail delivery, or investigating the potential for an offshore facility may obtain information from the following agencies:

U.S. Customs Service
1301 Constitution Avenue, N.W.
Washington, DC 20229
Telephone: (202) 566-8195

Maritime Administration
U.S. Department of Transportation
400 Seventh Street, S.W.
Washington, DC 20590
Telephone: (202) 366-5517

U.S. Postal Service
475 L'Enfant Plaza, S.W.
Washington, DC 20260
Telephone: (202) 268-2000

Overseas Private Investment Corporation (OPIC)
1615 M Street, N.W.
Washington, DC 20527
Telephone: (202) 457-7010 or (800) 424-6742

STATE AND LOCAL FOREIGN-TRADE ASSISTANCE

Nearly every state and many cities maintain active foreign-trade commissions with missions to assist local companies in getting into and expanding their export programs. The main objective, of course, is to foster business activity in that city or state, which in turn will create jobs and tax revenues. Although each state and city offers slightly different incentives and assistance, they do have common features.

In general, these local trade bureaus offer export counseling, coordination with federal export assistance programs, statistical data on the experience of local exporting firms, a modest amount of foreign market research information, technical assistance, and financing advice. Many states and some cities participate in Eximbank's City-State Agency Cooperation program to help finance exports (see Chapter 9).

State and city trade commissions work closely with local industry trade groups. Membership in your trade association may well bring added state and/or local foreign trade assistance. Specific advice and assistance in such matters as identification of reliable freight forwarders, trading companies, and export management firms are often relayed from local trade commissions to private trade associations or local trade groups.

Depending on your industry and city, trade associations and trade groups can be either very active or dormant. Several of the more active ones sponsor trade shows, trade missions, industry symposiums on foreign trade, and a wealth of other assistance programs. It can't hurt to check out what's available in your area.

State foreign trade bureaus also help companies or organizations set up local free-trade zones or, at a minimum, help local exporters identify existing zones that best serve their purposes.

PROFESSIONAL ADVISERS AND PRIVATE RESEARCH

Regardless of the volume of data supplied by federal, state, and local government agencies or industry trade associations and local trade groups, nothing beats doing your own market research. When you start gathering public data, it will become obvious that much of it has been sifted through and selected to meet the objectives of the particular agency or trade bureau. Furthermore, in many cases the data may be six months to a year old. International trade is very dynamic, and decisions should be made on the basis of current information, untainted by the supplier's mission or objectives. And the only way to get current, clean data is by gathering it yourself.

Most professional advisers, especially large public accounting firms and international consultants, have a wealth of current information in their possession, gathered from clients as well as their own research. All of the multinational accounting firms do an excellent job of maintaining up-to-date information from those foreign cities and countries in which they have offices.

Andersen Consulting (part of Arthur Andersen & Co.), McKinsey & Co., and Tower & Perrin are a few of the major consulting firms that are active in international circles. If you are interested in Latin American countries as potential markets, the main U.S. offices of Ernst & Young have proven to be excellent sources of information relayed from their Latin American branches.

Multinational banks are also invaluable resources. Citibank, Chase Manhattan, Bankers Trust, Chemical Bank, Bank of America, and American Express all have foreign branches scattered around the world that compile local economic, business, and political data. Depending on your choice of foreign markets, major foreign banks can also be helpful. British banks like Barclays, Midland, Lloyds, and National Westminster are especially helpful. German, French, and Japanese banks can provide current information on selected markets, provided you can get through to the right person.

Banks belonging to the Hong Kong and Shanghai Banking Group have worldwide contacts that can lead you to appropriate local joint venture partners, bureaucrats, or even potential customers. For foreign financing or merger and acquisition information, it's hard to beat investment banks such as Bear Stearns, Goldman Sachs, Merrill Lynch, and so on.

Accounting firms, consulting firms, banks, and investment banks all publish newsletters and other publications about international trade for their clients/customers. Most are happy to include your company on their mailing list if they think they might get business from you in the future.

In addition to gleaning foreign trade information from professional advisers and banks, it's essential to attend as many foreign trade seminars and conferences as possible. Many excellent ones sponsored by the federal agencies previously described are held in Washington. The Institute for International Research in New York is the largest conference sponsor in the world, with twenty five foreign offices. For Latin America and the Caribbean, it's hard to beat conferences and meetings sponsored by Caribbean/Latin America Action, a Washington, D.C. private organization. *LatinFinance* magazine, published in Miami, also sponsors some excellent seminars and conferences on Latin American financial topics.

Universities with active international departments, such as Wharton, Stanford, the University of Chicago, and the University of Miami, hold a flock of seminars every year on international trade topics. Regardless of which ones you choose, it's important to get into the habit of attending at least two or three a year, just to keep abreast of current happenings in international trade.

Reading is also an essential part of market research. Hopefully this book will lead you to acquire other exporting-related books. The more you can read, the better. International trade periodicals are also an important resource. There aren't very many that are worth subscribing to so expenditures should be minimal. I recommend the following:

- *The Economist* (a "must" read every week)
- *The Journal of Commerce,* (also a "must" read)
- *Export Today*

- *World Trade*
- *North American International Business*
- *LatinFinance* (for Latin America and the Caribbean)
- *Global Production* (for Latin American and the Caribbean)
- *Global Finance*

If you have time, *Current History* contains good political and economic background material, as does *Foreign Affairs*. Here are a few other periodicals that can be helpful:

- *Background News*, from the Bureau of Public Affairs, Department of State
- *Operational Information on Proposed Projects*, from the Asian Development Bank
- *United Nations Development Business,* included in the business edition of the Development Forum
- *International Business Outlook*, from the World Bank

The only way to get smart about international trade is to start digging. The amount of information and the number of sources may be overwhelming. Nevertheless, the worst mistake new exporters can make is to begin without knowing as many facts as possible about markets, trade barriers, costs, competition, distribution, financing, and any other topic that may affect either getting the order, delivering the shipment, or getting paid. Only by diligent market research and by arming yourself with as many current (and relevant) facts as possible can you be reasonably confident that your company can compete in global markets.

Chapter 5

The Administrative Country Survey

Under the best of circumstances, it's possible to be a successful exporter without much knowledge of the peculiar legal, economic, and political environment of your customer's country. Clearly, exporting to England holds far less uncertainty than exporting to Sri Lanka or Peru. Exporters can easily communicate with British customers, can rely on the British banking system, and can get more than sufficient information about the British business community from lawyers, accountants, and consultants. These same elements may not be so obvious, nor the answers to questions so readily available, for Sri Lanka or Peru. In either case, prudent strategic management dictates gathering as much information as possible about the peculiarities of doing business in your customer's country.

Moreover, as export marketing channels are opened, it may be in the best interest of strategic growth for you to begin sourcing materials, components, or labor offshore. This may seem like a far-fetched strategy if you're just beginning to export, but more than one company has learned that the complexities of offshore sourcing shrink as it gains knowledge through exporting. Should offshore sourcing be in the cards, however, additional information must be gathered about doing business in that country.

Chapter 4 outlined several sources of information about exporting in general and specific country market opportunities in particular. The next data-gathering activity is called a country survey. Country surveys advance the information-gathering process beyond generalities. Such surveys identify the various components of doing business in a specific country, whether such business involves exporting to that country, offshore sourcing, or establishing an overseas facility to tap local markets or to export to third countries.

Two types of country surveys are desirable for companies seeking offshore sourcing opportunities or production/distribution/sales facilities:

- An administrative survey (most of which can be done in the United States) to uncover the general business and legal characteristics of a specific country.

- A detailed country survey to uncover cultural, legal, market, and cost details of doing business in a specific country. This survey must be conducted on the premises, in the host country.

Although exporters who have no inclination to extend their international trade activities to offshore sourcing or facilities can often get by with just the administrative survey, even here, detailed, on-site surveys can be a big help in establishing long-term exporting strategies. Bear in mind that the major objectives of both the administrative and detailed country surveys are to

1. Gather enough hard data about doing business in a specific country to make intelligent marketing, financial, and production decisions.

2. Obtain facts about local customs and business practices to avoid making judgment errors.

3. Identify appropriate government and private-sector personnel who can be relied upon to open local doors and clear hurdles.

Chapter 6 describes the steps involved in a detailed country survey. The rest of this chapter covers administrative surveys.

The topics to be included in an administrative country survey are

1. Political and economic environment

2. Business structure requirements

3. Audit, tax, legal, and licensing rules

4. Banking affiliations

5. Communications bottlenecks

6. Professional advisers with local expertise

7. Personnel recruiting, training, travel, and safety protocol

8. Insurance coverage.

POLITICAL AND ECONOMIC ENVIRONMENT

A basic premise that underlies most export strategies is that once started, exporting should be viewed as a long-term marketing effort, not a one-shot chance to make a killing. Recruiting or training personnel to handle export marketing and transportation, negotiating agreements with overseas sales representatives, and perhaps initiating a joint venture with a host-country distributor are expensive, time-consuming activities. Only in rare situations does it make sense to incur these costs for a one-time export order. The whole idea behind exporting is to develop new markets for your products. And as with domestic marketing, this takes time and money.

That being the case, to develop markets in a country with an unstable political system or a shaky economic future can be suicidal. It's only prudent to make sure that your market will be accessible and growing over a reasonably long period of time. Although certainty is a luxury seldom present in international trade, specific facts and opinions about a country's future outlook that reduce the risk of market projections are generally available.

A wealth of data and prognostications for Western European markets, Japan, Canada, Australia, and Singapore are available for the asking. U.S.-based consular offices, trade bureaus, foreign chambers of commerce (usually fashioned after U.S. chambers of commerce), and federal agencies compile and distribute a wealth of current information about each country's political status and economic outlook. The Organisation for Economic Cooperation and Development (OECD) publishes reams of demographic and economic statistics and analyses for each member country (twenty four in number). Country desk officers at the Department of State can fill you in on current political and economic happenings. Articles about economic and political events in industrialized countries can be found in current issues of major city newspapers and international trade magazines.

Specific, up-to-date information about less developed countries is more difficult to come by. Aside from international trade periodicals, some of which provide excellent coverage of countries in a specific region (such as Latin America), the best sources of current political and economic data are U.S. and host-country offices of the American Chamber of Commerce, multinational banks with offices in the host country, multinational accounting and consulting firms with offices in the host country, and other American companies with facilities in that country.

Figure 5.1 lists a series of questions about a country's political and economic environment that should be answered.

Figure 5.1
Political and Economic Questions to Get Answered During Administrative Country Survey

1. Does the country have an elected government, or is it run by a dictator, monarch, or other form of central control?

2. If it has an elected government, when is the next election? What is the prognosis for change?

3. Is the current government favorably or unfavorably disposed toward Americans and especially toward American imports?

4. What is the current relationship with the U.S. government?

5. Are there other American companies doing business in the country? If so, which ones? If not, is there a good reason?

6. What is the official attitude toward foreign investment, especially from U.S. companies?

7. What is the *unofficial* attitude?

8. What is the country's main economic base made up of? Imports? Exports? Self-sufficient?

9. Are statistics available to show economic growth or decline (e.g., gross domestic product, interest rates, inflation rates, annual capital expendi-

---

tures, imports, exports, wage rates, unemployment rates)? If so, how reliable are they?

10. What are the country's demographic trends?

11. Are major businesses owned or controlled by the government?

12. If so, is there a privatization program underway and how many major businesses are being sold?

13. What trade barriers prevent foreign imports or foreign investment?

14. What are the barriers to distributing imported products?

BUSINESS STRUCTURE

Companies that restrict their involvement in international trade to exporting directly to customers or to intermediaries (such as distributors or trading companies that take immediate title to the goods) do not need to worry about host-country legal requirements relating to business structure. However, if you ship to sales representatives who do not take title but merely act as your local agent, if any type of joint venture is necessary, or if you decide to establish a local facility, then the form and capitalization of the local business entity must meet the legal requirements of the host country.

Some countries require import licenses that can be granted only to locally registered businesses. Others forbid foreign companies to hold a controlling interest in a local business. In some countries, a government agency must be the local partner in any joint venture with a foreign company.

The form of a business entity as well as its ownership is often decreed by local laws. In some countries, foreigners are permitted to incorporate a local business. In others, a joint venture partnership is required. Still others insist on hybrid structures that have some partnership and some corporate characteristics.

If permitted by local law, a joint venture with another U.S. company that is already established in the country might be the best way to go. On the other hand, a host-country partner usually has more clout with local bureaucrats—a valuable commodity for ensuring smooth passage through customs or settling banking, transport, or labor disputes. A host-country partner that has an "in" with local politicians also shields a U.S. partner from potential violations of the U.S. Foreign Corrupt Practices Act.

Rules governing host-country business structures and ownership, import licensing, tax clearances, business licenses, foreign exchange permits, and other operating approvals can easily be researched through that country's U.S. consulate or trade representative office. You can start the process through U.S. agencies, but it's always preferable to get the rules directly from the horse's mouth.

Figure 5.2 lists the types of questions about business structure that need to be answered during the administrative survey.

Figure 5.2
Business Structure/Ownership Question to Get Answered During Administrative Country Survey

1. What laws relate to foreign business ownership?
2. Is there a required business form? Corporation? Partnership? Hybrid?
3. Can or should tiered corporations be used?
4. What are the restrictions on each form?
5. Is a host-country partner necessary or desirable for a joint venture?
6. If a local partner is required, what percentage of ownership must be given up?
7. Should the host-country business carry the parent's name or be completely divorced from it?

AUDIT, TAX, LEGAL AND LICENSING REQUIREMENTS

Many questions involving audit requirements, tax laws, contract law, and licensing prerequisites can be answered only by visiting appropriate officials in the host country. Broad interpretations, however, can be obtained within the United States. It's generally a good idea to begin with multinational law firms and accounting firms.

Audit and Tax

Any multinational accounting firm—Ernst & Young, Arthur Andersen, KPMG Peat Marwick, Price Waterhouse, Coopers & Lybrand, or DTR International—can provide insights into countries in which it has offices. Special audit and tax reports on specific countries, changes in tax laws that have broad impact, and changes in reporting requirements are normally communicated to clients through newsletters, special reports, and information pamphlets. Most offices will send you what they have for a given country, just for the asking.

In addition, all multinational accounting firms maintain directories of their worldwide offices. Such a directory is an excellent resource when you travel to a foreign country. Most firms also produce booklets that give the current tax laws for individuals and corporations in every country in which the firm has offices.

In certain cases, especially for the twenty-four industrialized member countries of the OECD, consulates and trade promotion bureaus in the United States maintain a variety of booklets and pamphlets that describe their country's audit and tax laws applicable to foreign-owned facilities and to import licensing.

Figure 5.3 sets out questions to get answered relative to audit and tax requirements.

Figure 5.3
Audit and Tax Questions to Get Answered During Administrative Country Survey

1. What are the financial reporting requirements and when must financial reports be filed?
2. Are annual or quarterly audits required?
3. If so, must they be done by a locally registered firm, or can the parent company's audit firm do the job?
4. Must the audit firm be certified?
5. To what depth must an audit go to meet local requirements?
6. Will audited consolidated financial statements from the parent suffice, or must the local entity be audited separately?
7. Has a Tax Information Exchange Agreement been executed?
8. What tax rates apply to corporations and individuals?
9. What income is includable or excludable for corporate and individual tax purposes?
10. What other taxes apply to imports or direct sales?
11. Do any tax incentives apply to foreign direct investments?
12. How are intercompany transactions with the parent taxed?
13. Is there a withholding tax on repatriated earnings or royalties?
14. Does the country qualify under the IRS foreign sales corporation laws?

Legal and Licensing

Getting a firm handle on a host country's various contract and business laws is like shadowboxing: You can see the target, but you can't hit it. It's safe to say that no country in the world has as complicated a legal system as the United States. When each governmental body (village, town, city, township, county, state and the federal government) has its own set of duly authorized laws and a variety of virtually independent court systems interpret these laws, it seems a miracle that anyone can keep them straight. Yet our army of attorneys and courts seem to somehow get the job done.

However, I have yet to find a U.S. law firm willing to take on the task of interpreting or even reading the law of the land in foreign countries. About the only way to get a grasp on potential legal conflicts in a foreign country is to check with an attorney licensed to do business in that country. This doesn't necessarily mean that you have to wait for a detailed country survey to be completed before obtaining any information, however. Most large U.S. law firms have correspondent firms located around the world—at least in OECD member countries. And most are willing to extract much of the information you need from a correspondent—for a fee, of course.

In addition, several metropolitan-area law firms have sensed the advantage of having their own overseas offices and have either merged with local firms or set up their own offices—again, unfortunately, mostly in OECD countries. Still, these firms may provide at least some information that will make the detailed survey easier.

Figure 5.4 indicates the types of legal questions to try to get answered while still at home.

Figure 5.4
Legal Questions to Get Answered During Administrative Country Survey

1. Which correspondent firms in the host country does your attorney recommend?

2. Must business licensing laws be complied with?

3. Are export or import licenses required?

4. Will there be any ethical problems in dealing with a host-country law firm that you should be aware of?

5. What host country laws apply to incorporating a business there?

6. Are there any restrictions on or requirements for setting up joint ventures or partnerships with local firms?

7. What unique features of the host country's litigation laws pertain to American firms doing business there?

8. Is any advance planning necessary to obtain work permits or visas?

9. What liability do U.S. exporters have for actions taken by foreign representatives that may be in violation of the Foreign Corrupt Practices Act or other U.S. laws?

10. Do U.S. boycott laws affect shipments to the host country?

11. Which legal counsel (U.S. or host country) will review sales, countertrade, or other contractual agreements?

12. Who will handle arbitration cases if they arise?

13. Can the U.S. firm assist in contract negotiations, either in the host country or in the United States?

14. Does the firm have any Washington contacts to cut through red tape when your company applies for federal assistance?

BANKING AFFILIATIONS

As the chapters in Part 2 of this book point out, it's impossible to export, source foreign materials, or operate a foreign facility without using the U.S. banking system. Virtually all international transactions, regardless of how they may be structured, eventually involve the banking system. Wire transfers, letters of credit, foreign exchange conversion, documentary drafts, and a variety of other matters must clear through a bank.

This puts an added burden on exporters. International banking transactions handled by small regional banks or small local banks invariably cost more and take more time to complete. You also run the risk of having errors creep into the transaction. And, of course, when you put these transactions through a bank without solid international expertise, it's impossible to solicit advice about the best way to handle them. For these reasons, it only makes sense to strike up a relationship with a bank that is experienced in international financial matters.

Choosing the right bank can be a laborious task, especially for exporters located in rural areas, far removed from metropolitan banking centers. Even multinational banks are more proficient in one part of the world than in others. For example, in the Caribbean, Chase Manhattan, Citibank, and Bank of Nova Scotia (Canada) are all excellent choices; Citibank, Chase Manhattan, Bank of America, and Chemical have many branches in South America; Barclays (Britain) and Citicorp offer good coverage in the Middle East; all major French and British banks serve Africa; Hong Kong and Shanghai Banking Group has offices throughout the world, but is especially proficient in Southeast Asia, as are most multinational Japanese banks. German banks like Deutsche Bank, Dresdner Bank, and Commerzbank will be most helpful in Eastern Europe.

One thing to keep in mind, however: If you're going to solicit help from a multinational bank, U.S. or foreign, it's necessary to get a letter of introduction from your current bank. Without such a letter, few major banks will cooperate with smaller companies.

Figure 5.5 points out information to gather from your local bank or from any multinational bank you select.

Figure 5.5
Banking Questions to Get Answered During Administrative Country Survey

1. In what countries does the bank have branch offices?

2. If the bank has no branch banks in the country, which correspondent banks does it use?

3. Can the bank's international department issue L/Cs in one day and confirm customer L/Cs in two days or less?

4. Is the bank equipped to handle the verification of shipping documents?

5. Can you get reference and introductory letters from the bank for establishing host-country bank accounts?

---

6. Does the bank issue standby L/Cs or other performance guarantees?

7. How long does a money transfer take? It shouldn't take more than two days coming and going, and many banks can do it in one day.

8. What are the credentials of the manager of the bank's international department?

9. Can the bank handle currency conversions and exchange arbitrage, if necessary?

COMMUNICATIONS BOTTLENECKS

It can be very frustrating to try to communicate with foreign customers, sales representatives, local distributors, or overseas facilities, only to find that telephones lines are down, electricity is out, and mail delivery takes four weeks. Such bottlenecks seldom occur in Western Europe or Japan, but they are frequent annoyances in less developed countries. As far as OECD nations are concerned, efficient telephone systems are in place and functioning that permit virtual real-time communications via fax or electronic mail. Cable and telex lines are still in use in some countries, and regular mail delivery is reliable. Air transport makes emergency deliveries easy to manage. A wide range of shipping lines serve these countries.

In the rest of the world, however, communicating between the United States and local offices can be at best a trying experience. Although telecommunications are improving rapidly in less developed countries (a good example is the fiber-optic cable that now connects China and other East Asian nations with the United States), there are still glitches. In some cases, local telephone service is not interconnected with overseas lines. Undercapacity electric power plants frequently shut down (especially in certain Caribbean islands and Central America). Many African nations ration electricity, with long periods of complete shutdown.

Mail delivery is usually erratic. On more than one occasion, local mail handlers have opened mail and appropriated the contents, then "lost" the envelope or package. If this appears to be a danger in your customer's country, it's best to use international courier services. Even with a reputable courier like DHL, however, problems arise.

A good example occurred when a client urgently tried to contact its sales agent in Puerto Barrio, Guatemala, to relay changes in an important sales contract that I was negotiating with a potential buyer. Both DHL and Federal Express deliver to Guatemala, but only to their central offices in Guatemala City—some five hours by bus from Puerto Barrio. By the time the notice was delivered to the sales agent's office in Puerto Barrio, the sales contract had already been executed.

When gathering information about potential communications bottlenecks, it's a good idea to test out what you learn about telephones, courier service, and electronic mail. More often than not, the official line is vastly different from actual practice.

Nevertheless, certain questions set out in Figure 5.6 should be asked in the beginning.

Figure 5.6
Communications Questions to Get Answered During Administrative Country Survey

1. Does the country's telephone service provide direct dialing of international calls?

2. If not, are local operators (hopefully English-speaking) used for placing international calls, or do AT&T operators handle calls?

3. Can overseas calls be placed and received on private lines, or must a central telephone office be used?

4. How much do international calls to and from the United States cost?

5. Can U.S. credit cards be used to place calls from the host country?

6. Is telex used extensively?

7. Are fax machines reliable?

8. How reliable is the electric power system?

9. Is it practical to use computers? How does the local weather affect their performance?

10. Are local computer repair facilities and parts warehouses available?

11. How reliable is the local postal service, and what does mail between the United States and the host country cost?

12. How many days delivery from and to the United States?

13. Do major courier services deliver close to the offices of your sales representatives or facility?

PROFESSIONAL ADVISORS WITH LOCAL EXPERTISE

Although companies should already have retained competent legal counsel and auditors by the time they begin exporting, many times professionals who are fully capable of offering reliable advice about domestic matters may not be as well versed in the peculiarities of exporting or foreign direct investments. Nor do lawyers or accountants who handle only domestic matters usually have appropriate Washington contacts or know which state and city bureaus offer international trade assistance.

Most companies find it essential to engage lawyers, accountants, and perhaps consultants who have significant experience in international trade to provide assistance and advice on a wide range of matters, of which the most common are

- Putting together bid packages for foreign projects
- Assisting in the negotiation of sales contracts

- Arranging appointments with host-country professionals and bureaucrats
- Negotiating the lease or purchase of foreign property
- Preparing export documentation
- Advising about U.S. and foreign customs requirements
- Providing a roadmap to avoid pitfalls in the Foreign Corrupt Practices Act and boycott regulations
- Coordinating marketing, joint venture, and financing assistance through Eximbank, the SBA, the Overseas Private Investment Corporation, other federal agencies, and state and local trade bureaus
- Setting up or advising about foreign sales corporations (FSCs)
- Preparing federal export compliance reports
- Introducing company personnel to congressional representatives, governors, military liaison officers, U.S. trade representatives, and other federal and state officials whose backing is essential to cut through red tape
- Assisting in the selection of host-country advisers, when necessary
- Keeping company personnel up to date about changes in federal and state trade regulations, financing, and other assistance programs.

Although each exporter needs different professional assistance, these matters seem to be the most frequently encountered. If you try to enter or expand in international trade without the help of qualified advisers, the odds are very high that, at a minimum, you will incur significant extra costs—or, worse, fail completely.

The assistance of four types of advisers should be enlisted:

- International trade lawyers
- Multinational accounting firms
- Foreign-trade assistance organizations
- International management consultants.

In most cases, the services of all four should provide sufficient backing to get you up and running in the shortest time with the fewest errors.

It's important to select advisers that know the ins and outs of the specific country you plan to export to or invest in. An attorney with the right connections in the Department of Agriculture won't be much help if you're exporting corrugated containers to Argentina. However, if you're selling grain to Nigeria, such contacts could be priceless. An industry lobby group will be of little help in negotiating a sales contract in Argentina, but could be invaluable in pressuring a federal agency for export licenses to South Africa.

It can be difficult, however, to locate qualified international advisers. Most do not advertise, and the confidential nature of international transactions means that referrals are about the only way to make contact. Of all international professional advisers, multinational accounting firms are the most accessible. They all have competent consulting divisions with specialists in international trade, as well as worldwide office locations. About the best source for referrals to international lawyers is the International Law Institute, 1330 Connecticut Avenue, N.W., Washington, DC; telephone (202) 463-7979.

A few other potentially good sources of international advice are

1. Your industry trade association
2. State or municipal foreign-trade bureaus
3. International departments of universities
4. International departments of multinational banks
5. International managers in local multinational corporations.

Regardless of the sources of professional advice, it's important to ascertain the individual's level of competency before accepting suggestions or recommendations. Figure 5.7 lists the type of questions to ask.

Figure 5.7
Questions to Ask Potential Professional Advisers During Administrative Country Survey

1. What first hand experience does the individual have in your specific area?
2. Which companies has the person represented in international matters?
3. Will these companies verify the qualifications of the professional?
4. How much are the professional's fees? (If they are less than $1,800 per day, the chances are good that this is not the person you want to engage.)
5. Which federal and state foreign trade agencies does the professional work with and have personal contacts in?
6. Does the individual or firm specialize in a particular country or trading region?
7. Are there other people in the organization who can pick up the slack when this person is out of the office for extended periods?

Positive responses to most of these questions generally indicate that the person can be of assistance and that you can rely on the specific advice given.

PERSONNEL

One of the biggest mistakes new-to-exporting companies make is to push ahead using export management companies and professional advisers without first hiring a minimum number of experienced personnel. On-the-job training may be a satisfactory way to get up to speed in domestic markets; it most assuredly is not in the international arena. Inexperienced personnel nearly always make serious errors that can cost the company an enormous amount of money and create horrendous customer relations.

Moreover, if strategic plans call for an overseas sales office, distribution center, or production facility, it's crucial to recruit local nationals to fill key management positions. Company after company (including several Fortune 500 companies) has tried to manage offshore facilities with American executives, only to learn that the ground rules for interfacing with foreign employees, suppliers, customers, and government bureaucrats are entirely different from those in the United States. Especially in Third World countries, it's essential to lean on local managers to make and sustain appropriate local relationships.

Competent international personnel in your U.S. operation can usually be recruited through the normal channels (e.g., advertisements, employment firms, and personal references from banks, lawyers, accountants, and consultants). Recruiting overseas personnel is a different story. Here it's usually necessary to go through an international management recruiting firm. The large, experienced firms have offices both in the United States and overseas. For personnel experienced in European markets, the best source of advertising is the *London Sunday Times*.

A second step in the personnel part of the country survey involves taking care of travel details. People who have never traveled overseas, or who have traveled to parts of the world other than the country you intend to export to, may not be aware of various travel, health, and safety measures pertaining to that country.

Passports

The first step, of course, is to make sure that all personnel have current passports. This seems obvious, yet it's surprising how many times people allow their passports to lapse.

A good example occurred when the controller of a manufacturing company that I owned needed to visit Brazil to work out a sales finance hurdle. The controller had been an experienced international traveler twelve years before with a different company. After flashing his passport at the ticket counter, he boarded the plane, secure in the knowledge that he could wrap up the job in two days and be home in time for the first game of the World Series. As it turned out, that was the least of his concerns. His passport had expired, and he never made it through immigration at the Sao Paulo terminal.

New passports are easy to get at any county courthouse, by mail, or through any of the several passport services in any major city. Just submit an application form together with an original birth certificate, two passport-size photos, and a check for the appropriate fee. In thirty days (or less) you'll have your passport.

Driver's Licenses

International driver's licenses are another matter entirely. Very few countries, if any, now require such a license to rent a car. Nine times out of ten your state license is sufficient. However, just to be on the safe side, as part of the administrative survey, it can't hurt to get international licenses for anyone planning to travel overseas. Any office of the American Automobile Association will issue one for a small fee. State bureaus of motor vehicles will also oblige.

Medical

Several medical matters need attention during the administrative survey:

1. Vaccination certifications
2. Prescription drugs
3. Emergency kit
4. Health insurance
5. Emergency transport arrangements
6. English-speaking doctors.

Many countries, especially Third World countries, suffer from diseases long since conquered in the United States. Typhoid, malaria, diphtheria, cholera, and many other diseases pop up periodically throughout the world. The survey should include making sure that all overseas travelers have the appropriate vaccinations against diseases in the country they will be visiting.

Foreign consulate offices in the United States will tell you which vaccinations are required to enter their countries. The Department of Commerce, in cooperation with the Surgeon General, maintains a constantly updated list of contagious diseases by country. An even closer and easier way to find out what is required is to check with your local hospital. Many hospitals now have special departments dedicated to keeping track of diseases in foreign countries and providing appropriate vaccinations.

It's essential to make sure that all overseas travelers not only get the right vaccinations but carry an official International Vaccination Card, duly filled in by a physician, to prove that vaccinations have been obtained. All hospitals with international travel departments have these cards, as does the Department of Commerce. In some cases, it's necessary to show this card to immigration officials to get into the country. More important, it may be necessary to show it to U.S. immigration when returning home.

It's also a good idea for all overseas travelers to carry an emergency medical kit. It should contain all necessary physician-prescribed drugs (including a signed, officially stamped copy of the physician's prescription), aspirin, Band-Aids, diarrhea medication, and a toothache pain killer. Sleeping pills might also be desirable, especially for long flights. In many parts of the world, including parts of Europe and Japan, pharmacies are not readily accessible, and many do not carry what Americans consider basic products, such as aspirin or throat lozenges.

Health insurance and emergency transport are two areas frequently overlooked, even by experienced international travelers. Although most group health insurance programs carried by multinational companies include overseas coverage, policies carried by small companies seldom do. Popular Blue Cross/Blue Shield policies or HMO plans, for example, generally exclude hospital or physician charges incurred while out of the United States.

Part of the administrative survey should include verification of the coverages in your existing policies. If they exclude international care, many insurance companies will write separate riders.

THE ADMINISTRATIVE COUNTRY SURVEY

Another alternative is to arrange for a policy from one of the specialized health care bureaus dedicated to international care. Most of these policies also include air transport back to the United States if an emergency warrants it. The two best ones I have found are

1. Travel Assistance International, provided by Europe Assistance Worldwide Services, Inc., (202) 347-7113

2. Global Plus, obtained through Clemens & Company, (202) 872-0060

As a final health precaution, make sure that the names, addresses, and telephone numbers of English-speaking doctors in the host country accompany all travelers. Such a list can be obtained from the same medical office that administers vaccinations for foreign travelers.

Financial Emergencies

Financial emergencies can hit international travelers as easily and frequently as medical emergencies. One of the best precautions is to make sure that all travelers carry a letter of credit from your company bank. Such an L/C can be drawn against at virtually any local bank or used for collateral.

The dollar amount doesn't need to be large, but it should be sufficient to buy a new airline ticket home, pay emergency medical bills, post bail bond and pay fines, take care of extraneous customs/immigration charges, and pay hotel and food bills for at least a week. Many travel-related facilities—hotels, restaurants, rental car companies—in developing countries do not accept any credit cards, and a little extra cash can get your employees what they need to survive.

An interesting incident happened to me while on a business trip to Ecuador. While driving a rental car, I was sideswiped on a narrow mountain road. The local police were none too friendly, and I found myself spending the night in a roach-infested cell. The following morning the chief of police appeared and I pleaded my case—in vain, I might add. To prevent being locked up again for an indeterminate time, I offered my company's letter of credit (which I always carried) as assurance that I would appear in court three days hence. I was released, got a local lawyer, and beat the case. However, without the L/C, I might still be rotting in Ecuador!

If a letter of credit isn't appealing, at least make arrangements with a host-country bank to permit employees to draw cash advances. This usually requires maintaining a cash deposit or placing a standby L/C with the bank. More on this topic when we get to detailed surveys in Chapter 6.

Although they won't always be able to use it, it's still a good idea for all travelers to carry a company American Express or Visa card. In dire straits, one of these cards will usually get you a small cash advance at local banks or American Express offices. With Visa cards, however, be sure they are issued by a recognized multinational bank, such as Citibank, Chemical, or Chase Manhattan. Those from other banks are virtually useless in many countries.

Transport

If you're planning to export to Fortaleza or Salvador, Brazil, you'd better make sure your people can get there. The same goes for Kaimana, Indonesia; Xi'an, China; or Morelia, Mexico. Markets may look attractive and there may be overland freight service, but if your marketing people aren't able to visit customers, freight agents, or distributors, it's going to be very difficult to sustain long-term market relationships.

Therefore, part of the administrative survey should be to research the type of transport, frequency, and cost of getting people to your export destination. Normally, one thinks of flying to remote areas of the globe. That's fine, as long as reasonably convenient airline schedules will get you there. It may be, however, that one or more local commuter lines will have to be used. Or perhaps road travel from the entry city is the only way.

During the administrative survey, it's important to ascertain

- Which airlines fly to or near your export destination
- How much the fares are
- How frequently the planes fly.

Also, for remote locations, off the beaten track of international airlines, make a note to check out overland travel during the detailed survey.

Carnets

Customs regulations vary widely from country to country. Part of the personnel survey should be to determine what the rules are in the host country. Inexperienced travelers get quite upset when customs officials impound cigarettes, liquor, currency, or magazines with models in bathing suits on the cover (considered pornographic in certain Middle East countries).

Business travelers who plan to carry samples also need to know what they can carry into the country duty-free and what goods are taxed. In some countries, duties and extensive customs procedures covering sample products may be avoided by obtaining an ATA (Admission Temporaire) Carnet.

The ATA Carnet is a standardized international customs document used to obtain duty-free temporary admission of certain goods into countries that are signatories to the ATA Convention. Under the ATA Convention, commercial and professional travelers may take commercial samples; tools of the trade; advertising material; and cinematographic, audiovisual, medical, scientific, or other professional equipment into member countries temporarily without paying customs duties or taxes or posting a bond at the border of each country visited.

Clearly, it pays to check out whether your host country is a member of the ATA Convention! Applications for carnets can be made to

U.S. Council for International Business
1212 Avenue of the Americas
New York, NY 10036
Telephone: (212) 354-4480

Council offices are also located in Miami; Boston; Timonium, Maryland; Schaumberg, Illinois; Houston; Los Angeles; and San Francisco.

INSURANCE

The final step in the administrative survey is to make certain that appropriate insurance is available. At the same time, of course, research the cost of each policy.

Aside from medical coverage, discussed earlier in this chapter, one or a combination of five types of insurance coverage might be necessary: coverage for

- Losses due to work accidents
- Losses occurring in shipping
- Losses due to property destruction
- Losses due to product liability
- Auto and rental car property and liability.

Right off the bat, you can eliminate workers' compensation. Except in rare circumstances, such coverage is not available for offshore employees and must be purchased within the host country itself—assuming it's available at all.

Several marine insurance companies cover damage or loss of goods during ocean shipping. If you're having trouble locating one in your area, get help from your state insurance commission. If, for some reason, such help isn't forthcoming, you can always get a listing of marine insurers from ocean-bordering states (California, New York, Florida, Texas, Massachusetts, and so on).

Property insurers are a different story. AIG, a subsidiary of American International Group, is far and away the largest carrier in this business. Lloyd's and CIGNA also insure offshore property. If you plan to have an offshore facility, however, the federal government's Overseas Private Investment Corporation (OPIC) is hard to beat.

Product liability coverage can usually be obtained in the host country, provided it is one of the twenty four OECD countries. However, insurance companies in most developing nations have never heard of product liability coverage. It's doubtful that your U.S. carrier will cover claims from overseas customers; however, it certainly can't hurt to ask.

Company fleet policies may or may not cover overseas rental vehicles. Several U.S. insurers do, however. It's always a good idea to make sure you have coverage before leaving home because automobile rental insurance is usually several times more expensive overseas.

That's about all that can be done in a country survey without visiting the host country. Chapter 6 examines data to be gathered during such a visit. Before we get to that, however, the checklist in Figure 5.8 summarizes all the steps in the administrative survey.

Figure 5.8
Summary Checklist of Administrative Survey Data

Political/Economic
1. U.S. and host country trade barriers to exports, imports, and foreign direct investment.
2. Form of host country government (i.e., democracy, monarchy, dictatorship, military).
3. Implicit and explicit attitude toward Americans and American-made products.
4. Host country's major imports and exports.
5. Economic indicators showing growth or decline in economic base.
6. Government-controlled or free-market economy?
7. Ownership of host country businesses—state-owned or private?
8. Any privatization program underway?
9. List of American companies doing business in host country.
10. Current status of relationships between host-country government and U.S. government.
11. Host country demographic trends.
12. Barriers to distribution of imported products in host country.

Business Structure
1. Foreign business ownership laws.
2. Required business form? Corporation? Partnership? Hybrid?
3. Pros and cons of tiered corporations.
4. Pros and cons of structuring host country facility as division, subsidiary, or stand-alone entity.
5. Requirements for local business partners—government or private.

Audit, Tax, Legal, Licensing
1. Lists of correspondent law offices and accounting firms.
2. Business licensing and import license requirements.
3. Recommendations for coping with political graft.
4. Unique laws affecting American companies or products.
5. Restrictions or requirements for setting up joint ventures or partnerships with local firms.
6. Any U.S. exporter liability for actions of foreign representative?
7. Impact of current U.S. boycott laws on shipments to the host-country.
8. Work permit or visa restrictions.
9. Compliance requirements for pertinent U.S. laws.

10. Availability of legal assistance in host country.
11. Connections in Washington and host country to cut red tape.
12. U.S. and host country audit and financial reporting requirements.
13. Tax treaties with host country.
14. Host country personal and corporate income tax rates.
15. Other taxes applied to imports or direct sales.
16. Tax incentives in host country.
17. IRS qualification of host country for foreign sales corporation.

Banking

1. List of branch and correspondent banks and names of managers.
2. Ability of U.S. bank to handle L/Cs, shipping document verification, currency conversion, and exchange arbitrage.
3. Cost and timing of each of the bank's services.
4. Bank reference letters and assurances of guarantees.
5. Communications network with local U.S. bank if not a multinational bank.
6. Bank's participation in federal and state financing assistance programs.
7. English-speaking foreign branch managers.

Communications

1. Status of telephone service to and from the host country.
2. Cost of telephone service and long-distance calls.
3. Acceptance of AT&T or other international credit cards.
4. Status of telex communication systems in host country.
5. Reliability of electrical system for fax machines and computers.
6. Availability of local computer repair facilities and parts warehouses.
7. List of courier companies serving host country, including pickup and delivery points.
8. Status and reliability of mail service.

Professional Advisers

1. List and fee structures of Washington lawyers to assist in dealing with federal bureaucracy.
2. List and fee structures of lawyers in host country that can do the same.
3. List and fee structures of international management consultants.
4. Identification of multinational accounting firms in host country.
5. Services performed by industry trade association.
6. Professional references from American companies doing business in host country.

Personnel

1. Names and addresses of U.S. and foreign employment agencies listing international managers.
2. Staff all U.S. managerial positions with experienced personnel.
3. Use experienced nationals for foreign managerial positions.
4. Be certain everyone has a current passport.
5. Required and recommended vaccinations, including International Vaccination Cards.
6. List of English-speaking doctors in host country.
7. Emergency medical kits for everyone.
8. U.S. bank letters of credit for traveling executives.
9. Company American Express and Visa credit cards (Visa cards from bank recognized in host country).
10. Airline schedules and fares.
11. Host country member of ATA Convention?

Insurance

1. Review group health coverage and purchase special coverage if necessary.
2. Compare rates from private carriers with those from federal agencies.
3. Include foreign owned and rental cars in company policy if possible.
4. List of U.S. insurers of marine, property, product liability risks.

Chapter 6

The Detailed Country Survey

Companies that use the marketing and shipping services of export management or export trading companies can stop with the administrative country survey. Since these specialists handle all marketing efforts and shipping documentation, export sales can be treated in the same manner as domestic sales. Typically, such intermediaries not only undertake responsibility for sourcing customers, negotiating sales orders, and making shipping arrangements; they also collect customer payments. More often than not, they take title to the goods and resell them for their own account.

On the other hand, if your company plans to manage its own selling activities, distribution, shipping, and/or collections, further investigations into host-country business and political environments must be made. By their nature, these investigations must be performed within the host country, since very little, if any, pertinent information can be ferreted out from U.S. sources. Such in-country data gathering is called a *detailed country survey*.

Detailed surveys may include gathering data about such matters as available advertising media, alternative possibilities for distributing products, choices of sales agent-distributor arrangements, and business support activities (e.g., interpreters, safety/security features, banking and business permits, and informal trade barriers). Moreover, companies that intend to establish a manufacturing, distribution, or sales facility in the host country need to gather information about such matters as labor availability, sources of materials and supplies, inland transport, infrastructure conditions, and expatriate living conditions.

Most companies either do not have the experience to perform such a time-consuming investigation or do not want to be bothered with it. This is especially true when markets are located in Third World countries. The engagement of international management consultants is usually the answer. In fact, I have personally performed a number of detailed surveys in many countries of Latin America and the Caribbean, as well as in northern Africa, the Middle East, and east Asia.

If you decide to engage an international consultant, however, three steps will invariably keep expenses to a minimum:

1. Clearly define and communicate to the consultant the company's strategic objectives for entering that specific market.

2. Arm the consultant with as much data as possible about the company and its products, current markets, and personnel capabilities.

3. Perform the administrative survey *first* and turn over to the consultant names, addresses, and telephone numbers of host-country referrals that have been uncovered.

In other words, if a consultant knows specifically what your company is trying to achieve by entering a given market and has been given a dossier of referrals within the host country, the time involved in completing the investigation will be minimized. And with consultants, time is money.

Data to be gathered during the detailed survey depends on the amount of host-country involvement planned by a company. Although this chapter looks at the full array of data that might be necessary, most companies can get by with much less. A full detailed survey comprises three classes of data: that relating to business information, to support activities, and to personnel options.

BUSINESS INFORMATION

The amount of host-country business information that must be gathered and the difficulty of gathering it vary all over the lot. It is easiest for locations in industrialized countries. In Western Europe, Canada, Australia, and Japan, government agencies and trade bureaus accumulate vast amounts of data related to markets, demographics, labor, material availability, competition, government aid programs, and so on. Companies that export to or invest in the less-developed nations of Latin America, Eastern Europe, or elsewhere will have more difficulty ferreting out relevant trade and business statistics as well as authoritative opinions about current and future prospects.

The array of business information included in a typical detailed survey consists of

- Formal and informal marketing and distribution practices and restrictions
- Identification of competing companies
- Advertising and sales promotion options
- Government subsidies
- Sources of raw materials, parts, components, and supplies
- Labor/management resources and constraints
- Shipping and transport alternatives
- Infrastructure development (e.g., roads, telephone, electricity, water).

Marketing Practices and Restrictions

The first problem facing exporters who do their own marketing is to select or build a local sales organization. The main questions are

- What government restrictions inhibit foreign sales personnel?
- What regulations control contractual relationships with local sales agents?

- What business forms and restrictions govern sales agents and/or distributors? For example, can sales agents also distribute their own or competitors' products? Can distributors also sell retail? Do the same import licensing regulations apply to local sales agents, foreign-owned distribution centers, and end users?
- Does the government encourage countertrade arrangements? If yes, what incentives/restrictions apply?
- Do local trading companies handle imported goods? If yes, is this a predominant form of foreign sales representation?

Although much of this information can be obtained from government sources, it is vitally important to confirm the enforcement of official regulations with local merchants, producers, and sales agents. The most reliable confirmations are likely to come from managers of local subsidiaries of American companies. If anyone knows the ins and outs of local business norms, these people do. Most are more than willing to show a compatriot the ropes.

The detailed survey should also involve interviews with sales representatives of foreign companies and distributors who import products. Their answers aren't always straightforward, or necessarily reliable, but if your company plans to use such agents, interviews are one way to ferret out those who can be trusted. Also, confirmation of this information by local American managers can be invaluable.

During this part of the survey, it's important to learn the amount of power held by local business cartels. In some countries, such as Colombia, Egypt, France, and Germany, constraints on foreign competition imposed by local cartels can be fierce. Such informal barriers won't be sanctioned or even admitted by government officials. But if business cartels are powerful, it may be best to look at a different country for export markets.

The "good ol' boy" network prevalent in, for example, the U.S. defense and pharmaceutical industries, tends to be much more evident in other countries across a wide range of industries. You may find that personal relationships among sales agents, bankers, bureaucrats, lawyers, and accountants create a steady crosscurrent of preferential treatment and favors.

It's important to identify such power brokers early in the game so that appropriate groundwork can be laid to smooth the way through customs, financing, government regulations, and grievance settlements. This can usually be accomplished by asking government officials and sales agents for referrals to bankers, lawyers, and accountants (under the guise of needing to engage these professionals for other matters), and conversely, asking bankers, lawyers, and accountants for referrals to bureaucrats and sales agents.

When Citibank, Chase Manhattan, Chemical Bank, Bank of America or another American bank has branch offices in the country, or when a multinational accounting/consulting firm such as Ernst & Young or Price Waterhouse has a presence, these should be the banks and professionals recommended to foreigners. If they are not, then the opinions of bureaucrats and sales agents must be suspect.

It is more difficult to sort out relationships going the other way. However, in most cases, referrals from U.S.-affiliated banks, consultants, lawyers, and accountants can be trusted to be as straightforward as possible under the circumstances.

Competition

Business cartels also have a direct bearing on the severity of local competition and hence pricing. Very seldom can imported products compete with locally produced goods of similar quality, technology, or style. Even the sale of imported goods using higher technology or of better quality can be effectively stymied. The fate of personal computers in Brazil is a good example.

Brazilian computer manufacturers had made the same low-quality products for years, with little new technology. This computer cartel was powerful enough to get the Brazilian government to legislate stringent import controls over foreign-made computers, to the extent that higher-technology products were virtually shut out. IBM and Digital Equipment eventually penetrated the cartel by forming joint ventures with local manufacturers. However, local firms retained majority ownership in the joint ventures, and their brand names and logos continued to appear on all products.

Multinational competition can also deter foreign imports. The detailed survey should reveal the names of companies competing in the exporter's market, along with estimated market shares, growth prospects, and product development plans. This type of information is probably the most difficult to come by. The local American Chamber of Commerce office is a good place to start. U.S. commercial attaches also maintain extensive files on local companies. Interviews with potential competitors will quickly reveal the extent of their product lines and their pricing structures.

Finally, the detailed survey should identify any other imported products that compete in the exporter's markets. If such competition exists, it may be strategically desirable to join forces in some form of alliance—joint venture or other. If an agreement can be structured, it might be possible for two exporters to present a stronger force in the market, thereby capturing a larger market share than either could capture individually.

Advertising and Sales Promotion

Seldom do the same advertising and sales promotion tactics used in the United States work effectively in foreign markets. Demographics, cultural norms, infrastructure development, and a variety of other conditions make it necessary to design promotional schemes specifically suited to each foreign market.

It's almost impossible to determine the most effective advertising media from the United States. To make advertising and promotions effective, companies must recognize subtle market preferences, and the only way to ferret those out is to be present in the host country.

In some cases, the detailed survey should involve test marketing. In other cases, research alone will yield satisfactory answers. Pure observation produces invaluable insights. For instance, an aircraft parts manufacturer initiating an export program to Chile had planned to use the same television spots that had proved effective in American markets. I was asked to produce comparative analyses of the effectiveness of Chilean television, radio, newspaper, and direct mail advertising. Unfortunately, statistical data was very meager.

During my visits to Santiago, as well as Valparaiso to the north and the Talcahuano/Concepcion region to the south, I observed that radio, newspapers, and billboards seemed to reach a wide segment of the population. After verifying these observations with the Chilean-American Chamber of Commerce in Santiago and the managers of several Santiago-based branches of American and European companies, I relayed these findings to my client. The company dropped any thoughts of television commercials and hired a Chilean agency to produce newspaper advertisements and a series of billboard displays.

Government Subsidies

Many less-developed countries offer direct subsidies to local manufacturers and importers as incentives to attract foreign investment and trade. The form of subsidy varies, but most can be classified as

- Reimbursements for labor training costs
- Exemption from income and other taxes, often for periods of ten years or more
- Low-interest, long-term financing
- Exemption from import customs duties
- Rent-free housing for foreign managers.

Although certain subsidies are part of publicly announced economic reforms and are easily revealed during the administrative survey, others are less obvious and must be uncovered during an in-country investigation. Usually a visit to the country's minister of finance will produce the government's entire incentive package.

However, some incentives are not granted to foreigners across the board and must be negotiated case by case. Experience has shown that negotiating anything with government bureaucrats can be at best a nightmare. A far better tactic is to engage a local attorney with government connections to do it for you. Not infrequently, such well-placed influence can obtain desired incentives without ever sitting down at a negotiating table.

Seldom can American Chamber of Commerce offices, U.S. consular offices, or other American firms in the country be of much help. When it comes to government handouts or exemptions, foreign authority figures tend to be of little help. One exception, however, occurs when a country relies heavily on American aid to keep going, as is the case in most of Central America. In these situations, staying on the good side of U.S. embassies and other local American representatives is an integral part of the host government's efforts to sustain the goodwill of the U.S. Congress. In such U.S. cases, authority figures, either public or private, can help American companies obtain favorable treatment. Clearly, it pays to get a grip on the current status of government-to-government relationships during the detailed survey, if not before.

Sourcing, Labor/Management, Shipping, and Infrastructure Development

Obviously, if your company is interested only in exporting, not in establishing a local facility, such matters as local sourcing, the availability and cost of labor and management personnel, inland shipping, and infrastructure development are of little interest. On the other hand, companies that include a host-country production facility (either singly or as a joint venture) in their long-term strategic plans need to ascertain, as definitively as possible, the current status of these factors.

As far as materials, supplies, and production equipment are concerned, companies need to determine whether they are available locally or will have to be imported from the United States or other countries. If importing is necessary, the whole subject of import licensing and other trade barriers becomes a critical issue.

The detailed survey should include a clear description (hopefully derived from official government documents) of any import barriers. Normally, such information is fairly easy to obtain from government agencies. Most countries, even the less developed, make sure that official import requirements are fully documented. Also, government officials are usually eager to produce copies of such documentation to demonstrate how efficient they are.

Trading companies are a good source of information about unofficial import barriers. If you interview managers of local trading companies, it won't take long to find out the real (as opposed to the official) importing obstacles. Managers of host-country facilities of American companies are also an excellent source, especially if they have imported similar materials or equipment for their own operation.

In addition, if materials, components, or equipment are to be sourced locally, but from a location distant from your facility, it's important to ascertain the available modes of transport and the cost of getting the equipment or materials to the plant. Once again, trading companies and managers of American branches are often the best sources of information. Their opinions should be carefully solicited, and any forthcoming recommendations should be incorporated in your survey findings.

Labor/Management Resources and Constraints

If there is any possibility of your establishing a physical presence in the country you're exporting to, it makes sense to gather information about personnel availability and cost during the initial detailed survey. It doesn't make sense to incur extra costs for a second survey if everything can be accomplished at one time.

First, the question of labor. The initial stop should be the government's ministry of labor, or the comparable agency that administers workers' rights and benefits laws. Not only can you get a copy of pertinent labor laws, but the ministry can identify which jobs are covered under collective bargaining contracts.

In several European nations, as well as in Latin America, it is not unusual to find that nearly all skilled and unskilled workers are unionized. In that case, your next stop should be the union hall in the area in which you expect to set up facilities. Here you can gather data about hourly wage rates, vacation and holiday schedules, special benefits packages, and other labor related information. You can also get a good feel for the availability of the particular skills needed in your facility.

In certain countries it's necessary for foreign companies to recruit workers through labor brokers or to negotiate labor contracts through a local law firm. Names and addresses of both should be obtained during the detailed survey.

Determining the availability and salary scales of supervisory and management personnel is usually more difficult. In industrialized countries, quality employment agencies can be a big help. In England, France, Germany, and a few other European countries, help-wanted advertisements in local papers bring good results. The detailed survey should reveal which method is most appropriate under the circumstances. In the case of joint ventures, of course, your partner should be relied upon fto supply any required supervisory personnel.

Shipping and Transport

During the administrative survey, ocean shipping details should have been worked out. Now, it's just a matter of ascertaining whether any glitches can be expected at the port of entry. A visit to the customs office should provide information on official off loading procedures and duties to be paid. Unofficial payments may also be necessary. Host country trading companies are the best source of information about the amount of such payments and to whom and when they should be made.

If materials or equipment must be transported overland, the detailed survey should identify tariff rates, the availability of trucking lines, and onloading/offloading requirements. Any contract hauler can provide this information.

Infrastructure

The main infrastructure concerns center around the quality of roads and rail lines and the availability and reliability of telephone service, electricity, and water supplies. Take the matter of roads first. Typical questions that should be resolved include the following:

- Do toll roads connect your new facility with markets, suppliers, and ports of entry? If so, what are the tolls?
- Are roadways paved?
- Are roadways, bridges, and tunnels well maintained?
- Can company-leased trucks pass over bridges and through tunnels safely?
- What are the dangers of roadway bandits (mainly in less-developed countries)?

Local subsidiaries of American or other foreign companies that truck over these same roads are the best source of information. Be sure to ask about the status of new roads currently under construction that may affect the delivery of materials and equipment or, conversely, that will affect outgoing shipments. It's also important at this stage to gather information about the accessibility and cost of freight forwarders, containerization, and onloading facilities if your company anticipates exporting from the country.

Determining the availability and reliability of utilities (telephone service, electricity, and water) is one of the more crucial parts of the detailed survey. Too often, we assume that because such services are readily available and reasonably reliable in the United States, they must also be overseas. In recent years, vast improvements have been made in fiber optic telephone transmission in most developed nations. However, such advanced technology has not been absorbed by electric power and water utilities. Even in highly industrialized countries like Germany, France, Britain, and Japan, power outages and water shortages occur.

In less-developed countries, conditions are much worse. It is not uncommon, for example, to experience repeated breaks in telephone lines, more or less regular shortages of potable water, and frequent brownouts or even blackouts of electric power. To get a fix on all three of these matters, check with resident American Chamber of Commerce officials and local businesses. A short survey of businesses in the immediate area of the planned facility will quickly reveal utility problems that can be expected. The chamber of commerce should provide an historical perspective on recent adverse conditions affecting a broader area.

SUPPORT ACTIVITIES

In addition to business information, the detailed country survey should uncover all data pertaining to matters of a general nature that must be dealt with in order to move goods to market, move money in and out of the country, and provide for the safety and security of personnel and property. In addition, if interpreters are a necessary adjunct of doing business in the country, then appropriate arrangements should be made.

Wouldn't it be convenient if the entire world spoke English? Unfortunately, most of the world's population can't utter one word of English. Language hurdles continue to be one of the most frustrating impediments to international trade. Although in many developed and less developed countries, a sufficient number of people do speak English to permit foreign companies to conduct most business transactions, this is certainly not universally the case. And it would be a mistake to assume that you can get by with a few key words. More than one company has suffered the consequences of that ploy.

A case in point occurred when the sales manager of an American computer parts manufacturer made her first trip to Brazil. Confident that two years of college Spanish would get her through, she was aghast when, upon returning the States, she asked the local Berlitz office to translate the sales contract she had executed from Portuguese into English. Wonder of wonders! She had agreed to a total price for shipments extending over three years as planned—but for three times the quantity of parts she had intended.

If marketing personnel cannot speak the local language fluently, it only makes sense to bring an interpreter to key meetings. While performing the detailed country survey, line up two or three interpreters recommended by an American branch bank or the American Chamber of Commerce office. Then contract with the one that shows the best understanding of negotiating techniques for business contracts and speaks the most fluent English.

Safety and Security

A great deal can be done from your U.S. office during the administrative survey to establish some basic personnel safety guidelines. But nothing beats first-hand experience of the potential hazards that might confront your people. I realize it will be a bit uncomfortable, but try to intentionally create the types of conditions they will run into. Drive through some dark streets; try out some second-class bars and restaurants; look and act like a tourist; pop into the local police headquarters and ask to see the jail. Of course, it goes without saying that to run these tests without being duly prepared could be suicide. It certainly makes sense to have an influential national standing by, just in case you run into trouble.

Even if you don't want to take such risks, certain procedures should be followed so that you can pass on your reception to company travelers. Three steps should be taken as soon as possible after arriving in a foreign country:

1. *The American embassy*. Let them know exactly where you will be staying, for how long, and who to contact in the United States should an emergency occur. Don't expect any business help from embassy officials. And don't expect them to resolve your disputes with local government bureaucrats. However, in a genuine emergency (such as a coup d'etat or natural disaster), the American embassy may be the only place to get help.

2. *American Chamber of Commerce*. The local chamber office can be extremely helpful in less-serious emergencies. Officials always know who the power players are in the police department and government agencies. When push comes to shove, they will always try to help an American in distress. Tell your people to give the chamber office the same information they give the embassy.

3. *Local Police Department*. Let the police know who you are, why you are in their country, where you are staying, and who to contact in the event of an emergency. Be sure to include both local contacts and those in the United States.

In many countries, the best sources of emergency help are other expatriates—especially other Americans. In addition to the American embassy, the American Chamber of Commerce, and the local police, get to know the names and telephone numbers of expatriates in key business and banking positions. I have never seen an American or British expatriate turn away from helping one another.

During all my travels around the globe, I have learned one trick that has benefited me more than any other. I always keep on my person a typed letter that contains my name, U.S. address and telephone number, local address and telephone number, passport number, where I'm staying, special medication I may be on and what I am allergic to, blood type, and the names and addresses of at least three local people to contact in an emergency. Although at times it's difficult to arrange, I usually try to have this letter translated into the local language as well as English.

Security protection for company property can also be a problem in many countries—just as it is in the United States. It's better to be safe than sorry, and it's always a good idea to enclose any company property with at least a ten-foot metal fence topped with barbed wire. It may also be necessary to hire twenty-four-hour guards. Arrangements for such security measures should be made while in the country doing the detailed survey. Once equipment, vehicles, and other company property begin to arrive, it may be too late.

Moving Goods to Market

On the surface, it would seem that the data collected on freight forwarders, road conditions, local contract truckers, and so on, would be sufficient to make decisions about moving goods in and out of a facility. However, one more step may be necessary.

All industrialized countries and many less-developed ones operate free-trade zones. These are specific areas set aside by the government for duty-free storage of imported goods that will be transshipped out of the country or, in some cases, converted to finished products by assembly or other operations.

Since each country has different free-trade-zone laws, it is necessary, during the detailed survey, to assimilate all pertinent information about these zones, including

1. The location of free-trade zones

2. Facilities available within the zones and rental costs

3. Zone support activities (such as labor recruiting, bookkeeping, transport, utilities, and so on) and related costs

4. The character of goods that can be moved through the zones

5. The type of work (if any) that can be performed on the goods held in the zones

6. Restrictions on the destination of shipments out of the zones, such as sales to domestic markets, exports to specific countries, worldwide exports, and so on.

Moving Money into and out of the Country

It would be catastrophic if your company earned income from host-country sales and couldn't repatriate it. It would be just as harmful if you needed to transfer funds into the country but were either prevented from doing so or denied free access to them once they were in a host-country bank. One of the most serious steps of an in-country survey is to analyze currency exchange and repatriation laws and then make arrangements for the movement of company money in and out. At the same time, be sure to arrange for the conversion of U.S. dollars into local currency and assurances that you will have access to this currency for paying local bills.

Although government approval may be necessary, all currency travels through local banks. Therefore, it's necessary to establish relationships with a local bank, open appropriate company accounts, and obtain any government permits that may be required. It may take two or three months to get the required permits and get bank accounts opened, so waiting until transactions begin could delay both the repatriation of earnings and the conversion of currency.

To open a local bank account, virtually all countries require foreigners to present a reference letter from their home-country bank. They also require a duly authorized document from the company's board of directors giving you the authority to open the accounts. "Duly authorized" means stamped with the corporate seal, signed by the company treasurer, and possibly notarized. The more official-looking the document, the fewer questions will be asked. Also, don't make a deposit with a company check. This can take two to three months to clear. Instead, use letters of credit and wire transfers from your home-country bank.

Be aware that in many less-developed countries, bank checks are seldom used to pay bills. In many Latin American, African, and Middle East countries, for example, business is conducted almost entirely with cash, L/Cs, or wire transfers. Few local banks have the ability to manage volumes of checks, and if they do, it can take several weeks (or months) for checks to clear. Granted, many rapidly growing Latin countries have modernized their banking systems in conformity with the U.S. system, but some of them continue to use outdated methods. Nearly all African nations work with nineteenth century banking systems.

Here's another tip: While American, European, and Japanese banks are relatively safe, the same cannot be said of locally owned banks in less-developed countries. Corruption flourishes, bookkeeping mistakes are common, inflation quickly eats away at currency values, and banking rules keep changing. It's generally a good policy to keep as little cash on deposit in these banks as possible. In other words, wire transfer funds as needed, and repatriate funds as quickly as permitted.

When applying for permits to move or convert funds, take the time to also arrange for business licenses, labor hiring clearances, tax identification numbers, and any other permits necessary to conduct business in the country.

INFORMATION FOR PERSONNEL

If strategic plans call for company personnel to be traveling extensively or living in a country, it only makes sense to gather as much information as possible about four subjects:

1. Cost and availability of accommodations
2. Cost and availability of local transportation, either public transport or private automobiles
3. Educational facilities for families
4. Identification of as many American or English-speaking expatriates as possible that live in the country

Living Accommodations

Hotels are by far the most expensive way to house expatriates—whether in Ecuador or in England. Throughout Europe and Japan, the market for temporary expatriate housing is in full swing. In response, many former apartment buildings and suite-type hotels have been turned into temporary residence accommodations. Although prices for such at-home luxury are very high in metropolitan areas like London, Frankfurt, or Tokyo, prices are more reasonable in outlying areas. Even with seemingly exorbitant rents, however, such accommodations are far cheaper than putting up personnel in a hotel that charges daily rates.

One alternative to temporary residences is to buy an apartment or a house for use by key management personnel while in the country. Many companies have found this to be more cost-effective than renting temporary accommodations. Moreover, if the residence is large enough, several expatriates can live there together. Of course, if expatriates bring their families, then separate housing is probably necessary.

Much the same comparisons can be made in less-developed countries. Whether company managers travel to Nairobi, Kuala Lumpur, Colombo, or Lima, hotel rooms are always the most expensive accommodations, followed by temporary residence apartments and company-owned houses or apartments.

While performing the detailed survey, try to arrange for the approximate number of accommodations needed by your company. Leases will probably be required, however, so a fairly accurate expatriate count is necessary. Real estate agents abound in all metropolitan areas. They may go by strange-sounding titles, but nevertheless they are the best resources for locating nonhotel accommodations.

Even if it is impractical to execute leases during the survey, at least bring home descriptions of available accommodations, along with costs, probable lease terms, and availability.

Transportation

It is indeed surprising how many cities in the world have functioning public transportation. Services in European and Japanese cities are normally much cleaner, more efficient, and cheaper than U.S. buses, subways, or trains. They also cover a broader area than most U.S. city transport systems. Nearly all cities and towns in less-developed countries rely on bus transportation. Some systems are excellent, some abominable. But in a pinch, they always get you where you want to go—assuming you're not in a hurry.

If the country has public transportation with published schedules, it's a good idea to bring home the schedules that apply to the general location of the company's facility and/or living accommodations for company personnel. At least choices are then possible.

Most companies find that public transportation systems are fine for emergencies, but that expatriate managers nearly always want and need their own cars. In certain cases it may be more expedient and less costly to buy cars. However, insurance coverage may be either outlandishly expensive or not available. Generally, rental cars suffice and are a lot easier to maintain and dispose of than company-owned vehicles.

THE DETAILED COUNTRY SURVEY

Car rental companies flourish in nearly every country of the world. Some are franchises of American rental firms like Hertz or Avis; some are locally owned. This part of the survey should provide sufficient cost and availability data to permit home-office personnel to make a choice between buying and renting local cars.

One point about driving in foreign countries is often overlooked. More often than not, traffic laws are less well defined than in the United States, traffic congestion is immeasurably worse, and local police are less understanding if you get in an accident. In the long run, it may be more practical for companies to hire a driver with a car than to rent or buy their own.

Education Facilities

Expatriates who bring family members, especially school-age children, are vitally interested in the type and availability of educational facilities. In certain situations, public school systems are more than adequate; but in general, American expatriates tend to gravitate to private elementary and secondary institutions.

Moreover, in countries whose cultural and educational norms are vastly different from those of the United States and where there are many American expatriates living in the country (as in Saudi Arabia, Pakistan, China, and South Korea, for example), private schools that conform to U.S. teaching methods and curriculum standards have been set up by American Educators. This could be a very important consideration if your company plans to station personnel with families in the host country on a relatively permanent basis. In that case, all available data on locations, tuition, curriculum, and teaching standards of private schools should be assimilated during the survey.

Even expatriates without families may be interested in continuing education, language instruction, or other courses at the university level. Except for a few very backward countries—such as Myanmar, Central African Republic, or Afghanistan—major cities have one or more relatively modern universities.

It's not very difficult to track down the availability and cost of various educational institutions. American and British private schools are well known by the American Chamber of Commerce, as are all university facilities. Expatriates already stationed in the host country should also be well aware of what is available. Local telephone directories usually list both private elementary and secondary schools and universities.

Leisure-Time Activities

Although leisure-time activities are in the United States seldom considered a concern of businesses, employees posted to foreign positions often experience disappointment, low morale, and probably very short stays when they have few choices for absorbing their leisure hours. Staring at apartment or hotel walls every weekend can drive the most dedicated employee home.

Therefore, it's essential to accumulate as much information as possible about social activities available to expatriates. Access to sporting events, health clubs, athletic leagues, dramatic presentations, card clubs, cinemas, water sports, and so on, is an important aspect of expatriate living conditions.

A picture is worth a thousand words; so try to lay your hands on brochures, magazine or newspaper articles, photographs, or any other visual evidence of social activities. And don't forget club activities—golf clubs, tennis clubs, literary groups, travel clubs. They all offer newcomers a chance to meet people and socialize, and that's what expatriates need if they are to learn the ropes.

Although many other details could and probably should be assimilated during the detailed country survey, the items described in this chapter provide a good start. Since every survey, and every country, is different, it is likely that some of these items will be more relevant than others. It is just as likely that data that hasn't been mentioned will end up being the most important. However, we have to begin somewhere, and the topics discussed in this chapter are as good a place as any. Figure 6.1 summarizes the minimum data that should be gathered during this type of survey.

Figure 6.1
Checklist of Data to Be Gathered during Detailed Country Survey

Business Information
1. Government restrictions that make it difficult to use company employees as foreign sales personnel.
2. Regulations controlling contractual relationships with local sales agents.
3. Business forms and restrictions that govern sales agents and/or distributors.
4. Government's position on countertrade arrangements.
5. List and description of local trading companies that handle importing.
6. Relative strength of business cartels.
7. Reference checks on important government bureaucrats and local sales representatives from banks, lawyers, and public accountants.
8. Names and market shares of local and multinational competitors.
9. Description of imported products that directly compete.
10. Advantages of forming alliances with competing U.S. exporters.
11. Various advertising and sales promotion options.
12. Relevant government incentives or subsidies, separated into those that apply across the board and those that must be negotiated.
13. Availability and cost of skilled and unskilled labor, and management personnel.
14. Formal and informal barriers to the import of materials and production equipment.
15. Local sources of materials and supplies.
16. Port facilities and inland transport alternatives.
17. Reliability of electricity, water supplies, and telephone service.

Support Activities
1. Interview two or three interpreters and contract with the best one.
2. Test out potential personnel safety hazards.
3. Safety/security checklist for company personnel.
4. Property security fence and perhaps guards.
5. Location and availability of and restrictions on free-trade zones.
6. Legal requirements for currency conversion and repatriation of earnings.
7. Open bank accounts with banks that can handle L/Cs, wire transfers, and currency conversion.
8. Applications for business license, labor hiring clearances, tax identification number, and any other required permits.

Personnel Information
1. Expatriate housing accommodations, including availability, cost, and leasing arrangements.
2. Reliability, cost, and appropriateness of public transportation system.
3. Data to make automobile purchase-versus-lease decision.
4. Availability and cost of short-term and long-term rental cars.
5. Data about availability, curriculum, and cost of elementary, secondary, and college-level educational facilities.
6. Brochures, pictures, and descriptions of leisure time activities available to expatriates.

Chapter 7

Tips on Handling Different Cultural and Business Protocol

Over the years, employees of client companies in the initial stages of an export or import program or seriously considering a foreign direct investment have asked about a variety of personal and business subjects related to the peculiarities of doing business in foreign lands. At the personal level, concerns focus mainly on different cultural practices, language difficulties, safety hazards, health problems, the type and availability of accommodations and transportation, customs and immigration procedures, and international travel. At the business level, most questions center on insurance practices that differ from those in the United States and acceptable procedures for complying with the U.S. Foreign Corrupt Practices Act without losing business.

Clearly, unique cultural and business practices make doing business in every country slightly different. However, the tips offered in this chapter apply more or less generically worldwide, especially in less-developed nations. These tips are based on personal experiences that I have had while doing business in various corners of the world for more than twenty years. With the caveat that rapidly changing conditions may make some observations already out of date, here are a few tips on what to expect.

CULTURAL AND LANGUAGE DIFFERENCES

Regardless of the country, departures from American cultural norms seem to create the most confusion. Yet, in reality, cultural and language differences are the easiest to cope with.

To start with, do some research into the religious, political, and cultural heritage of the country you are planning to visit or export to. In many parts of the world, religious custom dictates many social norms that may appear to be entirely unreasonable to Westerners. Certain Islamic cultures follow a different work week, celebrate their beliefs at odd hours, and demand convoluted business practices, antiquated gender relationships, and ubiquitous favors that are completely at odds with a democratic Judeo-Christian heritage. First-time visitors to Haiti are generally overwhelmed by the cultural power of voodoo beliefs.

Different political systems also lead to divergent attitudes and practices. For example, people who have lived under dictatorships for seventy years—as in the erstwhile Soviet Union—cannot be expected to grasp the nuances of democratic free enterprise. Negotiating tactics, contract enforcement, and civil liberties may be at variance with our ways of doing business. Businesspeople who have grown up in social welfare states such as Germany or Japan find it difficult to accept our laissez-faire approach to just about everything. Taking the time to grasp these underlying cultural differences can make the difference between succeeding in international trade and failing.

A frequent error made by American business travelers is to forget that they are the visitors—and the minority—in a foreign land. That's a big mistake. As visitors, we are always in some sense the guests of local residents. We are welcome only so long as they are prepared to tolerate us. When foreigners forget that, they quickly become persona non grata.

During one of my frequent trips to the Caribbean, I was accompanied by the marketing vice president of a client that had recently decided to begin exporting chocolate candies to the region. This executive had never been outside the United States and had not taken the time to do any research about the cultures we were about to encounter, first in Jamaica and then in Trinidad. His parents were originally from South Africa and had suffered miserably under apartheid policies. He was thrilled to be doing business in the West Indies, believing that because of his heritage he would be readily accepted.

My warnings fell on deaf ears. No sooner had we landed at Montego Bay than this otherwise astute marketer began asserting himself, arguing with customs officials, and adopting what I considered an arrogant attitude. When we finished in Jamaica, he called his boss in New York, complaining that there were no opportunities in the Caribbean and that the trip was a waste of time. He neglected to mention that his arrogance during visits to several potential customers resulted in as cold a welcome as I have ever seen.

The lesson is obvious: Foreigners of any color or heritage are still foreigners. In the Caribbean, as elsewhere in the world, only the manners and mindset of a courteous visitor will make a person welcome and open opportunity's doors.

Most Americans have surprisingly little difficulty with foreign languages. One reason is that throughout the world, either local business is conducted by English-speaking people or interpreters are so readily available that no one needs to feel at a severe disadvantage. Although it always helps to know the local language and dialects, proficiency in either is definitely not required for being successful in international trade.

So many business leaders in countries from China to Russia and from Argentina to Germany get part of their education in the United States that you can make yourself understood in most business situations by speaking English slowly and articulately. Of course, negotiating and executing contracts is a different matter. Here the nuances of strange languages often put Americans at a disadvantage. Without fluency in local languages, we all need interpreters.

PERSONAL SURVIVAL TACTICS

Beyond cultural dissimilarities, first-time travelers may find local practices and institutions that are substantially different from those found at home difficult to cope with. Personal safety, health care, living accommodations, and transport arrangements seem to cause the greatest problems.

Excluding easily identified exceptions, most foreign countries are perfectly safe for Americans, provided one follows the same prudent rules that a stranger would practice in New York, Chicago, Toronto, Los Angeles, or Houston

- Don't walk alone on city streets at night.
- Don't drive alone on unlighted streets or back-country roads.
- Don't get intoxicated in public.
- Don't be rude.
- Don't flaunt jewelry or other expensive accessories.
- Stay away from decrepit neighborhoods, broken-down bars, and out-of-the-way restaurants.

One precaution described in Chapter 6 is worth mentioning a second time: Always carry on your person a clearly written document that contains your name, your local address, and a local American contact (chamber of commerce or embassy); the name, address, and local telephone number of persons to notify in case of accident or incarceration; blood type; and any medication you may need or are allergic to. It can be a frightening experience to be left at the mercy of local doctors or, worse yet, the local police. It's also a good idea to carry your passport wherever you go—in a safe (and hidden) place, of course.

Health Precautions

In less-developed countries, health hazards and the absence of good health care are common. In most cities, potable water and most food (except red meat) are generally safe, especially in first- or second-class hotels and restaurants (stay away from anything below second class!). Still, it can't hurt to avoid tap water (many countries have excellent local wine or beer as substitutes). And stay away from milk.

Although most countries are free of serious communicable diseases, outbreaks of cholera in some areas have caused health authorities to tighten immigration regulations. It's always best to carry the International Certificate of Vaccinations approved by the World Health Organization showing the dates and types of your latest vaccinations. Malaria pills and typhoid shots are a must if you are traveling off the beaten track.

In any country, developed or less-developed, professional health care must be regarded with skepticism. Many hospitals are government-run, with doctors and nurses on the government payroll. Basic pharmaceuticals are generally available, but not special prescription drugs.

Health Insurance

Except for some of the more advanced hospitals in large cities, most health care facilities will not accept standard U.S. health insurance (e.g., Blue Cross or HMO plans) in lieu of payment. Therefore, just to be on the safe side, before leaving home make provision for the transfer of funds via American Express or international banks in case of emergency. It's also a good idea to verify that your group or individual policy covers overseas health care so that, at a minimum, you can get reimbursed when you return home.

Many employee group policies are not valid overseas. The answer is a separate policy for each traveler. In many cases, such special international policies are accepted in local hospitals when a Blue Cross or other group policy isn't. These special policies also cover evacuation costs if it becomes necessary to fly home for treatment (see Chapter 6 for two excellent insurance providers).

Accommodations and Transport

As for living accommodations, nearly all countries have adequate housing, both short- and long-term. In less-developed countries, rents are substantially less than in the United States. In parts of Europe and Japan, rents are significantly higher. Major cities provide suburban living that matches U.S. standards. Even in smaller, less-developed areas, modest to elaborate homes owned by foreigners can usually be rented on short or long-term leases.

Transportation can easily be arranged through car rental agencies, although the rates are high. An international driver's license isn't essential; however, it doesn't hurt to carry one just for emergencies. All countries have bus service of one type or another that is inexpensive and convenient—albeit somewhat dirty, crowded, and in some locations downright decrepit. Throughout Europe and Japan extensive rail service is available.

Here are a few other tips for the unwary:

- Always dress in business attire when conducting business.
- If you are a woman, leave your slacks at home and restrict shorts and tops to the beach or pool.
- If you are a man, never wear shorts other than for leisure activities (except in Bermuda, or course).
- Register with the local American Chamber of Commerce upon arrival.
- For extended stays, register with the local police department.
- Try to learn some phrases in the local language—it's only common courtesy and it helps you get around.

CORRUPTION AT THE BORDER

Most of us like to believe that people are basically honest. In most situations, if we treat one another fairly and honestly, our actions will be reciprocated. In developed nations, this is just as true when passing through customs and immigration as it is in any other aspect of our lives.

In other parts of the world, however, bribing officials to get through customs is a way of life. Africa is far and away the worst, with the Middle East close behind. Some of the South and Southeast Asian countries also present serious problems. Like it or not, it is not unheard-of to offer uniformed customs and immigration officials something to avoid harassment. The traveler's demeanor also makes a big difference.

Here are a few tricks of the trade that should stand you in good stead:

- As often as possible, claim to be a tourist rather than a business traveler.
- Carry some loose change and dollar bills with you.
- Avoid wearing jewelry of any kind until you are safely in the country.
- Learn a few words of greeting in the local language.
- Be cheerful and businesslike.
- Create an air of being in command.
- If you get in a bind, call the local American embassy or consulate.

One final tip on personal survival: Invariably, once you clear customs and immigration, swarms of hawkers will clamor to offer you a taxi ride, especially in less-developed countries. Businesspeople are put upon the most. Don't get flustered. Look for a dispatcher. If one isn't available, pick out the taxi driver that looks the most presentable—not the one that is the most persistent.

Since metered cabs may not be available, be very certain to negotiate a fare before entering the taxi. When going to a new country, always ask airline personnel, police officials, or fellow business travelers about taxi rates to your hotel of choice. Without that information, negotiating a reasonable fare is impossible. Above all, don't panic. Stay in command.

BUSINESS PROTOCOL

"When in Rome, do as the Romans do!" applies to business dealings in virtually any country of the world. Very seldom is business protocol the same in two countries. Previous political associations (as with ex-colonies), religious beliefs, gender customs, government regulations, and prior experiences in dealing with Americans all affect the business demeanor of host-country sales representatives, customers, and government officials. If you try to break with these customs, either intentionally or inadvertently, chances are good that your business deal will fall through.

Negotiating contracts can often be one of the most confusing situations. Most international business transactions require some form of negotiation. Executing a sales contract necessitates the negotiation of prices, financing, payments terms, performance standards, and so on. Joint venture or partnership arrangements require the negotiation of liability limits, compensation, currency exchange, management responsibilities, and termination provisions. To effectively negotiate a contract with foreign parties, certain protocol should be followed, as outlined in Figure 7.1.

Figure 7.1
Outline of Negotiating Protocol

1. *Locations.* Given a choice, always hold negotiations in a formal setting, preferably an office. Unfortunately, at times the other party will prefer less formal surroundings, such as a hotel lobby, airport lounge, restau-

---

rant, or private club. Never force the issue. When this is a strong preference, go along with it. Perhaps that party doesn't have appropriate office space, or perhaps local protocol dictates an informal environment.

2. *Equal numbers on negotiating team.* Be sure to have the same number of participants as your opponent, with the same technical qualifications, such as lawyers, accountants, tax advisers, engineers, or marketing experts.

3. *Ending time.* Do not expect negotiations to end at a specific time. If you planned on three days and it takes three weeks, so be it. In many countries, hurrying through as important a matter as contract negotiations can signify lack of courtesy or worse, such as placing little importance on the outcome of the negotiation.

4. *Don't be in a hurry.* This is a corollary to avoiding a fixed ending time. Set a starting time, but if the other party shows up late, let it go. Each negotiating session should begin with a lot of small talk. Let the other party decide when to begin. Be patient.

5. *Courtesy.* Always be supercourteous, regardless of the demeanor of the other party. If tempers flare or negotiating points become emotional, stay cool. Be unflappable and chances are excellent that the other party will soon calm down.

6. *Maintain your position.* Don't switch from one negotiating position to another. This may be an excellent tactic for negotiating with another American, but it seldom works with foreigners. In other words, when negotiating price, don't start with a high number, expecting to come down. Don't begin with terms that are obviously unacceptable, expecting to restate your position later on. Once you take a position, stick to your guns. Wavering shows weakness in most foreign cultures.

7. *Clarify the meaning of words and phrases.* Stay away from clichés. Americans may know what you're talking about, foreigners invariably do not. Clarify the meaning of every word or phrase that could cause later confusion. And, most important, reduce every negotiated point to writing, clearly signed off on by both parties.

8. *Keep it formal.* Do not, under any circumstances, conduct negotiations with a jovial attitude. This is serious business. Jokes, snide remarks, and laughter only muddy your position with the other party. And be sure to wear business attire suitable to whatever the local customs prescribe. When in doubt, always overdress.

9. *Socialize when negotiating.* Keeping the meeting formal doesn't mean you should avoid all social contact with the other party. If that party suggests dinner, the theater, or a sporting event, by all means accept. It may be customary to work out sticky points during such an outing. Be very careful, however, of becoming too relaxed. Informality breeds mistakes, and more than one foreigner has won remarkable points simply by getting a visiting American's mind off business. If the social event is in the

United States or in your choice of location, then you pay the bill. If the other party suggests it or if it occurs in that party's location, let your opponent pick up the tab.

10. *Don't oversell.* When negotiations are completed leave. If you feel you have come out ahead, don't get the big head. Imply that there will always be a next time. Be humble. If you are unhappy with the results, don't show it. Let the negotiation end when it ends, even if you haven't achieved all your goals.

BUSINESS ETIQUETTE

When traveling or working overseas, four business etiquette situations seem to cause the most confusion:

- Determining courteous conduct
- Accepting and giving gifts
- Eating and drinking local fare
- Using idiomatic phrases.

Although few of us would admit to being discourteous in our daily demeanor, more often than not the hurrying, scurrying lifestyle common in the United States tends to make us forget common manners. Too often the art of conversation is relegated to the back burner. It's much easier to gulp our meals, commute solo to and from our jobs, and ignore strangers as if they come from a different planet. Very few other cultures live as frantically as we do. Even in countries where the value placed on human life is far below that in our country, people seem to take the time to at least notice other people, to help those in need, and to treat elders with respect. Throughout Europe and in many Asian countries, dinner is a social event, to be savored with good conversation and dinner partners.

Good basic manners, polite conversation, and courteous actions carry over to business dealings. If one's personal life is frenetic, business relationships tend to be as well. This can lead to major mistakes when conducting almost any form of international trade. The "ugly American" image is still portrayed on foreign television, in foreign movies, and in foreign theater. The more we forget proper etiquette when visiting foreign shores, the more we reinforce this image. And even though we find this hard to believe, such an image influences how foreign customers, partners, and bureaucrats deal with us.

About the only way to overcome the image many foreigners have of Americans as brash, discourteous, and frenetic is to bend over backwards to be just the opposite. If done with grace, a conscientious effort to follow local business etiquette will often turn adversaries into cooperative business partners.

A good example occurred on my first visit to Madras, India, on assignment to negotiate an agency contract with a local distributor. The atmosphere at our initial meeting was as thick as pea soup. I quickly determined that the distributor had been insulted twice by visiting American businessmen and wasn't about to take the same from me. Playing up to his choice of dinner menu and beverage and praising the Indian culture as being a model for the rest of the world won him over. My U.S. client was so pleased that I received double my normal fee.

The Matter of Gifts

In virtually every corner of the world except the United States, business gift giving is a way of life. Hosts frequently present gifts to visiting businesspeople, and generally expect something in return. Depending on the current rigidity of the U.S. government in enforcing the Foreign Corrupt Practices Act, such gift giving and receiving could become a major obstacle.

Pragmatically, as long as gifts are reasonably priced, no one is going to object. A bottle of champagne, perfume, or a basket of fruit won't raise any eyebrows. On the other hand, an automobile, a month-long ocean cruise, or a large deposit in a secret bank account probably would. Once again, as with any form of business etiquette, good taste should prevail. Keep gifts simple. Keep them inexpensive. But be prepared to give and receive them as required by local custom.

Local Food and Drink Customs

Other than first-class restaurants in highly developed countries that can afford to import food for foreign visitors, very few grocery stores or restaurants carry staples that meet American tastes. That doesn't mean that food served throughout the world isn't tasty or nourishing. Much of it is. It just means that you can't count on eating or drinking the same foods or beverages that you are accustomed to.

In some parts of the world, to refuse local delicacies is the epitome of discourteousness. When your host serves or recommends foods or beverages that you specifically do not like or have never heard of, it's only good manners to at least sample the fare. It is perfectly acceptable to decline large servings; it is not acceptable to refuse small portions.

During my last trip to the island of Yap in the Federated States of Micronesia, I was the guest of a village chieftain, whose wife slaved over an open fire all day to prepare our dinner. It consisted of fried fish heads, near-raw pork, two local vegetables (nearly inedible), greasy chicken, and a strange type of ocean fish that looked very much like a water snake—not exactly my idea of a gourmet meal, but I couldn't refuse the chief's hospitality. Breaking bread with the village chief opened the door to government approval of my client's bid on a roadway construction project.

Avoid Idiomatic Phrases

In another Micronesian case, I made the unconscious mistake of remarking, "This really bugs me," referring to the fact that my secretary in the States didn't return my phone call. The next thing I knew, my host had called a bug sprayer to decontaminate the office. Idiomatic phrases have become an acceptable way to communicate, not only in the United States, but in other parts of the world as well. Obviously, this exacerbates the language problem. Not only must we cope with unfamiliar languages and dialects, we must try to decipher the meaning of colloquialisms native to a special social class, community, or industry. There is no easy solution, except to ask enough questions to clarify the meaning of both spoken and written phrases.

On the other hand, just because our customers use idiomatic phrases doesn't mean that we must reciprocate. The more one travels internationally, the more conscious one becomes of clear verbal communication. It's just a matter of concentration.

Try a short experiment to see how many colloquialisms you use in your everyday speech. Keep a recorder next to your phone for three days. Carry a pocket recorder to three business meetings, dinners, or lunches. At your next formal presentation, use both a video camera and a sound recording. Then have the recordings typed up and see how many times you have used phrases that violate acceptable English grammar. As an alternative, hire an English major from a local university to do the critique. Once we realize how poor our verbal communication skills are, we can begin to concentrate on what we say and how we say it.

A SYNOPSIS OF TRAVEL TIPS

Every experienced international traveler has a drawer full of horror stories about goof-ups, bloopers (how's that for an idiomatic word?), and strange encounters: near misses in the air, crazies on the plane, lost luggage, nonexistent hotel reservations, bribing customs officials, getting sick on two beers while crossing the Atlantic, being too ill to get out of bed, or arriving home after a ten-hour flight and a month's stay overseas only to learn that your luggage is on its way to either South Africa or South Dakota—airline personnel don't seem to know which.

To my knowledge, no one has found a sure-fire way to avoid these annoying situations. However, those of us who have spent several years in strange ports of call have developed all sorts of tricks and gimmicks to cope with them. Figure 7.2 lists a few tips I can offer from years of trying to find a way to survive the varied headaches of global travel.

Figure 7.2
Tips for Making International Travel Easier

1. Schedule a flight that arrives in the evening. Airlines seem to think that businesspeople like to fly all night so that they can work the next day. This is crazy. At least some airlines have one or two daytime flights to Europe and Latin America. When traveling to East Asia, schedule a twenty four-hour stopover in Hawaii or Guam if you're going north, Hawaii or Australia if you're heading south.

2. Sleep at least twenty-four hours after arrival. Converted airline seats that let you stretch out are helpful, but very few people are able to sleep soundly with the plane's engines purring and people moving about in the

aisles. Remember that your host will be refreshed and ready to make decisions. After a long overseas flight, it takes a superhuman effort to be that fresh. There are enough problems to be faced without adding a foggy brain and cloudy reasoning.

3. Don't drink alcohol or eat heavy meals while in the air, regardless of the meals or drinks offered by the airline. Both alcohol and large meals will rob you of much-needed energy and sleep.

4. Take only carry-on luggage, if possible. New lightweight bags that hold twice as much as the old-fashioned suitcases can usually be brought on board, provided you have only one. At a minimum, carry on enough clothing and emergency supplies to get through three days. In other words, count on your luggage being misplaced.

5. Carry your own medicine chest. A letter, duly notarized and officially stamped by your doctor, will get the drugs through customs. Be sure to include lots of aspirin, Band-Aids, mosquito repellent (for tropical destinations), calamine lotion, sunscreen lotion (also for the tropics), scissors, gauze, tape, safety pins, rubber bands, paper clips, and glue—all of which are difficult to find in foreign locations when you need them.

6. Be sure to get all recommended vaccinations before you leave: also, as an added precaution, get preventive medicines and perhaps extra vaccinations that are not strongly recommended but might be helpful. Cholera vaccinations come to mind as one example. Carry an IAMA International Vaccination Card and a list of names, addresses, and phone numbers of English-speaking doctors for all countries in which you will be traveling.

7. Carry an international driver's license—available from all state bureaus of motor vehicles.

8. Don't drink tap water anywhere for the first two days, regardless of who says it's safe. Use bottled water, even to brush your teeth. And be sure to stay away from milk during your entire stay. Local beers and wines are usually safe, however.

9. Don't eat meat anywhere in the world for the first week, even if it's frozen and imported from the United States. Also stay away from seafood of any type, unless your destination is a seaside location. You can normally tell by looking at fruits and vegetables whether they are safe. It's a good idea, however, to refrain from eating them in very backward countries like Bangladesh and most of sub-Sahara Africa.

10. When traveling to tropical countries, carry plenty of mosquito repellent and roach poison.

11. Always carry on your person a letter explaining who you are and who to contact in the host country and in the United States in case of emergency.

This letter should also list any medication you may be allergic to or that you must have, along with your blood type.

12. Do not leave the United States without a confirmed hotel reservation at your destination. Also, check ahead to find out how much local taxi fares are to hotels.

13. Carry a small amount of host country currency from home. This saves a lot of time and trouble when trying to get a taxi at the airport.

14. Convert only a minimum amount of dollars to local currency at the arriving airport. Invariably, banks will have better exchange rates.

15. Regardless of advertisements, don't count on using your credit cards overseas, especially in less-developed countries. Carry plenty of U.S. dollars and travelers checks. Those credit cards that you do carry should be American Express and Visa, but be sure your Visa card is from Citibank, Chase Manhattan, Chemical Bank, or Bank of America. Many foreign areas do not recognize Visa cards from less-well-known American banks. American Express still has the best coverage worldwide.

16. Never appear to be a tourist. Dress and act like you have authority. This is especially relevant in less-developed countries.

17. **Most important of all:** Carry a small stock of gold pens, U.S. coins, cigarettes, and inexpensive jewelry in case you need a hand out to get through customs. This is essential, especially in more backward countries. Regardless of U.S. morals or laws, such payoffs may be the only way to get into (and out of) a country.

BUSINESS INSURANCE

Although few companies have difficulty protecting their assets and employees at home, the reverse is true overseas. The problem arises partly from a lack of understanding of local laws and regulations and partly from an inability to adjust to different cultural practices. The biggest obstacles seem to arise in less-developed countries, primarily because of hazards not encountered at home. A comprehensive insurance program is one of the best ways to guard against such hazards.

Comprehensive insurance coverage is a relatively inexpensive way to avoid monetary losses and the extraneous bureaucratic paperwork that invariably follows an accident or other mishap. Because business insurance is not as popular overseas as in the United States, there are many fewer insurers available to choose from.

Most companies find it easier and less expensive to place insurance with home-country carriers than to sort out options in a foreign environment. Many poorer or smaller nations do not have any insurance companies. In others, the few small carriers that do exist frequently shun foreign customers or charge prohibitive premiums.

Types of Coverage

The Foreign Credit Insurance Association (FCIA), a branch of Eximbank, is the most prominent insurer of export credit risk. American International Group (AIG) is the largest private-sector insurer, although CIGNA and Lloyd's also offer good coverage. The best coverage for political risk can be purchased from the Overseas Private Investment Corporation (OPIC).

In addition to credit and political risk, both exporters and investors should include product liability, property protection, and lost-income-reimbursement coverage. Although domestic policies usually exclude overseas property or activities, a few carriers will issue riders or additional policies for an increased premium.

When leasing a car, it may be necessary to prove that your U.S. automobile policy covers overseas rentals. Even if auto insurance can be purchased locally (which is impossible in many countries), it is substantially more expensive than in the United States.

The risk of damage to or complete loss of shipments to poorer countries is very real. Inland transit to rural areas frequently results in broken containers and damaged or lost goods. The solution lies in a good cargo-in-transit policy from a home-country carrier. Cargo-in-transit coverage, which protects against loss or damage of shipments between point of embarkation and point of debarkation, is required by Eximbank and most commercial banks involved in trade finance. Full-package policies can be purchased from AIG, CIGNA, Continental Insurance, and several other major business insurers. At a minimum, in addition to standard coverage, it's a good idea to include four special occurrences:

- Refused or returned shipments
- Concealed damage
- Brand and label removal
- Control of damaged goods.

Most companies prefer to go through a qualified insurance broker who knows which carriers offer the best deals. Two of the biggest and most reliable are Alexander & Alexander and Frank B. Hall & Co. Both have offices in metropolitan areas nationwide.

Captive Insurers

Wholly-owned insurance subsidiaries, or "captives," are the self-insurance wave of the future. With premiums skyrocketing and large competitors able to charge lower product prices by self-insuring, smaller companies have no choice but to do the same. Captives are usually set up to self-insure a portion of property, liability, and marine exposure. Some companies even include employee coverages.

In its simplest form, a captive agrees to take back a portion of the normal coverage from the major insurer, perhaps assuming the first U.S.$250,000 of annual losses. This reduces the premium and permits a company to invest the savings until they are needed to pay for losses. Rather than paying high premiums to outsiders for predictable, noncatastrophic losses, the company keeps the cash in-house and earns income on it.

Chapter 15 describes the effective use of tax havens as domiciles for captive insurance subsidiaries.

DEALING WITH THE FOREIGN CORRUPT PRACTICES ACT

The twenty-year-old U.S. Foreign Corrupt Practices Act, among other provisions, prohibits U.S. companies or employees from accepting or giving bribes, payoffs, kickbacks, or other favors in exchange for favored treatment from foreign government officials relating to contracts, financing, or assistance that

1. Affects the U.S. government (including Eximbank, OPIC, USAID, and all other agencies) in any way
2. Could be detrimental to the security of the United States
3. Is against U.S. public policy

Strict adherence to this law puts U.S. companies at an extreme competitive disadvantage in world markets. Recognizing that such payments are a normal part of doing business in less-developed nations, as well as in many industrialized ones, companies from Europe and Asia are less shackled. Corruption is a way of life in international trade. Companies that try to ignore it usually lose out to more flexible European and Japanese competitors.

Since U.S. multinationals have been competing in global markets for decades (and very successfully), they must have found a way to compensate. They have. The answer lies in using intermediaries. All multinationals do it; smaller companies must do it if they wish to compete.

Intermediaries flourish in virtually every country. They go by different titles: labor brokers, import houses, commissioned agents, consultants, trading companies, audit firms, and attorneys. Since many practices forbidden to U.S. firms are perfectly legal, or at least acceptable, under foreign laws, intermediaries are more than willing to assist American companies through the bureaucratic maze—many times the corrupt bureaucratic maze.

Part II
Financing Exports and Foreign Direct Investments

Chapter 8
Short-Term Trade Finance

Except under very unusual circumstances, in a free-market economy such as the United States, sellers of goods and services do not finance customers other than through normal trade credit channels. Moreover, highly selective federal and state financial aid programs apply only to restricted markets and certain categories of companies, such as urban redevelopment projects and minority-owned businesses. For example, the Small Business Administration (SBA) offers bank guarantees of up to $750,000 for companies meeting the SBA definition of a small business. The Economic Development Authority (EDA) provides partial financial assistance for the development of economically depressed areas. The Department of Agriculture subsidizes farmers with price platforms and payments for land not used. The Department of Defense assists government contractors with progress payments. And so on. In general, however, customers finance their own purchases and sellers finance their own production of goods.

Exporting is a different ball game. Between federal and state agencies, private organizations, international banks, and special insurance programs, exporters can, for all practical purposes, fund their export orders with outside financing, thereby eliminating the need to use their own capital or lines of credit.

Before going any further, some definitions are probably in order. The funding of export orders is referred to as *export sales finance*, or just *sales finance*. The term "trade finance" is used in a much broader sense, denoting the complete funding of export orders—from the time production begins until the goods have been accepted by the customer. Sales finance is a marketing tool, and in many companies under the jurisdiction of the marketing department. The financing of production orders with short- or long-term capital is clearly a finance department responsibility.

As a marketing tool, sales finance can be used as effectively as price discounts, after-sale customer service, or free deliveries to gain a competitive edge. In international trade, the form of sales finance offered to customers frequently determines which competitor gets the order. Customized sales finance strategies are crucial to success regardless of your customer's country. To demonstrate the point, here are two examples of companies that failed to regard sales finance as a competitive weapon and thereby killed orders that would have been profitable.

The first case involved one of our consortium clients. This $75 million manufacturer of solar-energy monitoring systems received an inquiry from a state-owned power company that was installing new lines in the remote Patagonia region of Argentina. Buenos Aires negotiations yielded a contract valued at more than $15 million, delivery schedules that extended over a three-year period, and installation assistance. Power company officials then announced that they expected the U.S. exporter to arrange buyer credit and performance guarantees.

Taken aback, the marketing executive returned home and assigned the problem to his controller. Six months later, financing arrangements were still in progress. Tired of waiting, the customer canceled the order and negotiated a fully financed deal with a competitor. Needless to say, the exporter's marketing executive and controller began looking for new jobs.

In another case, a client chose to take on a well-entrenched local cartel in Colombia without developing a sales finance strategy. This $250 million manufacturer decided to begin exporting a line of graphite-based gaskets used in heavy-duty agricultural and industrial equipment. No Colombian company made such a high-tensile product, so the vice president of marketing believed that a competitive edge was inevitable. He scoffed at my recommendation that he offer three-year payment terms and went to market demanding irrevocable, confirmed L/Cs.

Playing on buy-Colombia nationalism, a cartel of small local manufacturers overwhelmed my client with word-of-mouth sabotage, and within eighteen months all efforts to develop this market were abandoned. I later heard from my Bogotá contacts that money talked, and that if my client had offered attractive payment terms, the cartel would have been beaten before it could get started.

As a colleague once said, "Appropriate sales finance won't always carry the day, but more times than not it will pave the way."

These cases demonstrate that sales finance strategies should be as much a part of an international marketing plan as product/market strategies, distribution strategies, and sales promotion strategies. Why? For two reasons. First, because most private- and public-sector customers expect U.S. exporters to help arrange financing for them to pay for the goods. And second, because the cost of capital is a major element in competitive pricing, especially for large orders or those with payment terms extending over one or more years.

This second reason probably needs clarification. Somebody—either exporter or customer—must finance the shipment of goods from the port of embarkation to the port of debarkation. Shipping to many destinations, such as Bombay, Buenos Aires, or Pretoria, can involve a significant period of time. Moreover, somebody—either exporter or customer—must "hold the paper," during any deferred payment period. In both cases, capital is tied up that could be used for other purposes. And the cost of that capital should be factored into the selling price of the order.

When selling into highly competitive markets, sales financing costs can easily put your company in an unfavorable competitive position. It is the high cost of capital, more than any other factor, that causes many U.S. companies to seriously consider producing products for local markets in the host country rather than exporting them from the United States.

CHOOSING A BANK FOR EXPORT TRADE CREDIT

Commercial banks play a critical role in global trade finance. This is especially true when exporting from the United States. Commercial banks participate in nearly every aspect of export financing, either as a lender or as an intermediary for letters of credit, wire transfers, and currency conversions. Foreign customers, as well as Eximbank and the SBA, work through the banking system, not around it. This means that choosing the right bank is a critical first step.

History has shown that companies just beginning an export program too often assume that because their local bank satisfies their domestic needs, this same bank must be capable of providing export banking services. In some instances this assumption may prove correct, but in the majority of cases, local or regional banks, especially the smaller ones, do not even begin to measure up to global trade finance standards. A commercial bank with little or no experience in international finance often creates more difficulties than it helps resolve.

Therefore, one of the first steps for new-to-exporting companies is to locate a commercial bank capable of providing competitive services in the international finance marketplace. To do this, a bank should have the following:

1. An experienced, diversified international department. Without this expertise, the bank will be nothing more than an intermediary for another larger bank. This only confuses the issue, adds significant time to clearing transactions, and makes exporting more costly.

2. Decision-making bank executives familiar with the role letters of credit (L/Cs) play in international trade.

3. A willingness to accept Eximbank and SBA guarantees without insisting on additional collateral or personal guarantees to cover the bank's 10 to 20 percent of the loan balance.

4. Recognition in foreign banking circles and solid relationships with correspondent banks in foreign countries. Acting as an intermediary for money center banks diminishes the bank's financial credibility in the eyes of foreign traders, leading to higher operating costs.

5. An organization that can handle foreign currency translations, currency hedging (if necessary), and wire transfers directly to and from other banks around the world without going through a money center bank.

EXPORT CREDIT TERMS AND BANK INSTRUMENTS

Domestically, trade credit refers to buying or selling "on time." Payments against open account transactions are made in thirty days, sixty days, or some other mutually agreed upon time frame. The term "trade credit" has an entirely different meaning when applied to global trade. Here there are two types of trade credit: supplier credit and buyer credit.

Supplier credit refers to credit extended to the buyer by the seller (exporter). An exporter may extend credit directly, or it may obtain outside financing from banks, government agencies, or any other source. If an exporter records a receivable on its books, even temporarily, the credit extension is regarded as supplier credit.

Buyer credit refers to credit extended to the buyer by someone other than the exporter. Credit may be extended by an American bank, a foreign bank, a U.S. government agency, a foreign government agency, or another third party. The credit can carry guarantees, or it can stand alone. Exporters do not record receivables because cash, or cash equivalents, are received as the products are shipped.

Credit terms, or payment terms, for export sales are also different from those traditionally used for domestic sales. In the latter, the buyer obtains possession of the goods without executing a formal declaration indicating an obligation to pay. Credit terms are normally on open account, with payment made upon presentation of a commercial invoice, bill of lading, or promissory note. Export sales, on the other hand, are normally settled with drafts or bills of exchange together with supporting shipping documentation.

Drafts and Bills of Exchange

Traditional export payment terms specify a formal promise to pay, known as a Document against Acceptance (D/A) of a bill or draft, or against payment in full, referred to as a Document against Payment (D/P), before a customer takes possession of the goods. This typically occurs when the original on-board ocean bill of lading and other supporting documents are presented by the exporter to a U.S. correspondent bank of the buyer's home-country bank.

Many types of payment terms can be used in conjunction with bills and drafts:

- *Sales on consignment or open account.* Both similar to domestic sales.
- *Cash against documents, goods, or payment* (CAD, CAG, and CAP, respectively). Since drafts are not required, CADs are frequently used by European companies to avoid stamp taxes on sight or time drafts.
- *Clean drafts.* These are presented to a bank for collection simultaneously with the transfer of the shipping documents to the customer (similar to open account terms).
- *Time drafts.* Drawn on a foreign customer, these drafts require that the customer accept the draft on arrival of the goods, otherwise known as a trade acceptance (T/A). The customer then promises to pay the draft at its maturity, usually ninety days.
- *Sight drafts.* These drafts are similar to time drafts, except that they are payable upon "sight" by the customer, not after an extended time period.

This chapter and the next explore a variety of export trade finance methods as well as ways to guarantee the timely collection of customer accounts. Some methods are available only through government-sponsored programs, some are available from states and cities, and others can be arranged through private means.

In an attempt to bring some order to the vast array of options, it helps to divide trade finance strategies into three groupings, according to the time period granted in the terms of sale:

- Short-term trade finance, which applies when payment terms are less than 180 days
- Intermediate-term trade finance for sales with payment terms running from six months to five years
- Long-term financing, which involves payment periods greater than five years

LETTERS OF CREDIT

The most common forms of short-term trade finance, documentary letters of credit and banker's acceptances, place the collection burden on American banks. Occasionally open account terms may be used, but that is the exception rather than the rule. Unless you know the customer very well, it has an excellent credit rating, and you keep some leverage over the transaction as security, open account sales should rarely be considered.

Documentary Letters of Credit

A documentary letter of credit (L/C) is an instrument that will reduce the risk of nonpayment (or delay of payment) as a result of the buyer's financial difficulties and, at the same time, mitigate political risk from the buyer's country of origin. It is called documentary because the terms of the letter specify payment against the presentation of certain sales and shipping documents. Nearly all letters of credit used in international trade are documentary. Payment terms may involve sight or time drafts or other demands for payment. Time drafts are also referred to as usance drafts.

Many new-to-exporting managers mistakenly believe that L/Cs guarantee payment from banks and rely on L/Cs as a substitute for common sense credit judgment. L/Cs do not, in and of themselves, guarantee payment. It is the instructions embodied in the L/C that determine the payment security. Therefore, it is crucial to be certain that specific instructions are included to positively ensure payment in compliance with the sales contract.

Letters of credit come in many forms and carry a wide range of provisions. They can be revocable or irrevocable, confirmed or advised, straight or negotiated, payable at sight or over an extended period of time, transferable, assignable, or restricted. They can be written to cover partial shipments, full shipments, or transshipments. An L/C can cover one shipment, or it may be revolving, covering several subsequent shipments.

Regardless of other provisions, it's important to insist that L/Cs be irrevocable and confirmed on an American bank. *Irrevocable* means that the issuer cannot change the terms of the L/C, and *confirmed* means that an American bank is obligated to make payment upon presentation of proper documentation. The confirmation by an American bank also means that a host-country (or other) bank has extended your customer sufficient credit to purchase the goods.

Banks honor L/Cs upon presentation of bills of lading or other transport documents proving that the goods have in fact been delivered as specified in the order. However, L/Cs must be properly prepared and executed to be valid. A bank will not honor an L/C unless all supporting documentation accompanies a payment request.

Although the variety of terms and conditions is virtually limitless, most L/Cs contain the following:

- Payment terms
- Terms of sale
- Expiration date
- Shipment date(s)
- Presentation date at a later time (if applicable)
- Revocability
- The opening bank
- Advising or confirming bank
- Minimum documentary requirements
- Amount of credit carried by the letter
- Opening date of the letter
- Whether partial shipments are allowed and in what quantities
- How the letter will be transmitted to the beneficiary.

Here is an example of what happens when payment is made against an irrevocable letter of credit confirmed by a U.S. bank.

1. After the exporter (Foreign Sales, Ltd.) and its customer (Chilean Markets, S.A.) agree on the terms of a sale, Chilean Markets arranges for its bank, Banco Secundo, to open a letter of credit.

2. Banco Secundo prepares an irrevocable L/C in favor of Foreign Sales, including all negotiated instructions covering the shipment.

3. Banco Secundo sends the L/C to a U.S. bank, Chase Manhattan, requesting confirmation.

4. Chase Manhattan prepares a letter of confirmation and sends it to Foreign Sales along with the L/C.

5. Foreign Sales carefully reviews all conditions in the L/C to be certain that they agree with the negotiated terms. Foreign Sales' freight forwarder should then be contacted to make sure the shipping date can be met. If Foreign Sales cannot comply with one or more of the conditions, Chilean Markets should be immediately contacted to arrange new language in the L/C.

6. Foreign Sales arranges with its freight forwarder to deliver the goods to the appropriate port or air terminal.

7. When the goods are loaded, the forwarder completes the necessary documents, including the bill of lading.

8. Foreign Sales, or its freight forwarder, presents the documentation to Chase Manhattan.

9. Chase reviews the documents and, if they are in order, airmails them to Banco Secundo for review and transmittal to Chilean Markets.

10. Chilean Markets, or its agent, then uses the documents to claim its goods upon arrival in Chile.

11. At the time specified in the L/C, Chase Manhattan honors the draft that accompanies the letter of credit. As an alternative, Chase may discount the draft for payment at an earlier date.

No matter how carefully an L/C is prepared, errors seem to creep in that prevent payment. Figure 8.1 lists the errors that seem to be the most common.

Figure 8.1
Common Errors in Letters of Credit

1. Omission of the statement "irrevocable" or "confirmed by _____ bank" (an American bank), or both

2. Misspelled name and/or address of exporter or customer

3. Credit insufficient to cover full cost of shipment—i.e., forwarding fees, consular fees, insurance, inspection charges, etc.

4. Incomplete or inaccurate description of merchandise, prices, and terms of payment

5. No allowance for variations in shipping quantity resulting from shrinkage, damaged goods, etc.

6. Omission of the word "about" or "approximately" (which allows for 10 percent variance) preceding the amount of credit

7. Marks and numbers on invoice different from those on other documents

8. Wording in customer's draft different from that in the letter of credit

9. Inappropriate or incomplete markings on the bill of lading that do not conform to L/C instructions

10. Bill of lading shipping date later than that allowed in L/C

11. Drafts and other documents not all dated within the expiration date of the L/C

12. Instructions in L/C that are different from those specified on the invoice

Variations of Documentary Letters of Credit

Many variations on a straightforward documentary letter of credit are used in international trade finance—far too many to be inclusive here, although there are several excellent books are available that provide comprehensive treatment of the subject. Following are the more common variations.

1. *Back-to-back L/Cs.* Back-to-back L/Cs are used when vendors or subcontractors demand payment from the exporter before collections are re-

ceived from the customer. For example, assume that a manufacturing company gets an order to ship 1,000 bicycles to a buyer in Norway. Payment will be made against the buyer's L/C placed on a New York bank. The order calls for shipments of 100 bicycles every month for ten months. The L/C allows for payments against partial shipments.

The manufacturing company subcontracts the assembly gear mechanism and the subcontractor wants payment for all 1,000 gear sets in thirty days, refusing to wait for payment until all ten orders have been shipped to Norway.

The manufacturer merely presents the buyer's L/C to the bank and asks the bank to issue a new L/C to the subcontractor, payable in thirty days. The new L/C is from the manufacturer to the subcontractor, but it uses the Norwegian customer's L/C as collateral. The manufacturer's L/C and the buyer's L/C are called back-to-back L/Cs.

The manufacturer remains obligated to perform fully against the buyer's L/C. If default occurs, the bank is left holding worthless collateral. This causes many banks to refuse an exporter's request to issue back-to-back L/Cs, although those with solid international experience and a good relationship with the exporter normally will oblige.

2. *Off-balance-sheet credit extension.* Off-balance-sheet credit is a variation on the back-to-back L/C theme. By extending off-balance-sheet credit, a bank does not use the buyer's L/C as collateral. This eliminates the risk of the exporter's not performing.

Rather than collateralizing its L/Cs with letters of credit against a shipping order, the bank issues new L/Cs directly to an exporter's vendors. The general credit of the exporter secures these L/Cs, which become an addition to the exporter's line of credit. This procedure is not as gratuitous as it appears at first glance. Once a drawdown occurs against the buyer's L/C, the bank expects the exporter to deposit these funds and to grant the bank authority to use them to pay down other outstanding loans, keeping everything in balance.

Many times banks demand additional security from exporters against the credit extension. In that case, the bank always has the option of filing a lien against the goods to be exported under the Uniform Commercial Code (a UCC filing). This ensures that the proceeds will be deposited when the buyer's L/C is drawn down.

Both back-to-back L/Cs and off-balance-sheet credit extensions cost money. Rates vary considerably, but normal fees range from 0.5 to 2 percent of the value of the L/C. Some banks charge as much as 5 percent. In addition, many banks extract an additional commitment fee ranging from 0.5 to 5 percent.

3. *Assigned proceeds.* Exporters can also use their buyer's credit to raise working capital. This is achieved by assigning the proceeds from the buyer's L/C. Any L/C can be assigned without permission from the

buyer, a bank, or anyone else. Assigning an L/C is easy. It merely involves telling the bank holding the L/C that it should pay either the entire proceeds or a percentage of the proceeds drawn on the L/C to a specified third party.

If a vendor doesn't believe in the authenticity of a foreign buyer's letter of credit, a copy of the L/C can be forwarded. To prevent a vendor from knowing the identity of the buyer, the buyer's name is blacked out on the L/C and all supporting documentation. The only time a vendor or subcontractor really gets hurt by accepting an assignment is if the shipment gets held up for reasons outside of anyone's control. Obviously, when that occurs, payment against the L/C will also be withheld.

In rare cases, an imperfection in the customer's L/C prevents drawdowns. If the L/C carries nonrecourse terms, the assignee has no option but to try to collect directly from the exporter or the exporter's customer.

Assigning an L/C involves no additional cost or addition to credit lines—merely the completion of a simple assignment form.

4. *Transferred L/C*. When an exporter requires that certain materials or products be shipped directly from its supplier to the foreign customer rather than being relayed to the exporter for inclusion in the complete order, it can use *transferred letters of credit*. In this case, the exporter acts as an intermediary. With high value goods, the supplier might demand that the exporter actually transfer the customer's L/C intact, avoiding reliance on the exporter's performance as a condition of getting paid.

Permission must be obtained from the buyer to transfer an L/C, either partially or in its entirety. Obviously, the foreign buyer then knows that a third party, not the exporter, is the original supplier of these goods. This might raise questions about the exporter's financial viability, potentially hurting additional business.

A foreign buyer has the right to refuse permission to transfer the L/C. This seldom occurs, however, unless the relationship between buyer and exporter rested on shaky ground to begin with.

Terms of payment, shipping instructions, insurance provisions, product markings, drawdown documentation, and all other terms and conditions stipulated in the letter of credit remain intact when transferring it. If part of the order is manufactured and shipped by the exporter and part by the exporter's vendor or subcontractor, the exporter can still avoid negotiating an entirely new L/C for its share of the order. It accomplishes this by instructing the paying bank to limit payment on the transferred L/C to the amounts due the vendor or subcontractor, then substituting export invoices for the balance of the L/C.

This sounds complicated, but it really isn't. It is fairly common practice, and banks seldom blink when an exporter initiates the transaction. It does involve more paperwork, however, and therefore added cost, although bank fees for this service tend to be reasonable and shouldn't influence the decision.

The identity of the foreign buyer can be kept confidential in a transferred letter of credit as easily as with an assignment. Merely include instructions in the documentation that the paying bank should notify the exporter rather than the buyer when both shipment and payment have been made. Again this is not an unusual request, and most banks and buyers go along with it.

Standby Letter of Credit

American commercial banks cannot, under the law, issue guarantees of performance or payment except under two circumstances:

1. If the bank has a substantial interest in the performance of the transaction

2. If the bank has sufficient segregated funds on deposit to cover any potential loss.

Overseas branches of American banks can issue guarantees where permitted by local law, although they must conform to restrictions spelled out by the Federal Reserve System.

As an alternative to a straightforward bank guarantee, banks are allowed to issue standby letters of credit. Standby letters of credit serve a number of uses. The most common uses are as guarantees for

- Contractor bid and performance bonds
- Performance guarantees against advance payments
- Guarantees against payments on open account
- Guarantees against payment of other financial obligations.

A standby L/C is essentially an unsecured line of credit to a customer. Whereas a documentary L/C cannot be drawn against without documentary proof of shipment and compliance with all other terms of the letter, payments against standby L/Cs are made against a simple statement of default or nonperformance.

When a foreign buyer does not have sufficient credit or capital to warrant the issuance of a confirmed, irrevocable L/C as immediate payment, other financing tools can be used. A documentary banker's acceptance is one such tool.

DOCUMENTARY BANKER'S ACCEPTANCE

A documentary banker's acceptance (BA) is a form of payment that uses the exporter's credit (supplier credit) to complete a sale. Once the products have been shipped and the sale is concluded, the exporter sells the receivable to a bank—at a discount, of course. The process includes steps similar to factoring a domestic receivable and works as follows:

1. The buyer executes a time letter of credit for the full amount of the sale price. Instructions included in the L/C authorize payment a specified number of days after the exporter presents shipping documentation. An exporter should insist on a fixed date not in excess of 180 days from the date of sight, the maximum time frame for a BA.

2. When the exporter presents the shipping documentation, the bank issues a BA in place of cash. The BA consists of the exporter's draft with a bank marking "accepted" stamped across its face. This marking means that the bank promises to pay the exporter, or any other holder of the BA, on the fixed date of the L/C.

3. The exporter presents this BA to the issuing bank and requests that bank to discount the document. The bank pays the face value minus the discount interest, which the exporter merely adds to the invoice price. Documentary BAs allow both sides to win. The buyer conserves cash for up to six months, and the exporter gets cash immediately.

Banks charge a very low discount rate for BAs, making this instrument the practically the least costly form of trade credit. However, to compensate for the low discount rate, issuing banks charge an acceptance fee for handling the transaction. This ranges from 0.5 to 2 percent per annum of the face amount of the L/C. Foreign buyers will often pay this acceptance fee directly even if they won't allow it to be factored into a higher price for the goods.

Clean Banker's Acceptance

A clean BA differs from a documentary BA in that it does not have the buyer's letter of credit as collateral. Instead, the exporter must use its own credit as security.

A clean BA applies to a specific transaction or shipment, just like a documentary BA. The BA is discounted with the exporter's bank. The bank then takes this readily negotiable instrument and sells it in the secondary bond market. Banks like this instrument for two reasons: It does not get recorded on the bank's balance sheet, and it is always readily negotiable.

As can be expected, large corporations are the main users of clean BAs. Smaller exporters must have very good credit to use clean BAs. However, if they have a good track record of shipping quality products on schedule over a period of time, smaller companies stand a reasonable chance of getting a bank to go along.

Clean BAs usually run about $500,000, although they can be as low as $100,000. Clean BAs are the province of very large regional banks and money center banks. Smaller banks prefer other instruments. Interest rates on clean BAs run less than LIBOR (London Interbank Offered Rate), which is nearly always less than the prime rate. Acceptance fees range up to 2 percent per annum on the face amount of the BA.

Both sides win with banker's acceptances. Customers conserve cash for up to six months. You get your cash immediately.

OVERSEAS BRANCHES OF U.S. BANKS

In addition to documentary drafts, L/Cs, and banker's acceptances, it may be possible to arrange customer financing directly from your U.S. bank. This can be a viable strategy when your bank has branch facilities or a line of credit with a bank in the customer's country.

In many cases, the U.S. office and the foreign branch office of the same bank work in tandem to secure import lines of credit for local companies. Such lines are usually secured by guarantees or insurance from Eximbank or from other commercial and political risk insurers.

Your customer may also be able to arrange financing with a host country bank that has offices in the United States.

CASE STUDY: INVOICE TIMING

This chapter has covered six types of short-term export trade finance:

1. Open account

2. Documentary drafts

3. Letters of credit

4. Banker's acceptances

5. Exporter's bank line of credit

6. Customer's bank line of credit.

All six methods potentially create the same timing problem: When do you book the sale and, therefore, when is payment due?

For domestic sales, typical terms and conditions call for the collection period to begin on the date of the invoice, which is also the date on which accountants assume that title has passed and therefore the sale can be booked. For instance, if a domestic invoice calls for thirty-day terms and the invoice date is March 31, your accounting department will book the sale in March and begin dunning the customer April 30 if payment has not been received.

Export sales aren't as straightforward. The following example demonstrates two types of timing problems frequently encountered.

Assume the following:

Amount of export order:	$150,000
Payment terms:	Ninety-days dated draft from bill of lading (B/L) date
Terms of sale:	FAS, New Orleans, Louisiana
Shipped from:	Knoxville, Tennessee on April 1
Transport time:	10 days from Knoxville to New Orleans
	60 days from New Orleans to Salvador, Brazil
Estimated on-board B/L date:	April 15
Estimated time of arrival (ETA):	June 15

The first question that arises is: Which date should be used when booking the sale?

1. Should the sale be booked and invoiced April 1? Marketing personnel would certainly prefer to get credit for the sale as early as possible, which would be April 1. But then collection from the customer would be expected by July 1, only fifteen days after receipt of goods.

2. Should the sale be booked and invoiced April 15? Accounting departments prefer this date. Since the time interval in ocean shipping is indeterminate, accountants assume that title to the goods has passed when they have been loaded on the ship. However, if payments are not received by July 15 (only thirty days after the customer's receipt of goods), the credit department will begin the dunning process.

3. Should the sale be booked and invoiced June 15? Clearly, customers prefer this date, since payment can then be delayed. However, using this date to record the sale means that payment won't be due until September 15, a full 165 days after shipment!

The solution in this example is straightforward. Since the order include FAS terms, the invoice must be dated when the bill of lading (B/L) is prepared, presumably April 15. Payment will then be due ninety days from this date, or July 15.

It should be noted that FAS means "free alongside ship," which obligates the exporter to place the goods alongside the overseas vessel and within reach of its loading tackle. Responsibility for obtaining shipping space and marine insurance then rests with the buyer. This is the most common means of handling export shipments.

But booking the sale on the bill of lading date creates a second timing problem. You won't know for certain that April 15 was the date that title passed until you receive the B/L from the freight forwarder. It is not uncommon for freight forwarders to miss an expected B/L date by as much as ten days—or more. Also, mailing time from a New Orleans freight forwarder to Knoxville could add another three or four days.

When a company has many export shipments, all with different B/L dates, such uncertainties can easily delay both the marketing department's credit for the sale and the receipt of customer payments.

One solution would be to install a direct computer link-up with your freight forwarder. Such a link-up is called an *electronic data interchange*, or EDI. It coordinates bills of lading and other export documents

1. Between your accounting department and freight forwarders

2. Between freight forwarders and ocean carriers

3. Between carriers and port authorities.

This effectively eliminates mail time, provides precise B/L dates, and gives you better control over invoicing dates. If your company is not hooked up to an EDI system, it may pay to ask your controller to investigate it.

GETTING PAID

In addition to assisting customers to finance the purchase of goods, exporters need to be certain that they will get paid. An army of lawyers and a flotilla of courts are only too eager to enforce U.S. contract terms. In international trade, however, there is no court from which an exporter may seek recourse. Therefore, other means must be used to ensure timely payment.

Three major factors affect the ability of foreign customers to pay for imported products:

1. The country's *hard currency reserves*. There will be scant chance of getting paid in U.S. dollars if your customer's country has a shortage of hard currency reserves. In that case, a countertrade deal may be the only logical possibility.

2. *Exchange controls* that relate to the use of hard currency. From time to time, most less-developed countries enact protective exchange controls—especially when hard currency reserves run low. Local government import approval, usually in the form of import licenses, is then necessary. And import licenses can be hard to get.

3. The country's *inflation rate and U.S. dollar exchange rate*. Inflation rates and exchange rates go hand in hand. In countries with skyrocketing inflation, such as Brazil, the selling price of imported goods paid for in hard currency can easily place them out of the reach of local customers.

If all countries had stable economies with controllable inflation rates, surplus hard currency reserves, and continuity in their political systems, financing exports would be relatively straightforward. The fact is, however, that although local conditions may seem stable when an order is placed, they could change radically by the time payments are due.

Creditworthiness

The starting point in any sales transaction (domestic or foreign) should be to establish the customer's creditworthiness. Fortunately, there are several organizations, both federal and private, that can provide assistance in this matter.

On the federal side, the Department of Commerce will sell you World Trader Data Reports, prepared by U.S. commercial attachés. These reports include information about a company's business activities, reputation, number of employees, ownership, products, and general operations, but they do not include financial information. They do, however, include the attachés' opinion as to the company's general creditworthiness and its reliability as a trade contact.

Eximbank and its insurance arm, the Foreign Credit Insurance Association, also furnish credit data on foreign companies that they have done business with, or whose credit they have checked for other American companies.

Dun & Bradstreet and a few smaller American credit bureaus provide reports on mostly larger foreign companies. However, foreign credit agencies are more familiar with local companies. They respond more quickly to individual requests, and usually produce reports that are far more comprehensive than those from D & B, and at a lower cost. However, be aware they will still be incomplete.

Finally, all major banks maintain their own credit departments. Chances are good that your bank can get credit information on virtually any foreign customer that has purchased goods from an American company in the past.

The Foreign Credit Insurance Association

Even though credit reports give an important indication of a customer's ability to pay, it only makes sense to also purchase credit insurance. Insurance against both political and commercial risk is available from private carriers or from Eximbank's Foreign Credit Insurance Association, referred to as FCIA.

FCIA policies cover a wide range of risks, including expropriation, customers' failure to pay, and currency fluctuations. Here is a brief summary of the various policies.

New-to-Exporting Policy

This is a one-year blanket policy that insures the collectibility of short-term credit sales for companies that are just beginning to export or that have had average annual export sales of less than $750,000 for the past two years. Policy terms are

- Coverage of 100 percent of political risk and 95 percent of commercial risk (this drops to 90 percent after two years).
- Interest payments of up to prime rate minus 0.5 point due on debt obligations.
- Export order credit terms must be 180 days or less, except for agricultural commodities and consumer durables, which are covered for 360 days.
- Premium schedule available for the asking.
- Mandatory minimum annual premium of $500.
- If commercial risk insurance is not needed, political risk alone may be covered.

Umbrella Coverage

Umbrella coverage is provided to export agents—such as export management firms, commercial lenders, state agencies, finance companies, insurance brokers, export trading companies, and similar agencies—who administer the policy on behalf of multiple exporters. Umbrella policy terms are

- One-year coverage for short-term export sales from exporters with average annual export sales of less than $2 million for the past two years and who have not used FCIA during this period.
- Coverage of 100 percent of political risk and 90 percent of commercial risk.
- Interest coverage, maximum payment terms, and assignability are the same as for the new-to-exporting policy.
- Minimum annual premium of $500 must be paid by the policy administrator.

Multibuyer Coverage

This is a one-year blanket policy for either short-term or medium-term credit sales, or a combination of both, that covers all export transactions from a single exporter to multiple foreign buyers.

Coverage, repayment periods, minimum annual fee, and assignability follow those for other coverages. No cash down payment from the buyer is required under short-term coverage, but a 15 percent down payment must be made for medium-term.

Short-Term and Medium-Term Single-Buyer Coverage

These policies cover groups of exporters that ship to a single buyer, frequently a government-owned project or business. Premiums by type of customer are

- Sovereign buyers: $2,500
- Nonsovereign public-sector buyers: $5,000
- Private-sector buyers: $10,000.

Premiums for medium-term export orders are based on the type of buyer and the country of destination. In addition, all buyers must make a 15 percent down payment before shipment.

Lease Coverage

Lease coverage is offered to cover both the stream of lease payments and the fair market value of leased products. Loss coverage may be obtained on both new and used capital equipment and services, including aircraft, construction, medical, and communications equipment. All covered products must have been manufactured in the United States and be physically located overseas.

Coverage normally extends for five years; however, different terms may be negotiated case by case, depending on the type of product, the contract values, and the form of the lease. Premiums are determined individually by country, lease term, and type of lease, and must be paid in full in advance of shipment.

PRIVATE INSURANCE COMPANIES

Very few private insurance companies cover export risks. AIG Political Risks, Inc. (a subsidiary of American International Group, Inc.) is one of the few that does. AIG insures against political risk for export transactions, expropriation, money transfer, and contract repudiation by foreign governments, and provides performance bonds required in bidding arrangements. This carrier also insures export orders and projects that fall under government restrictions. In addition to AIG, Lloyd's and CIGNA offer export insurance coverage.

Chapter 9

Intermediate- and Long-Term Trade Finance

Although documentary drafts, letters of credit, banker's acceptances, and straightforward lines of credit work well when customers need short-term credit, they do not fill the financing need for export orders that have payment terms in excess of 180 days, such as those involving capital equipment or multiple shipments. Such large orders normally carry payment terms of three to eight years, although shorter or longer periods may be negotiated. In any case, orders with terms beyond 180 days must be financed differently from short-term sales.

When a sales order calls for payments over periods of from 180 days to five years, intermediate-term financing is necessary. When payments extend beyond five years, long-term trade financing is in order. Intermediate-term trade finance may be accomplished through forfaiting, factoring, leasing, or alternative transaction financing. Long-term financing usually involves greater risk, with buyer credit extended by either the Private Export Funding Corporation (PEFCO) or Eximbank. Both PEFCO and Eximbank also handle intermediate-term trade finance, but the terms and conditions of their programs are generally better suited to long-term orders.

FORFAITING

How would you like to negotiate sales contracts with payment terms well beyond one year (perhaps as much as ten years), eliminate all credit and political risk as well as the attendant problems of collecting against a time letter of credit, get paid 100 percent of the selling price at the time of shipment, and have your customer pay all financing costs?

Too good to be true? Not at all. It can be done with *forfaiting*. Although forfaiting remains a relatively new technique in the United States, European exporters have used it for decades as an effective sales finance tool. With forfaiting, an exporter gives away, or forfeits, its right to receive future payments in exchange for immediate cash—a more ingenious financing scheme than straightforward trade credit for high-value, intermediate-term transactions.

The term *forfait* originates from the French *à forfait*, which means a surrendering of rights. The process is called *le forfaitage* in traditional French, *la forfetizacion* in Spanish, and *fortaitierung* in German.

The intermediary, or middleman in a forfaiting transaction, called a forfaiter, is usually a specialized type of bank or lending institution that deals in the nonrecourse financing of export sales. Several transaction finance organizations (described later in this chapter) offer forfaiting services, as do a half-dozen or so U.S. money center banks and virtually all foreign multinational banks. As an aside, major international banks and specialized forfait houses buy and sell forfaited paper (drafts, bills of exchange, or promissory notes) in a highly specialized capital market. Gradually, outside investors are being admitted to this market, but to date, banks and forfait houses are the principal players.

International banks do not usually forfait export transactions of less than $250,000; however, specialized transaction finance houses will go as low as $100,000. Nor is forfaiting generally used for transactions of more than $5 million, although under certain circumstances transactions up to $10 million have been managed. The ideal export order runs between $500,000 and $2 million. Forfait transactions usually range from one to ten years, with five to six years being the most common.

Forfaiting cannot be used for short-term trade finance. It is best suited for customers that need medium-term credit, from three to eight years, when other forms of buyer credit are not available. Forfaiting is also popular when

- Direct buyer credit is too complex or unavailable.
- Export credit insurance is not available.
- Competitors offer forfaiting.
- Fixed-rate financing is necessary to close the order.

Forfaiting is a relatively simple concept. Every forfait transaction involves an exporter, an importer, a forfaiter, and, most important, the importer's guarantor (usually the importer's bank).

An exporter sells its receivable obligation to a forfaiter, who assumes all commercial and political risks of collection. In return, the exporter receives cash equal to the discounted face value of the receivable (that is, the discounted present value of the stream of future payments to be made by the importer over the life of the obligation). The forfait discount is calculated as the cost of the forfaiter's capital plus a premium for profit. This premium ranges from 0.5 to 6 points over LIBOR (which is typically 1 to 2 percentage points below the U.S. prime rate). Commitment fees run about 0.75 percent per annum.

The forfaiting process works as follows:

1. Assume that a Brazilian customer wants six-year credit terms for an order totaling $500,000, to be delivered in five semiannual shipments. Of course, this customer must be sufficiently creditworthy to get a Brazilian bank to grant one of the following:

   a. An unconditional bank guarantee to pay the forfaiter.

   b. An endorsement, called an *aval* on your export International Bill of Exchange that guarantees payment.

c. A term letter of credit (L/C), also called a usance, time L/C, or deferred-payment L/C. However, it must be a clean L/C; that is, one against which payment will be made without any extraneous conditions.

2. The forfaiter and the Brazilian customer together negotiate directly with the customer's bank to determine instrument will be used. The simplicity of this transaction has great appeal to bankers and customers alike because no contracts are involved that could require litigation in the event of default.

3. The forfaiter then discounts the L/C. Since the amount of the discount will be known ahead of time, it can be included in the selling price of the order.

4. When the exporter presents a complete set of documentation proving that the shipment has left, the forfaiter pays the exporter 100 percent of the selling price—less the discount, of course, if it was included in the selling price. Such payment is made within two days of the presentation of shipping documents.

5. The forfaiter then collects against the L/C directly from the Brazilian customer or from the customer's bank.

The broker's commission and commitment of funds fee (if these are paid by the exporter when funds are committed and the exporter adds the charges into the selling price) will be returned to the exporter at the time the L/C is discounted. In its simplest form, forfaiting is very much like traditional accounts receivable factoring, except that forfaiting requires the customer to arrange bank guarantees.

Forfaiting has three broad advantages:

- It provides medium- to long-term financing when short-term credit won't work.
- It covers the entire sale, not just 85 percent of the contract value (the maximum covered by Eximbank).
- It costs less than borrowing from a bank.

However, forfaiting also has two major disadvantages for smaller companies: First, it cannot be used for short-term credit, and second, many American banks just don't understand the mechanics yet. Furthermore, banks in some developing countries remain reluctant to handle the guarantee portion of the deal for the buyer.

As with any financing arrangement, you can run into logistical hurdles with forfaiting. Here are three examples, along with possible solutions for each.

1. *Problem:* A customer in a high-risk country, such as Peru or Surinam, cannot provide a guarantee from a bank acceptable to the forfaiter. *Solution:* Help the customer locate a foreign multinational bank—Dutch banks often bend the rules for Surinam (a former Dutch colony), and Japanese and Taiwanese banks might be interested in helping a Peruvian

company. Also, local government-sponsored export credit agencies should be willing to back local companies.

2. *Problem:* The customer's Brazilian bank is squeamish about issuing a letter of guarantee, doesn't understand aval bills of exchange, and won't issue a usance L/C. *Solution:* Ask the customer to investigate standby L/Cs to guarantee the payment. In most cases, forfaiters will accept standby L/Cs as a substitute.

3. *Problem:* A customer in Paraguay needs a $50 million credit, but no forfaiter will touch any form of guarantees from Paraguayan banks or the government. *Solution:* Use a forfait broker—possibly one of the transaction finance houses—that knows how to arrange *project finance.* The customer's import order could then be financed as a local project with equity capital.

Clearly, forfaiting isn't for everyone. But if it does fit your needs, it is the fastest and cheapest way to finance a medium-term export order. If forfaiting seems like a viable choice, try a foreign bank with offices in the United States rather than an American bank. As the years pass, more and more American banks of various sizes will inevitably begin to support forfaiting. As of this writing, however, only money center banks (such as Chase, Citicorp, Bank of America, and Chemical), a few larger regional banks, and specialized nonbank transaction finance organizations handle forfait deals.

An interesting variation on the forfaiting theme is offered by a few of these transaction finance organizations. Under certain conditions, they will act as brokers of forfait transactions, serving as a liaison between U.S. exporters on the one hand and forfait houses and underwriters on the other. Most (although not all) forfait brokers are based in Europe, however, making the logistics somewhat cumbersome for U.S. exporters.

EXPORT FACTORING

Since 1945, factoring receivables in domestic trade (that is, selling receivables to a factor with recourse to the company for collection defaults) has usually been associated with high credit-risk sellers who cannot obtain normal working capital bank financing. The stigma of failure has kept otherwise viable companies from even considering factoring as a financing tool.

Export factoring is an entirely different story. The process is different, the benefits are different, and the tool is not reserved for poor-credit-risk exporters. Export factoring does involve selling receivables at a discount—usually 70 to 90 percent of the invoice value. But there the similarity to domestic factoring ends. With export factoring, the exporter is off the hook for any collection default; both commercial and political risks are assumed by the factor. The factor also performs collection activities. And there is no upper or lower limit on the dollar amount of receivables.

In addition, export factors provide a variety of other services if the exporter so desires. These services include buyer credit investigation; all bookkeeping functions, with monthly reports issued to the exporter; a choice of three payment cycles to the exporter—based on total collections, average collections, or collections at maturity—and collateral for bank loans. The latter benefit warrants further explanation.

When a factor's services (credit approval, bookkeeping, collections) are used, the factor guarantees 100 percent nonrecourse protection against most risks. The exporter assigns the receipt of funds or credit balances due from the factor to a bank. Banks are generally willing to loan against these future collections as long as they can look to the factor and not the exporter for collection.

Factors charge a commission of 1.5 to 2 percent for this service, and banks charge interest of prime plus 1 to 2 percentage points. This can be extremely beneficial if the exporter has already used up existing credit lines. Also, factors tend to collect receivables faster than commercial sellers.

There are four major international factoring organizations:

1. Factors Chain International, whose members are independent factoring companies in various countries around the world.

2. International Factors, originated by First Bank of Boston, the world's oldest export factoring organization. Its members are located in twenty-two countries.

3. Walter Heller Overseas Corp., the largest export factoring company. It also has subsidiaries located throughout the world.

4. Credit Factoring International, a subsidiary of National Westminster Bank in London. It operates subsidiaries in ten countries.

LEASING

Capital equipment exporters often find leasing to be a viable alternative form of supplier credit. Recognizing the profitability of foreign leasing, many exporters have set up separate companies to handle the leases internally, rather than selling the equipment to third-party lessors.

As described in Chapters 8 and 11, insurance coverage provided by the Foreign Credit Insurance Association (FCIA) significantly diminishes the risk of entering into a long-term lease with a foreign buyer. The FCIA insures against both commercial and foreign-government expropriation losses. With such minimal risk and an opportunity to increase profits beyond normal sales transactions, leasing may be an attractive alternative to either private trade finance or government-supported aid programs.

When exporting to a less-developed country that uses soft currency, leasing is frequently the only feasible way to finance sales. Lease payment terms can be very flexible, arranged to suit the needs of both the exporter and the customer. Several companies have found leasing so profitable that they finance entire export programs with leases and countertrade arrangements. The use of countertrade to convert soft-currency lease payments into hard currency or goods is rapidly becoming a popular method for avoiding restrictive currency exchange controls. (See Chapter 10 for a full description of countertrade techniques.)

Export leasing (also known as cross-border leasing) involves complex agreements that stipulate secondary collateral guarantees from suppliers and contractual arrangements between a leasing company in country A and a lessee in country B. It gets more complicated when leased assets reside in country B but the lessee is domiciled in a third country, C.

A wide range of legal and tax problems also arise, including customs and contractual constraints, collateral rights, foreign taxes, creditor/debtor rights, and government expropriation risks. By and large, cross-border leasing works well for transactions between large buyers (frequently foreign governments) and large exporters; however, smaller companies generally find the process too complex.

If you decide to use international leasing, it usually makes sense to go with a third-party leasing company located in the host country. Local lessors know the local rules. They can take advantage of local tax regulations. And (by far the most important consideration) they will source their own funds to purchase assets to be leased. This reduces both the risk and the cost of capital built into rental payments.

In addition to handling trade finance, international leasing companies absorb much of the exporter's administrative burden. They perform lessee credit checks in foreign countries; manage all customs duties, licenses, and tax requirements for selling in the host country; and relieve exporters of arranging and then administering complex insurance and collection procedures. Moreover, since ownership of leased products is transferred to the international leasing company upon shipment, exporters are immediately off the hook.

Although most multinational investment banks have leasing subsidiaries, commercial and merchant banks are the main originators of international leases. Working with major Japanese, French, British, Dutch, or German merchant banks is the quickest way to get the ball rolling. Within the United States, most money center banks and large investment banks can also help in arranging appropriate leasing terms and executing lease contracts.

In addition, names and addresses of active international leasing companies can be obtained from

- The American Association of Equipment Lessors (AAEL) membership roster, which includes most active equipment leasing companies based in the United States. This list identifies both domestic lessors and companies handling international leases.
- The *World Leasing Yearbook*, published by Hawkins Publishers, Ltd, London, which identifies many foreign leasing companies. Leasing industry descriptions from more than forty countries are covered, as well as leasing companies that operate in over sixty countries.

ALTERNATIVE TRANSACTION FINANCE

The reluctance of commercial banks to look beyond a company's balance sheet has opened the door to a variety of nonbank organizations that specialize in export trade finance. These organizations finance export *transactions* rather than an entire company. In other words, their level of interest is determined by the viability of a specific export order, not by a company's profitability or debt/equity ratio.

Some trade finance organizations are outgrowths of state foreign-trade programs. Others are subsidiaries of manufacturing, shipping, distribution, or trading companies. Still others are owned by major international commercial and investment banks.

California has one of the most aggressive state-sponsored trade finance organizations, called World Trade Finance, Inc. World Trade Finance specializes in what it calls preshipment financing to small manufacturers located in California. The following description of how it works appeared in the World Trade Finance newsletter, *Transactions*, Summer 1993 edition:

> A small company that manufacturers equipment receives a foreign order for several hundred thousand dollars. The equipment, having a production cycle of several months, will potentially drain the company of its already limited working capital.

The newsletter goes on to explain that "World Trade will grant a production loan to cover the direct expenses related to the foreign order."

World Trade Finance warns potential applicants, however, that a letter of credit in hand will not necessarily qualify as collateral for preshipment financing. This state-sponsored organization considers it more important that the exporter have the ability to perform against an export order.

Most private-sector trade finance organizations specialize in a particular form of trade credit or in specific industries, and offer a variety of finance services, including factoring, forfaiting, foreign exchange management, loans, and equity contributions, the latter primarily for companies interested in establishing *maquiladora* or "twin" plants.

One such specialized private organization, British-American Forfaiting Company, Inc., of St. Louis, considers its forfaiting brokerage service as "analogous to that of an independent insurance agent." In addition to brokering forfait deals, this company offers such transaction finance services as discounted, back-to-back, and standby letters of credit; coordination of Eximbank financing; project financing; countertrade assistance; currency swaps; and merchant banking services.

Midland International Trade Services of New York is one example of a bank-owned transaction trade finance organization. It is a subsidiary of Midland Montagu, which, in turn, is the international and investment banking arm of the Midland Bank Group of Great Britain. Midland offers sales finance designed to meet specific exporter needs and has fully staffed offices throughout Latin America, as well as in many other regions of the world.

These examples point out how far export trade finance in the United States has progressed. The plethora of private financing sources refutes the contention by domestically oriented smaller companies that lack of commercial bank credit prevents their expansion into global trade. As the globalization of trade escalates and an increasing number of American businesses recognize worldwide opportunities, both banking and nonbanking institutions will continue to devise new, creative means to provide trade finance.

That wraps up intermediate-term trade finance. Although very few companies will need all of these methods, one or more will probably be necessary to finance any export order with terms beyond 180 days. Pragmatically, forfaiting, export factoring, leasing, and transaction finance should all be seriously considered as part of your strategic trade finance plans.

Financing more extended-term orders, however, is usually less expensive and easier to arrange through one of the long-term financing sources.

LONG-TERM TRADE FINANCE

There are six prominent sources of long-term trade finance:

- Eximbank
- The Trade and Development Program
- Department of Agriculture programs
- The Private Export Funding Corporation
- Joint ventures
- Countertrade.

In addition, several states and cities have started export finance and development agencies that operate under Eximbank's City-State Agency Cooperation Program.

Although joint ventures and other forms of strategic alliances have become a popular vehicle for financing export sales, they are mainly useful for establishing overseas facilities. The same holds true for countertrade. While it unquestionably can be used for export trade finance, it is most frequently used in conjunction with foreign direct investments. Because of the peculiarities of joint ventures and countertrade, they will be treated in later chapters: countertrade in Chapter 10 and joint ventures in Chapter 17.

Eximbank

Although documentary drafts, letters of credit, banker's acceptances, or one of the transaction finance methods may be all you need to close an order, the Export-Import Bank of the United States, otherwise known as Eximbank, offers both medium- and long-term trade finance that goes beyond what banks can offer.

Eximbank coordinates its policies with other government agencies to ensure consistency with overall foreign policy and objectives, and it will not support exports to communist countries or finance the sale of military products or services. All U.S. exports must have at least 50 percent U.S. content to be eligible.

The bank charges initiation fees and interest charges, both based on the perceived risks of doing business in a specific country. Even though the U.S. Congress does not appropriate funding, it does set Eximbank's annual authorization ceilings. Through fees and interest charges, recoveries on previous claims, and borrowings from the U.S Treasury and the Federal Financing Bank, Eximbank continues to be largely self-sufficient. Because it is self-sustaining, it cannot always compete effectively with the rates and terms offered by foreign export credit agencies, although in most instances it remains in the running.

Although any U.S. exporter of any size and in any industry can utilize Eximbank services, in the past most funding had gone to larger companies exporting high-value, high-volume orders. In an attempt to answer critics of this policy, within the last few years Eximbank has initiated programs especially designed for small and midsize exporters. One such program is a hotline counseling service to answer questions from smaller businesses about financing and other export matters. The toll-free number is (800) 424-5201.

Two of the principal obstacles that smaller companies encounter with Eximbank are the inordinate amount of paperwork required to process an application and the time it takes to actually receive funding. As the federal bureaucracy continues to expand, it seems doubtful that relief from either roadblock will be forthcoming in the foreseeable future. Nevertheless, once a company learns to cope with federal procedures and manage its export schedule to put up with funding time lags, Eximbank programs can be very helpful.

Among smaller exporters, the most popular financing programs are

- The commercial bank guarantee program
- The foreign credit insurance program (see Chapter 8).

Eximbank also has two programs used exclusively by intermediary lenders:

- A cooperative financing facility with overseas banks
- The discount loan program with U.S. banks.

The Application Process

When making application to Eximbank, the following questions must be answered in the manner stated:

1. Is a U.S. export involved? (Yes)
2. Does the export order include military products? (No)
3. If foreign competition exists, is it officially subsidized? (Yes)
4. Is the transaction economically feasible? (Yes)
5. Is there reasonable assurance of repayment? (Yes)
6. Would there be an adverse effect on the domestic U.S. economy from the transaction? (No)

The only exception granted small business exporters (as defined by Eximbank) is that evidence of foreign competition is not required, provided Eximbank's guarantees or loans are less than $2.5 million. A preliminary commitment is the starting point regardless of the type of funding requested.

Eximbank Preliminary Commitment

A preliminary commitment consists of an offer from Eximbank to finance a specific export sale in advance of the transaction. It outlines the bank's willingness to participate and the terms and conditions of loans or guarantees. Any business may apply for a preliminary commitment, provided it pays a $100 processing fee. Preliminary commitments remain valid for 180 days, although Eximbank then may extend them.

Eximbank Working Capital Guarantee

The Eximbank Working Capital Guarantee program was designed specifically to help smaller U.S. exporters obtain preshipment working capital loans from commercial lenders. These loans go to the exporter directly, not the foreign buyer.

Any commercial lender willing to extend such export-related credit to small businesses qualifies for Eximbank loan guarantees. The guarantee covers up to 90 percent of the principal balance, and interest rates range up to one point over the U.S. Treasury rate. Repayment must occur within twelve months, unless previous arrangements are made with both the lender and Eximbank. The exporter pays for this guarantee. Eximbank also charges an up-front facility fee of 0.5 percent of the loan and quarterly usage fees of 0.25 percent of the loan's average outstanding balance.

The guarantee is with recourse to the exporter, who must provide the lender with adequate collateral (e.g., inventory used to produce the products, accounts receivable, or other appropriate security) so that the loan balance never exceeds 90 percent of the collateral value. The Eximbank Working Capital Guarantee may be used either for a single export transaction loan or for an export revolving line of credit. It can also be combined with the SBA's Export Revolving Line of Credit program. Eximbank guarantees loans up to $300,000 under this program.

Eximbank Medium- and Long-Term Guarantees and Loans

Eximbank's medium-term (one to seven years) and long-term (seven to ten years) guarantees and loans are designed to provide buyer credit for the purchase of U.S.-manufactured capital equipment and apply only to the U.S. content. The guarantee has two restrictive provisions:

1. The U.S. content does not exceed 85 percent of the contract price of each item.

2. The total U.S. content is not less than 50 percent of the total contract value.

Medium- and long-term guarantees serve as collateral for loans made by U.S. and foreign lenders directly to a foreign borrower for the purchase of American goods. The buyer must pay 15 percent of the contract value as a down payment, either in the form of cash or with an irrevocable, confirmed L/C. Furthermore, these guarantees cannot be used to collateralize direct loans to American exporters.

Guarantees cover up to 100 percent of the financed portion of the order. For medium-term loans, the guarantee extends to balances up to $10 million. Either the exporter or the lender must counterguarantee Eximbank for 2 percent of the commercial risk. Eximbank charges the lender 1/8 percent per annum on the undisbursed balance of a guaranteed loan. In the event of default, the guaranteed lender must file a claim no less than 30 and no more than 150 days after the default. The claim will be paid within five business days after receipt.

In addition to collateralizing the principal of a loan, Eximbank guarantees dollar-loan interest charges, provided repayment terms comply with the following schedule:

Contract Value	Maximum Term
$50,000 or less	2 years
$50,000 to $100,000	3 years
$100,000 to $200,000	4 years

For loans of more than $200,000, repayment periods may extend from five to ten years, depending on the nature of the project and the OECD classification of the buyer country.

Medium- and long-term guarantees are unconditional, are freely transferable, and can be combined with Eximbank loans to financial intermediaries. The costs of such guarantees must be borne by U.S. exporting companies and are

1. A $100 processing fee

2. An up-front exposure fee based on the term of the loan, country risk, and category of borrower, paid on each disbursement

3. A commitment fee of 0.5 percent per annum on the undisbursed balance of the guaranteed loan.

Eximbank Direct Loans

Eximbank provides two types of direct loans:

1. Loans to foreign buyers of U.S. goods

2. Loans to intermediaries (usually financial institutions, either American or foreign), who in turn fund foreign buyers.

Medium-term intermediary loans (less than $10 million and seven years) are structured as standby loan commitments, permitting lenders to borrow against the remaining undisbursed loan at any time during the term of the underlying debt obligation. A prepayment fee is triggered by the early repayment of the loan by the foreign borrower. Maximum coverages and repayment terms are the same as for the Eximbank guarantee program.

Both foreign-buyer loans and intermediary loans require a 15 percent down payment by the buyer. Interest is based on fixed rates established by the OECD. Exporters must also pay an exposure fee, the amount of which is based on the classification of buyer and country risk. Currently, exposure fees range from 0.5 percent to 8 percent.

Engineering Multiplier Program

The Engineering Multiplier Program (EMP) funds feasibility studies by architectural, design, engineering, and other preconstruction service companies. Financial aid is also available for the export of goods used in the construction of these projects. Moreover, medium-term loans of up to $10 million are provided directly to foreign buyers.

EMP loans may be rolled into long-term project loans when contracts result in the export of American-made goods for the project. The export contract must be the greater of $10 million or twice the value of the engineering contract. Rates, repayment terms, and fees are similar to those of other programs previously described. Eximbank also finances U.S. firms that operate and maintain foreign projects.

U.S. Department of Agriculture

Through its Foreign Agricultural Service (FAS), the Department of Agriculture (DOA) administers several specialized assistance programs for the export of agricultural products. Programs vary depending on the specific product being sold.

The following describes one FAS program that flows through the Commodity Credit Corporation (CCC):

The CCC offers buyer credits based on government-to-government agreements. It also assists exporters directly through its Export Credit Guarantee (ECG) program and its Intermediate Credit Guarantee (ICG) program. Both programs provide CCC guarantees against a foreign letter of credit for up to 98 percent of the value of the exported product. The ECG program provides credit guarantees for up to three years. The ICG program extends credit to ten years. Both types of guarantees cover an unlimited amount of credit and are intended to aid purchases by those countries with major economic problems.

The Bonus Incentive Commodity Export Program (BICEP) is triggered when the CCC determines that an American exporter must be subsidized to compete effectively with foreign companies subsidized by their respective governments. The BICEP subsidy takes the form of an Export Enhancement Program (EEP) bonus certificate. This certificate carries a value equal to the difference between the price an exporter can charge for products and the price foreign competitors charge.

EEP certificates are redeemable for any surplus commodity held by the CCC. These certificates can also be sold or traded in secondary markets, making them as good as cash. If the sale or trade value exceeds the certificate value, the exporter makes a profit on this transaction as well as on the original export sale.

Information about FAS programs, can be obtained directly from

Director of High Value Products Division
FAS
Room 4647
South Building
U.S. Department of Agriculture
Washington, DC 20250;
Telephone: (202) 447-6343

For further information about all Department of Agriculture export finance programs, contact

General Sales Manager, Export Credits
Foreign Agricultural Service
14th Street and Independence Avenue, S.W.
Washington, DC 20250
Telephone: (202) 447-5173

Small Business Administration Export Financing

Provisions included in the Omnibus Trade Bill of 1988 modified SBA programs to provide a source of export financing for small businesses. Although SBA facilities are frequently used for domestic financing, the agency's participation in export trade finance has been minimal to date.

The Export Revolving Line of Credit (ERLC) is the only program specifically designed for export business. It has been in effect for years but has received little emphasis from SBA offices, hardly any publicity, and very little use by exporters. Exporters may make any number of withdrawals and repayments against ERLC funds as long as the dollar limit of the credit is not exceeded and disbursements are made within the stated maturity period. Proceeds can be used only to finance labor and materials needed to manufacture products for export or to penetrate and develop foreign markets. The maximum maturity of an ERLC guarantee is eighteen months.

In the mid-1980s, in an effort to reach more small businesses with its Working Capital Guarantee program, Eximbank reached an agreement with the SBA to extend coguarantees under the ERLC program. This risk sharing raised the loan limit to $1 million. Thus, if an exporter qualifies as a small business under SBA criteria and needs $1 million or less, the resources of both the SBA and Eximbank are available.

SBA continues to handle amounts below $200,000 solely through its ERLC program, and Eximbank funds the balance up to $1 million. Other qualifying criteria and definitions are the same as those established for domestic SBA programs.

The SBA continues to suffer from a lack of qualified staff personnel with export trade finance expertise. This, coupled with stringent budget cuts over more than ten years, makes SBA participation in trade finance meager at best. If increased allocations become available and more qualified staff are hired, the SBA could eventually become a good starting point for smaller exporters. In the meantime, other facilities are more helpful.

To learn more about the status of SBA export trade finance, contact

Office of International Trade
U.S. Small Business Administration
Room 501A
1441 L Street, N.W.
Washington, DC 20416
Telephone: (800) 368-5855 or (202) 653-7794

Eximbank's City-State Agency Cooperation Program

In 1989, Eximbank launched its City-State Agency Cooperation program. The idea was to use city and state export finance and development agencies to help small and midsize businesses understand and use Eximbank's programs. As of 1993, a significant number of cities and states have signed up to participate.

The theory behind this program is that by working with Eximbank as the funding medium, state and local government agencies can offer export counseling and financial assistance to small and midsize companies for the creation of new jobs developed by export orders.

Although the program started as an Eximbank marketing tool, since 1989 it has expanded into direct trade finance assistance. In addition, participating city and state agencies offer export seminars and provide technical support to new-to-exporting companies. According to Eximbank officials, this "makes exporting more accessible and creates less confusion and wasted time for local banks." Although each city and state promotes a slightly different program, they all have the same objective: involving more companies and lenders in export trade.

Trade and Development Program

The Trade and Development Program (TDP) is an independent agency of the federal government. Its primary goal is to fund feasibility studies for public- and private-sector projects in developing countries, thereby helping U.S. engineering and planning firms win major overseas contracts.

Feasibility studies falling into the domain of TDP include large-scale energy generation and conservation projects, infrastructure development, mineral exploration and development, agribusiness projects, and the construction of basic industrial facilities.

Further information can be obtained from

U.S. Trade and Development Program
Room 304, SA 16
Department of State
Washington, DC 20523-1602
Telephone: (703) 875-4357

Private Export Funding Corporation

The Private Export Funding Corporation (PEFCO) is a private organization closely associated with Eximbank. Formed by several U.S banks and large corporations, PEFCO generates investment funds by selling Eximbank-guaranteed negotiable debt instruments on the open market. PEFCO's primary mission is to bridge the gap, assisting projects that require longer-term financing than commercial banks will handle, but shorter than that provided by Eximbank. Loans are made directly to foreign buyers of American exports or to intermediary financial institutions. Although financing packages with unique interest-rate and repayment terms can be structured on a case-by-case basis, nearly all require Eximbank guarantees.

PEFCO is considered a supplemental lender, which means that it makes loans only when financing is not available from traditional sources. Its principal contribution to the world of exporting has been that it can make long-term loans with fixed interest rates during periods of tight credit—as we have recently experienced.

Funding is somewhat restrictive, however. PEFCO will not participate in projects valued at less than $1 million, and repayment terms must exceed five years. Although it is clearly not for smaller transactions, PEFCO does provide another alternative to either Eximbank or private trade finance for larger projects.

Chapter 10

Countertrade

No one would argue that hard currency is not the preferred payment medium for any export sale. However, to compete in foreign markets, it may be necessary to take payment in soft currency or in goods or services. That's where countertrade comes in. With countertrade, the form and substance of remuneration can be structured to meet individual customer needs. Moreover, if a joint venture is in the cards, the odds are high that a countertrade arrangement will be mandatory.

As José Luis Yulo, president of the International Association of Trading Organizations of Developing Countries, stated at a countertrade conference in 1992:

> No one denies that it [countertrade] is not as efficient a system as the free, multilateral system. No one denies that it is complex, risky, and sometimes costly. No one denies that it is not everyone's cup of tea. However, most people agree that it is a rational and practical approach to difficult international economic circumstances, such as lack of foreign exchange, protectionism, and structural limitations facing many developing countries in the global economy.[1]

Countertrade is no longer the exclusive domain of military hardware suppliers, nor is it restricted to currency-poor countries. In 1992, Paul Labbe, president of the Ottawa-based Export Development Corporation, estimated that countertrade accounts for the equivalent of more than $600 billion of world trade annually.[2] Throughout the world, countertrade is an essential selling tool for booking large export orders. Although its marketing features often overshadow its financing benefits, financing exports is still a primary function.

What, then, is countertrade? Countertrade is a contractual arrangement that links exports from one country and imports to another country, with limited use or no use of currency. Although many have tried to be more succinct, countertrade defies pigeonholing. Barter, offset, compensation, coproduction, counterpurchase, compensating trade, switch trade, evidence accounts, buybacks, and so on, all describe one form or another of the same concept: that of giving up something of value (namely, exported products) in exchange for something of value (cash, products, or services).

---

[1]"Countertrade: It's as Epidemic as Capitalism in This Decade," *Global Production*, Summer 1992, p. 5.
[2]Ibid.

Countertrade contracts vary with each deal and from customer to customer, with form and content limited only by the imagination of the parties. Some contracts involve only the exporter and the customer. Others involve third or even fourth parties. Any given contract may call for full payment in goods or services or part payment in goods and services and part in cash. The cash portion may be denominated in the currency of the buyer or that of the exporter. Moreover, a contract may require additional services to be performed by either exporter or buyer beyond the mere delivery of goods.

In all cases, however, countertrade transactions create their own financing, independent of a company's balance sheet or outstanding debt obligations. In that sense, countertrade is one of the original transaction finance mediums.

In recent years, the opening of markets in currency-poor developing nations has fostered a rebirth of countertrade, once the sole domain of military hardware suppliers. Today it is almost impossible to develop international trade strategies without including countertrade as an important marketing and financing tool. Pragmatically, it is the only way exporters can sell to customers that cannot raise hard currency to pay for the goods.

By and large, countertrade is a relatively new concept in the United States. It is so new, in fact, that the IRS, the Department of Commerce, and other U.S. regulatory bodies are generally opposed to it, although in a free-market economy they can do little to stop it. The U.S. government recognizes that countertrade is necessary if American firms are to compete in world markets, yet refuses to officially sanction it.

The Securities and Exchange Commission, the Internal Revenue Service, and the Justice Department have yet to figure out how to establish rules to control this strange beast. And the American Institute of Certified Public Accountants seems befuddled by the nonconformity of these trade practices with generally accepted accounting principles.

It seems obvious that as the U.S. business community comes to accept countertrade as a necessary feature of global competition, both public and private regulatory organizations will begin to devise methods for coping with it. During the transition period, however, further confusion and misunderstandings can be expected. Nevertheless, companies must learn to use this tool as a viable means of meeting competition. With that end in mind, this chapter examines broad countertrade techniques and then outlines steps to achieve proficiency in this complex but essential form of transaction finance.

TYPES OF COUNTERTRADE ARRANGEMENTS

The many variations of countertrade preclude inclusive descriptions. In general, however, countertrade transactions can be logically grouped under three broad headings: barter, parallel trade, and buybacks.

Barter

Barter is the oldest form of countertrade and involves exchanging one type of goods or services for another. The amount exchanged by each party is determined by negotiation. And there is no invoicing or exchange of money. Obviously, both parties must be able to use the goods or to sell them at a profit.

Compensation is merely a variation on the barter theme. In this case, the exporter is paid a combination of goods and currency. The currency may be either U.S. dollars or the buyer's home currency. In the latter case, the exporter must either convert the soft currency to a hard currency or use it in the buyer's country.

As with all countertrade arrangements that involve the exchange of goods, unless the merchandise received can be used directly by the receiving parties, it must be sold in the marketplace. This usually means contracting with a third party, a countertrade broker, who has the ability to dispose of the merchandise at the best price.

To be certain that the transaction will not result in a loss, it's a good idea to check out the market price of the goods to be exchanged prior to executing any countertrade contract. Furthermore, it only makes sense to verify the quality, condition, and quantity of goods to be received in payment before they are shipped.

Creative countertraders have come up with several methods for handling these peculiarities of barter trade. Here are a few examples:

1. Exporter (seller) and customer (buyer) negotiate provisions for the inspection of each other's products at the port of embarkation prior to shipping. As a variation on this theme, one party, usually the buyer, ships first and then inspects the seller's products prior to their shipment.

2. Seller and buyer each place in escrow an amount of cash or a confirmed, irrevocable letter of credit equal to the party's profit from the sale. Upon presenting mutually acceptable shipping and receiving documentation, the funds or the L/Cs can be withdrawn.

3. The buyer arranges for a bank guarantee against which the seller can draw if the goods are not shipped on time or if any variation from the negotiated quantity and quality occurs.

4. If a seller anticipates difficulty in finding an appropriate third-party buyer for the goods received in exchange, the buyer might agree to handle the sale (usually in the buyer's home country) and forward collections to the seller.

Parallel Trade

Parallel trade involves the execution of two separate contracts: one contract for the sale of goods by party A to party B and one contract for the sale of goods by party B to party A. Insurance carriers and financial institutions normally require that two contracts be used so that each can be enforced individually.

Counterpurchase is one of the terms used to describe a parallel-trade transaction that involves actual cash transfers. Under such an arrangement, exporter and customer each pay the other for the goods received, either with drafts, L/Cs, or wire transfers. These payments may both be in one currency, or they may be denominated in the home currency of each party.

The governments of less-developed countries in Eastern Europe, Latin America, and Africa encourage counterpurchase arrangements as a way to balance imports and exports, as well as to stabilize their currencies and control inflationary pressures.

When soft currency is part of a counterpurchase transaction, U.S. exporters face two hurdles. First, the currency itself must be used, disposed of, or converted to hard currency, and second, the purchased goods must be sold.

A *soft currency* is so defined for one or both of two reasons:

1. It cannot be readily exchanged for U.S. dollars, British pounds sterling, Japanese yen, or other hard currency on the world's currency exchanges.

2. Its value is so far beneath hard-currency rates that accepting such currency for goods and services becomes uneconomical.

More complex parallel trade arrangements call for third or even fourth parties to enter a transaction. In this case, exchanged goods originate from a company other than the exporter's customer, and frequently from a different country entirely. These arrangements are typically called *offset* transactions.

Most offset transactions involve large corporate sellers and sovereign purchasers. Products typically include aircraft, military equipment, or large infrastructure equipment (turbines, boilers, smelting furnaces, and so on). In addition to receiving much-needed capital goods, sovereign purchasers use offsets to improve their foreign exchange position. The deal normally involves a package of transactions, carried out over a defined period of time, that—theoretically, at least—compensates the acquiring or importing country for loss of jobs, currency, and local development of technologies.

This is how an offset transaction might be structured:

1. Assume that you want to sell mining equipment to the Peruvian government, which doesn't have enough hard currency to pay for it.

2. Your company agrees to finance the building of a state-owned fertilizer plant in Peru in exchange for a 40 percent equity interest.

3. Fertilizer is then exported to Argentina for pesos, which are used by the Peruvian government to pay you for the mining equipment.

4. Your company, in turn, uses the pesos to pay operating expenses in your Argentine plant that produces components for mining equipment to be assembled in your U.S. plant.

Everyone wins! The Peruvian government creates jobs, foreign exchange, and a viable industry. Most of the funding for the building of the fertilizer plant comes from the U.S. Agency for International Development. As the fertilizer business grows, you should be able to reap profits from your 40 percent equity ownership. And, of course, you succeed in closing the original export order.

Disposing of Soft Currency

One unorthodox way to dispose of soft currency is through secondary money markets that bypass the host country's banking system. In an effort to attract hard currency, several poorer countries quietly promote this process. Off-system money markets run by street vendors exchange local currency for hard currency. These moneychangers may either be licensed by the government (as in the Philippines) or operate in nonlegal "gray markets." In both cases, if the currency part of the counterpurchase transaction is relatively small, it's a simple matter to negotiate exchange rates with a moneychanger and make the conversion.

Clearly this process would be considered surreptitious in the United States or Western Europe; however, in many developing countries, local officials either officially support such a secondary market or close their eyes to it. In any case, it's an off-system way to convert relatively small amounts of local currency to U.S. dollars.

Another, relatively new method of converting soft to hard currency has come into being as a result of the billions of dollars being poured into developing countries by humanitarian and conservation foundations and funds, such as CARE, Save the Children Fund, Rainforest Network, Christian Children's Fund, and so on. The procedure is somewhat convoluted, but as time goes by it will inevitably smooth out.

This is how it works: Americans donate dollars to a charity. The charity must convert dollars to local soft currency (say, in Guatemala) to provide food, shelter, and so on to the needy. An American capital goods exporter works a counterpurchase deal for Guatemalan bananas. The Guatemalan company pays quetzels into a local bank account owned by the American charity. The charity exchanges its dollar contributions for the quetzels. The bank forwards the dollars to the American capital goods manufacturer.

Of course, current exchange rates must be negotiated and approved by the bank, the charity, and in most cases local government officials. However, as long as the government authorizes the imported products, the deal is relatively easy to arrange even though the terms may be complex. Because of the complexities, working through an American international consulting firm or trade finance organization that has experience in such transactions is about the only way to get the job done.

Selling goods received in a counterpurchase transaction can be a bit stickier, especially when the contract permits the foreign customer to designate the specific goods to be exchanged. Nine times out of ten, such goods cannot be disposed of locally. Not infrequently, they are below the quality standards of similar products in the United States, making a resale virtually impossible to arrange.

In other cases, exporters can get stuck with a loss, or at best a diminished profit, if market prices for goods shipped at a later date end up being less than anticipated when the original transaction was contracted. Clearly, it makes sense to leave the identification of goods to be taken in exchange until the shipping date, at which time acceptable goods can be negotiated.

Buybacks

Buyback arrangements are quite common in the sale of technology, licenses, production lines, or even complete factories. Payment is made in full or in part either by products manufactured in the new facility or by production from the new license or technology. Buyback transactions are frequently used for importing subassemblies, components, or parts that your company may need for its finished products or can sell on the open market.

Buyback countertrade is especially popular for turnkey infrastructure projects. For example, the customer pays for the project with government-backed long-term credit. The exporting contractor first guarantees that the telecommunications network, electric utility, water purification plant, or other project will work when completed; then agrees either to buyback products or services from the completed facility or to serve as a distributor for products exported from the host country. The host-country buyer uses these hard currency payments to liquidate the original long-term credit.

In a variation on this scheme, no cash changes hands and no credit arrangements are necessary. The countertrade contract merely states that the output from the newly constructed facility is to be applied to the original price of the exports. However, when using this arrangement, it's a good idea to demand a bank guarantee as assurance that the customer will produce and ship the products on schedule.

Buyback products are normally priced at manufacturing cost plus an add-on for interest accrued during the period. A five-year amortization period is not uncommon.

Buybacks can be used successfully by smaller contractors that may not enjoy sufficient political influence, either at home or in the host country, to negotiate a standard progress payment contract. Buybacks have been especially effective when selling turnkey manufacturing facilities to China and Eastern European countries.

For example, a contractor agrees to take a certain percentage of the production back to the United States or other hard-currency country, thus creating an export market and hard currency flow for the host country. The contractor also transfers valuable production know-how to host-country buyers. To ensure currency translation, the agreement may combine a buyback agreement with other forms of countertrade.

Co-production is a specialized form of buyback countertrade used principally for the transfer of technology or management expertise. Here's how it works:

1. Assume that you want to sell desktop printers in Venezuela.

2. A Venezuelan company wants to purchase the printers but also wants the technology for producing them at home.

3. The two companies form a joint venture to build a plant in Maracaibo to manufacture the printers.

4. Your company takes an equity interest in the project and may also furnish management support to run the facility. In either case, the facility is usually co-constructed by exporter and customer.

Since both parties remain responsible for the operation of the facility, manufacturing the printers is known as coproduction. The benefits of such an arrangement are as follows:

1. With equity interests, both parties profit from printer sales.

2. The Venezuelan customer gains new technology.

3. Most important, your company has made an export sale.

Co-production is used throughout the developing world as a method for bringing technology and management know-how into a country. On the other hand, U.S. firms, both large and small, use this technique to acquire direct investment interests in foreign countries, thereby avoiding the difficulties associated with starting a business from scratch.

One point needs clarification. The terms used to define countertrade transactions—compensation, counterpurchase, coproduction, and so on—are not germane to the structuring of a countertrade deal. Call the deal whatever you want, as long as it benefits both your company and your customer.

BARRIERS TO COUNTERTRADE FOR SMALLER COMPANIES

Countertrade is an extremely complex form of international trade. Very seldom does a countertrade deal involve a simple buy/sell transaction. Many recent deals have specified that a portion of the transaction be structured with money payments. On the other hand, countertrade can be an effective method for achieving a competitive edge in new markets, either through exporting or when used in conjunction with a direct investment.

Countertrade benefits depend on five factors:

- The objectives expected to be achieved
- The products or services involved
- The degree to which the purchaser wants or needs the goods or services
- The level of support the purchaser gets from its home country government
- Whether the customer is from the private sector or government-owned.

Objectives

Two objectives push companies into countertrade deals:

1. The need to finance a specific export transaction when other, more conventional means are not available

2. The need to finance a foreign direct investment when other means are not available.

Exporters should use countertrade only as a last resort, when other financing means are not available for a specific export transaction to a specific customer. Nearly every other conceivable method promises higher cash throw-off, faster collections, and, in most cases, greater profits. If an export transaction can be financed through a federal assistance program (such as Eximbank), with state-sponsored assistance, through a trade finance organization, or with a joint venture, countertrade is a poor alternative. A first-time exporter can practically be assured of problems. Here are the major ones:

- Countertrade transactions cover long time periods.
- Exchanged goods must be disposed of for at least the value traded, and this usually means incurring the cost of a third-party broker.
- The administration of countertrade contracts nearly always requires the addition of qualified staff personnel.
- Countertrade is costly, time-consuming, and allows plenty of room for errors in judgment and execution.

Despite these obstacles, an increasing number of smaller companies have learned that countertrade is the only feasible way to compete in foreign markets, especially in Third World countries. Executives of companies engaged in countertrade offer five simple rules for overcoming the most difficult hurdles. Although certainly not inclusive, these rules are a good starting point:

1. Establish a risk threshold, measurable in money terms, time required, and difficulty of administering the contract, beyond which the transaction becomes uneconomical and must be terminated.

2. Identify a trading broker capable of disposing of the exchanged goods, then accept the broker's evaluation of the likelihood of recovering at least the value of the exported goods.

3. Insist on adequate shipping and collection insurance as well as bank guarantees against customer performance.

4. Get a clear interpretation of the terms of the countertrade contract(s) from a competent professional.

5. Structure the deal as simply as possible to reduce the risk of an unmanageable contract.

Most smaller companies that do use countertrade successfully engage a qualified third-party broker who provides assistance throughout the entire transaction. A competent broker protects the exporter not only by arranging a manageable contract but also by identifying exchange products that can be sold in other countries.

One way to locate such third-party brokers in your area or industry is through the International Reciprocal Trade Association of Alexandria, Virginia. The association's members specialize in transactions involving the purchase of a company's excess inventory or unproductive assets for cash or credit and remarketing them in the United States and abroad.

Although countertrade has evolved primarily as an export strategy, smaller companies reap the greatest benefits when they use the technique to establish a foreign facility. Any of the buyback arrangements previously described fills the bill, as do certain variations of parallel trade. But using countertrade for this purpose requires a long-term strategic game plan. If it is viewed as a short-term tactic, countertrade becomes an end in itself rather than a means to an end. And it usually results in less profits than other, less complex marketing or financing methods.

Companies looking for long-term relationships might find that accepting a lower selling price gets them in the door. Or they might have to provide management training for buyer personnel. The deal might require a joint venture or an equal partnership with a buyer, or perhaps taking a minority interest in a coproduction facility with an option to increase ownership in the future.

Bearing in mind the long-term nature of the transaction, experienced countertraders recommend negotiating a getting-out position at the time the countertrade contract is executed. Some companies find that negotiating a barter arrangement to swap ownership in one facility for a stake in a different one at a later date serves their long-term objectives best. Others have followed different approaches to ending the relationship. Regardless of the method used, when structuring a getting-out position, it's important to keep in mind the strategic intent of establishing a foreign presence in the first place.

Products or Services

Although buyback arrangements lend themselves particularly well to construction or construction-related projects, companies selling products or services can also benefit from them. The secret lies in structuring the right contract. One of the same problems that exists with international licensing agreements, loss of product rights, also occurs with buyback or coproduction agreements. Once the product technology, management skill, or process is put in place with joint ownership, products are no longer proprietary. Joint ventures with a sovereign customer can also be dangerous for the same reason, especially in less-developed nations.

How Much Are the Products Needed?

Another element to consider when deciding whether to pursue a countertrade transaction is the market growth potential. In other words, how great is the market demand for the products and what impact do government trade barriers or incentives have on customer choice?

Even though the customer may be a private company, actions that it takes and agreements that it reaches are frequently controlled by its government's policies. It's only through the government that business licenses, import approvals, and foreign currency conversions can be sanctioned. Consequently, the ease of making a countertrade deal and the potential benefits of the transaction depend to a large extent on how much the customer's government needs or wants the products or project in the country.

If demand is there and the host-country government doesn't interfere, the parties can freely negotiate price, terms, delivery schedules, and a host of other matters. Also, customers more readily accept terms calling for cash or negotiable credit instruments as a major portion of the transaction. On the other hand, for many consumer luxury items, the likelihood of benefiting from a significant amount of negotiating leverage is remote.

Ownership of the Customer

Whether a customer is a public- or private-sector firm frequently influences the desirability of entering into a countertrade transaction in the first place. Contracts with sovereign customers tend to be far more complex. There is much less negotiating room for structuring beneficial terms. Political favors usually count as much as or more than equitable prices and terms. These peculiarities tend to keep smaller companies away from countertrade deals that involve public-sector projects or companies.

Trying to arrange a countertrade deal with a large corporation can be equally maddening. Unless your products or technologies happen to be in great demand and face weak competition, negotiating a favorable countertrade deal with a large corporate customer is nearly as difficult as it is with a sovereign. Successful countertraders nearly always recommend that beginners concentrate on smaller countertrade deals with similar-sized private-sector customers. Once experience has been gained and competent countertrade staff and third-party brokers are in place, it's easier to venture farther afield into more complex transactions.

Cost Considerations

Countertrade is significantly more costly than traditional trade finance. Companies handling the sale of exchanged goods internally find that the disposal cost can easily reach 10 percent or more of the value of the goods. Using a third-party broker (a countertrade house or trading company) can double the cost. Furthermore, third-party brokers seldom handle deals of less than $1 million, which automatically excludes many smaller companies.

Time is another cost, although one that is hard to measure. Any countertrade transaction slows the selling process. With potentially lengthy negotiations and complex side arrangements, a countertrade transaction can easily take four to six months to close. And if it doesn't close, the time spent on it has been wasted.

Accounting and Tax Difficulties

The American accounting profession is still trying to figure out how to account for countertrade transactions. A variety of questions remain unanswered, such as

- At what point in time does the exporter record a sale?
- At what value is the sale recorded?
- When and at what value are exchanged goods recorded?
- How are unsold exchanged goods shown on a company's balance sheet?
- How can companies record transactions that extend over several years?
- Are credit transactions recorded in the currency of the exporter's country, the importer's, or that of a third party to the transaction?
- How does a company record exchanged goods used internally?

While the accounting profession struggles with financial statement niceties, taxing authorities wrestle with issues involving the timing and the amount of countertrade taxable income and deductible expenses:

- What constitutes taxable income?
- When is taxable income recognized?
- What expenses can be offset against revenues?
- What income or expenses arise from exchanged goods that are used internally? Or sold in a third country?
- When is an asset an asset? And when and how much is it depreciable?

Although this is certainly not openly acknowledged, one of the reasons that the U.S. government, and specifically the federal budget office, frowns on countertrade transactions must be that no one can figure out how to effectively tax them. Although no moves have been made to stop countertrade, and in fact such moves would probably be ignored by the international community, the U.S. government has gone on record as denouncing countertrade as an improper way for American companies to conduct business.

INTERNATIONAL CONSULTANTS

Most companies, large and small, find international consultants useful in one phase or another of countertrade transactions. Intermediaries always play an important role as arrangers, negotiators, and coordinators in international markets. Nowhere is this more apparent than in countertrade deals.

Acting as independent intermediaries, consultants assist marketing, contract administration, and financial executives to break logjams, not only with customers but with host-country bureaucrats. Smoothing the way through the maze of strange cultural and trade barriers, international consultants more than pay their way, especially for smaller companies or those unfamiliar with countertrade. In many first-time countertrade deals, consultants provide the only reasonable safeguard against being outsmarted by far more savvy customers.

International consultants perform five services in a typical countertrade transaction. They help a client to

- Structure and negotiate the countertrade transaction.
- Recruit and train internal staff to source countertrade customers and then to administer contracts.
- Locate appropriate third parties to dispose of traded goods, either in the exporter's country or the host-country.
- Monitor the performance of countertrade partners.
- Develop strategies to utilize countertrade goods for expansion into other product lines or businesses.

More than one small business that has gone the countertrade route has learned that consulting intermediaries add very little extra cost to the overall transaction and, in fact, offer the only feasible, cost-effective means to master constantly changing countertrade techniques.

PROS AND CONS OF COUNTERTRADE

The basic countertrade philosophy is to create a transaction that benefits both trading parties beyond the single transaction itself and that can be accomplished with a minimum amount of currency exchange. Russia needs wheat from the United States. The United States needs electronic products from Japan. Japan needs oil from Russia. Private companies, government agencies, or a combination of both from each country benefit from countertrade agreements.

Regardless of its form, the essence of countertrade is the exchange of one type of product or service for another. Although the process began with straight barter deals, today international finance and trade have grown considerably more sophisticated. The same advantages of a barter system continue to flourish; however, modern competitive market forces make the process more complicated.

As a financing tool, countertrade offers four major benefits:

1. *Only option.* Trade can be financed with countertrade when other means are unavailable. Either supplier or buyer credit may be impossible to arrange. Performance or payment bank guarantees may be too costly. The project might call for longer term financing than government-supported export credit facilities allow. The political situation in host countries might preclude other government financial aid. The host country might not permit currency repatriation.

2. *Competition.* Exporters from the United States must use countertrade to remain competitive with companies from other industrialized nations. Japanese and European trading companies have used countertrade for centuries. Their techniques for arranging deals and disposing of exchanged goods are well honed. If one of these experienced global traders really wants an order, a U.S. company will not stand a chance with traditional financing. With countertrade, it can at least stay in the race.

3. *Foreign presence.* Countertrade provides a way to make a foreign direct investment without starting from scratch or going through the difficult process of buying a going business. If structured properly, a coproduction arrangement puts a company directly into new foreign markets. This might be in addition to exporting or, in some cases, take the place of further exporting. In either case, access to distribution channels gained through a direct investment is an obvious advantage.

4. *Nontrade benefits.* Long-range management and technical benefits from joint venture partnerships can often be achieved through buyback countertrade arrangements, specifically coproduction transactions. In most cases a host-country partner brings to the partnership local management techniques and protocol that might take a foreign company years to develop on its own. In some cases, the partner brings technical or application techniques unique to the host-country cultural environment.

Countertrade also involves significant risks:

1 *Disposal of goods.* Countertrade contracts involving the exchange of goods that cannot be consumed internally require the sale or trade of these goods on the open market. Even with an in-house trading specialist and assistance from an international consultant, the process is time-consuming and costly. Using a third-party broker doubles or even trebles the cost of disposing of the goods. Added profits on their resale might compensate somewhat, but the net effect is often a loss.

2. *Internal expertise.* To achieve long-term success in countertrade transactions, a company must establish internal expertise. This means setting up a department dedicated to arranging and managing countertrade deals. This can be a costly addition for a smaller company, and unless it engages in several countertrade deals, these personnel add unabsorbed overhead.

3. *Length of time.* Countertrade deals require a long time to negotiate and close. Many months and dollars can be spent trying to arrange a transaction, only to have the deal fall through at the end.

4. *Results uncertain.* The end results from countertrade transactions are usually very uncertain. In most cases the final result—that is, the recognition of profits—won't be realized for many years. Political and economic conditions change rapidly in world markets, and it's entirely possible that when the deal is finally completed, the results may be different from those originally intended.

CRITERIA FOR CHOOSING COUNTERTRADE

No one can say precisely what types of products or services are adaptable to countertrade. Neither is it possible to say with any certainty which companies will succeed and which will fail. Or to determine which country or region of the world may be more amenable to countertrade than others. Too many variables keep changing.

Most companies, regardless of their size or industry, do not consciously solicit countertrade transactions in preference to straightforward exporting or direct investment projects. Other methods for financing exports or foreign direct investments are usually less costly and less complex, and bring better results. Even if countertrade is the only viable means of conducting business in a given area, most companies find it preferable to let countertrade deals come to them than to actively solicit them.

On the other hand, to engage in international trade, companies must be prepared to compete wherever and however they can. And that means using countertrade if it is the only way to make a sale. The questionnaire in Figure 10.1 has consistently helped companies determine the advisability of entering a countertrade transaction. If the answers are predominantly affirmative, the complexities of the transaction should be manageable.

Figure 10.1
Questionnaire for Determining When to Use Countertrade

For Exporting Purposes:
1. Is the transaction valued at more than $1 million?
2. Do competitors offer countertrade as an inducement to buy?
3. Does the customer have good credit references?
4. Does the customer have good banking relationships?
5. Is the customer located in a soft-currency country?
6. Is the customer privately owned or sovereign?
7. Does the customer have products to be exchanged that the exporter can use internally?
8. If so, is the value of products taken in exchange roughly equivalent to that demanded in a countertrade?
9. If exchanged products cannot be used internally, can a resale deal be consummated prior to closing the countertrade transaction?
10. Would such a resale open additional markets for further exports?
11. Can the company afford to add a complement of countertrade personnel?
12. Can such personnel be recruited in a reasonable time period?
13. Have all possibilities for alternative financing sources been exhausted?
14. Will the company remain financially viable if the deal falls through?
15. Do banking relationships support a countertrade arrangement?

For Foreign Direct Investment
1. Will importing products produced in the foreign facility add value to other company products or product lines?
2. Has sufficient country research been done to determine that this is the best location for a facility?
3. Has sufficient market research been done to make the same decision?
4. Does the foreign partner have sufficient technical expertise to carry out that side of the arrangement or can additional consultants or brokers be brought in at a reasonable cost to ensure success?
5. If a private company, does the customer/partner have the right political connections?
6. If a sovereign, have connections been made with the right bureaucrats?
7. Does the customer/partner have good market connections, or will a whole new sales force have to be established?
8. Will the facility be flexible enough to change product lines and emphasis as market demand changes?

9. Do both trading partners have the same objectives?

10. Does the trading partner have local banking connections?

11. Will any additional money be required, either for working capital or for equity?

12. Is the company's current bank in agreement with the transaction?

13. Will the bank continue to support the company?

14. Is the company strong enough financially to withstand start-up expenses and lost time?

15. Can the company use products from this facility to augment its own products or markets?

16. Are there any host-country prohibitions against exporting to other countries?

17. Will the facility produce standardized products?

18. Does the company have spare management talent to help manage an overseas facility?

19. Is it certain that there are no local patent infringement problems?

COUNTERTRADE SURVIVAL TACTICS

In addition to establishing clearly defined company objectives, certain other features peculiar to countertrade must be recognized. Companies that have been involved in these transactions caution newcomers to be especially mindful of the countertrade process itself, host-country objectives, host-country legal and trade regulations, and finance and insurance options.

Countertrade Contract Peculiarities

To succeed in countertrade, a clear grasp of the process is crucial. First demands from customers, such as penalties for nonperformance, ratios of export volume to current consumption, delivery schedules, and deadlines, nearly always sound unreasonable. Such conditions should be negotiable, however, if both parties want to proceed with the transaction.

Most countertrade transactions beyond straight barter require three separate agreements. One contract stipulates the terms and conditions of the originating export transaction (primary agreement). A second agreement covers the terms and conditions of the exchanged goods exported from the host country (counterpurchase, offset, or buyback agreement). It is that you include two elements in this contract: (1) the right to cancel the contract if the primary agreement is canceled, and (2) the broadest possible range of goods, without regard to restrictions on resale.

The third agreement, often referred to as a protocol agreement, specifies specific responsibilities and relationships between buyer and seller.

Host-Country Conditions

Every country has its own national objectives that influence trade. The political, commercial, economic, and social ambitions of the ruling bureaucracy together with the bureaucratic hierarchy that oversees trade policies will in the end determine the potential success or failure of any countertrade transaction.

Before entering a countertrade contract, it is crucial to get as thorough a grasp as possible of current government policies and attitudes. Whether the government's objective is to stabilize prices, reduce inflation, attract hard currency, pay off debt obligations, develop the country's infrastructure, bring in foreign technology, or effect an overall improvement in the general economy, countertrade transactions that fall outside the government's agenda invariably fail.

Host-Country Legal and Trade Regulations

Along with a firm grasp of the host country's objectives, an exporting or investing company should thoroughly research the country's laws and trade barriers and incentives before executing a contract. (See Chapters 5 and 6 for instructions for performing country surveys.) Every country has its own set of import and export regulations. Some are restrictive, some add incentive. These regulations have been initiated to either protect or stimulate certain aspects of the country's economy. Countertrade agreements that do not comply with these regulations face certain failure.

Finance and Insurance Options

A popular misconception of newcomers to countertrade is that these transactions do not involve cash, credit, or insurance considerations. Nothing could be further from the truth. Whereas a great many choices exist for export trade finance, these methods won't work for countertrade transactions. Banks and many government export agencies insist on a verifiable, binding trade contract before they grant credit. In a countertrade transaction, however, collectibility against a contract is conditional upon performance by both parties.

Most U.S. banks won't touch this type of transaction. However, development banks and other funding sources within the host country, especially in Third World nations, will at least grant performance guarantees.

Government-backed export insurance agencies like the FCIA also stay clear of countertrade contracts. As an alternative, since insurance against political risk and nonperformance is such an important element in any international transaction, policies from private carriers should be purchased.

There can be little doubt that countertrade is here to stay and will continue to play a major role in financing international trade well into the next century. Although most smaller companies are still learning how to use the technique, many that have tried it remain convinced that in one form or another, countertrade makes both export sales and a foreign presence possible when other financing methods are cost prohibitive or unavailable. In some cases, countertrade is the only feasible way to gain access to host-country markets.

Companies that have achieved success guard their methodologies as valuable secrets; however, new trade associations are beginning to sift through reams of data about countertrade successes—and failures. Eventually they will offer technical and probably management assistance to smaller companies that want to participate in countertrade transactions. The two trade groups formed so far are the Defense Industries Offset Association (obviously sponsored and controlled by major defense contractors) and the American Countertrade Association (supported by nondefense firms). Regional offices can be located through the auspices of local chambers of commerce.

In addition, the world is full of countertrade intermediaries, or middlemen, who, for a fee, will help any company arrange and manage a transaction. Because of their advantageous locations between East and West, both Switzerland and Austria are important venues for these countertrade middlemen. Ten years ago, one Austrian bank estimated that 20 to 30 percent of world trade involved countertrade and that most of that passed through Austria or Switzerland. Today, that percentage has probably doubled, although with the cloak of secrecy surrounding countertrade, no one really knows. Press releases from the IMF and the World Bank indicate that 40 to 50 percent is probably not a bad estimate. In any event, there is little doubt that countertrade flourishes worldwide and will for many years to come.

Chapter 11

Financing Foreign Direct Investments

In the vernacular of international trade, making a *foreign direct investment* refers to establishing a presence on foreign soil, either with a manufacturing, distribution, or research facility or by opening sales and administrative offices. Ten years ago few companies other than corporate giants looked at offshore expansion as a viable growth strategy. Exporting maybe; a foreign facility, never! The risk was considered unmanageable, cultural and language barriers impenetrable, and financing impracticable.

Today, globalization has hit home in virtually every industry. No longer can U.S. companies rely exclusively on domestic sources of materials and parts, home-bred labor and management talent, or U.S. markets. Competition from Europe, East Asia, Canada, and Latin America is forcing new long-term strategies that include sourcing materials and labor from the least-cost, highest-quality location anywhere in the world. Shrinking local markets and the seemingly inexhaustible resources of multinationals now force smaller companies to seriously consider burgeoning overseas markets as viable alternatives.

In most cases, a foreign direct investment should not be viewed as a stand-alone strategy, but rather as an adjunct to an exporting program. Trade deficits in most countries have spawned local tax, financing, and other incentives to entice foreign exporters to help local companies adopt new technologies and learn new management techniques—which, of course, is the hallmark of countertrade.

Especially in less-developed countries, governments are making it increasingly clear that selling foreign-made products in their countries is not enough. Local labor, technology, and facilities must be developed simultaneously. In other words, if you want to sell your products in overseas markets, you had better be prepared to also invest in the host country's economic future.

So far so good. Foreign sourcing of cheap labor and plentiful resources is a viable long-term strategy. But that's only half the story. The big question is how to finance such an investment.

Nine times out of ten, companies that have concentrated exclusively on domestic markets, and perhaps experimented with a small export program, hit a stone wall when they try to finance offshore expansion. Commercial banks, secured lenders, and other financial institutions that have traditionally supplied capital for domestic business turn the other way when confronted with a request to fund a foreign direct investment.

This chapter bridges the gap between raising long-term capital for domestic expansion and sourcing funds for offshore facilities. It examines financing programs from several classes of major bilateral and multilateral organizations:

- U.S. Agency for International Development
- Puerto Rico's 936 program
- United Nations agencies
- Regional development banks
- Overseas Private Investment Corporation
- Foreign government bilateral aid programs.

In addition, the latter part of this chapter looks at the potential for financing overseas trade and investments through foreign clearing and merchant banks.

Multilateral aid programs from United Nations organizations, bilateral aid programs from development banks, and special U.S. government financing programs run the gamut from low risk to high risk, from inexpensive to costly, and from relatively simple to arrange and administer to complex undertakings. Several programs are applicable only to investments in specific regions of the world. Matching available financing with a company's specific objectives tends to be the most difficult part of the entire exercise.

Some agencies are more helpful than others. Offices in one city may be more helpful than offices of the same agency in another city. Unfortunately, the size and strength of the company seeking assistance often determines the amount of cooperation received from public institutions—the larger the company, the more assistance. Although smaller companies can also get help, it takes more persistence.

Space limits the coverage of the hundreds of financial institutions that offer offshore financing assistance. However, substantially more detailed information can be obtained from my book *The McGraw-Hill Handbook of Global Trade and Investment Financing*.

As the cost of doing business in Europe and East Asia escalates, competition tightens, and capital sources increasingly favor national firms, more and more U.S. companies of all sizes are turning to opportunities in Latin America, the Caribbean, and Canada. And with good reason. The easing of cross-border trade and investment restrictions that has resulted from a variety of regional trade accords has made U.S. foreign direct investment in the Western Hemisphere more profitable and less expensive than investment in any other region of the world. For this reason, the description in this chapter of assistance programs from multilateral and bilateral agencies focuses on superior funding programs applicable to this region.

A wide variety of public and private organizations stand ready to provide assistance to any company, large or small, wishing to do business in Latin America or the Caribbean. In addition to providing trade finance and investment capital, these agencies are excellent sources of information on demographic trends, market demand, competition, and product pricing. They supply information on the availability of raw materials and labor. They help identify joint venture partners. And they provide the names and addresses of foreign government agencies that can be of service.

U.S. AGENCY FOR INTERNATIONAL DEVELOPMENT

The mission of the U.S. Agency for International Development (USAID), an agency within the Department of State, is "to assist foreign governments in economically disadvantaged areas to stimulate economic growth, promote higher standards of living, and improve foreign exchange earnings."

Seventy offices worldwide administer USAID programs. Special private-sector offices offer assistance to private businesses that includes:

1. Financing imports of raw materials and intermediate goods that help in the short-term stabilization and economic recovery of the host country.

2. Improving the business climate by supporting host country policy reforms and incentives to restore domestic business confidence, rationalize interest and foreign exchange rates, attract foreign investment, upgrade the infrastructure (roads, port facilities, irrigation projects, free-zone facilities), and develop new trading programs.

3. Funding programs that upgrade human resource skills and managerial capabilities, overcome technical marketing and export obstacles, and capitalize financial intermediaries that provide credits to businesses in the host country. This includes capital for private-sector development banks and other credit facilities for small and medium sized businesses.

USAID is a government-to-government agency. However, although it does not provide any direct financial assistance to U.S. companies, either overseas or domestically, it does provide indirect assistance by funding foreign projects that include U.S.-produced goods and services.

Moreover, when local governments receive funding from USAID, American companies bidding on projects receive preferential consideration. In poor, underdeveloped countries where political connections are far more important than the lowest price, USAID influence may be, and frequently is, the only way to get in.

USAID has been very supportive of companies participating in private sector economic development projects in the Caribbean and Central America under the Caribbean Basin Initiative (CBI) program, and more recently in Bolivia, Colombia, Ecuador, and Peru under the Andean Trade Preference Act. Through its Private Enterprise Bureau (PEB), USAID arranges medium- and long-term loans to joint ventures between American companies and either public or private companies from the host country. USAID tailors these loans case by case. Contact the PEB directly for an application and current qualification criteria.

Given the U.S. government's roller-coaster approach to foreign policy, the only certain way to get in on USAID or any other government financing program is to stay in touch with your congressional representative or with USAID offices.

PUERTO RICO'S 936 FINANCING

Section 936 of the Internal Revenue Code designates certain U.S. corporations that derive a significant portion of their income from Puerto Rican business activities as "936 companies." These companies are exempt from U.S. income tax on a percentage of their income derived from sources within Puerto Rico.

Such favorable tax treatment has resulted in large amounts of Section 936 funds, referred to as *qualified possession source investment income* or QPSII (quipsy) funds, remaining on deposit in Puerto Rican financial institutions. This money is available for funding foreign direct investments in Puerto Rico or in any CBI country that has executed a Tax Information Exchange Agreement with the United States. Loans from Section 936 funds carry below-market interest rates that approximate 85 percent of LIBOR (London Interbank Offered Rate). Many U.S. companies use this financing to set up "twin plants" in Puerto Rico and in qualified CBI countries such as Jamaica, Grenada, or the U.S. Virgin Islands—similar to the Mexican-U.S. *maquiladora* program.

Either new business or expansion projects in manufacturing, information processing, agro-processing, hotels, or tourism are eligible for 936 funding. Section 936 funds may also be used for the development of roads, airports, telecommunications, and low-cost housing. Although current estimates place the quipsy pool at more than US$10 billion, private placements against 936 collateral continue to augment the original pool.

The following countries qualify for investment of Section 936 funds: Jamaica, Barbados, Grenada, Dominica, Trinidad and Tobago, the Dominican Republic, Costa Rica, Honduras, and the U.S. Virgin Islands. Nicaragua, El Salvador, and other CBI countries are in various stages of consideration.

Applicants must meet the same criteria used by mainland banks: namely, a sound credit history, a capable management team, and a demonstrable ability to repay. Furthermore, 936 applicants must provide guarantees from home-country banks. This can be a major headache for smaller companies. In fact, as many have already learned, U.S. banks normally refuse to grant guarantees for offshore projects.

To circumvent the problem, several public agencies stand ready to offer guarantees, albeit each with its own restrictions:

- OPIC offers guarantees up to US$50 million provided the investment project is at least 25 percent U.S.-owned and the loan/equity ratio does not exceed 60 percent.

- A World Bank agency, MIGA (discussed later in this chapter), issues loan guarantees providing it also issues equity guarantees in the same project. Also, the borrower must either be from a country that has joined MIGA or be a national of a developing country bringing equity from a foreign source. Unfortunately, most countries have not yet ratified MIGA, and of course MIGA cannot grant loans without participating in equity guarantees.

- The USAID Small Business Loan Portfolio Guarantee program covers up to 50 percent of the commercial risk for projec˙s in the US$1 to US$3 million range

The primary advantage of using Section 936 funds is not that loans are easier to obtain, but that the interest rate is substantially lower than that charged on conventional bank loans. Although no minimum loan value is prescribed, the larger the loan, the greater the benefits. With interest rates of approximately 85 percent of LIBOR, a five-year term loan for $500,000 saves the borrower at least $8,000 per year; a $50 million loan results in savings of more than $800,000 each year.

Caribbean Basin Partners for Progress

Smaller companies, or those needing lesser amounts, might do better working through a private Puerto Rican venture capital fund: the Caribbean Basin Partners for Progress, Ltd. (CBPP). This venture fund is a partnership of 936 companies formed specifically to invest up to US$100 million of quipsy funds in small and midsize private-sector projects with job-creating potential.

CBPP grants loans of $1 million to $10 million for up to 75 percent of the financing requirement. Terms extend to ten years. According to Andrew Markey, international treasurer of Johnson & Johnson, a large majority of the loans have been under US$1 million. During 1991, its first year of operations, CBPP financed four projects: a US$300,000 manufacturing plant in Barbados, a US$600,000 banana farm and a US$900,000 tourism project in Costa Rica, and a US$520,000 apparel project in the Dominican Republic.

Caribbean Basin Projects Financing Authority

To further expedite the flow of 936 funds, the Puerto Rican government has established a bond-issuing agency, the Caribbean Basin Projects Financing Authority (CARIFA). By tailoring a bond issue to the needs of a qualified borrower and selling the bonds to 936 companies, CARIFA provides a mechanism by which companies can invest directly in specific projects. Banks holding 936 funds can also invest in CARIFA bonds.

It should be noted that during 1993, the U.S. Congress changed some of the 936 rules. As the program stood at the end of 1993, only a percentage of Puerto Rican-derived income is exempt from U.S. taxes (or alternatively, companies are allowed tax credits), as opposed to full exemption prior to 1993. It seems likely that additional changes will be made to Section 936 regulations as the new Puerto Rican government and the Clinton administration engage in further dialogue about U.S. subsidies to Puerto Rico.

Further information can be obtained from

Caribbean Development Program
Economic Development Administration
1290 Avenue of the Americas
New York, NY 10104-0092
Telephone: (212) 245-1200
Fax: (212) 581-2667

Or

Caribbean Development Program
Economic Development Administration
Department of State
P.O. Box 3271
Old San Juan, PR 00902
Telephone: (809) 758-4747
Fax: (809) 723-3305

UNITED NATIONS AGENCIES

The United Nations' World Bank and International Monetary Fund (IMF) are the primary multilateral lenders to foreign governments and private-sector enterprises for economic development in developing countries.

Evolving over fifty years, the IMF is today one of the most powerful and important financial institutions in the world. Its major thrust is to encourage the building of infrastructures in developing countries by exercising approval authority over specific projects and developers prior to the awarding of financial assistance by development banks.

The World Bank's mission has also shifted. Today it is the primary source of funding for projects in developing nations when private capital cannot be raised. The World Bank's annual lending commitments in 1993 hit $23.7 billion, a 9.2 percent increase over the previous year—and four times that of the Inter-American Development Bank (discussed later in this chapter).

Yet, recent criticism of World Bank lending policies has forced a new look at the bank's evaluation criteria. As one critic notes, the funding of a "flood action plan" for the Brahmaputra river in Bangladesh "has nothing to do with Bangladesh. It's all about dollars," or, as Paul Sweeny put it more precisely in *Global Finance*, it is "about creating employment for Western engineers using World Bank money."[1]

Be that as it may, the World Bank continues to play an important role in financing foreign direct investments. In addition to lending medium- and long-term funds directly to developing-country governments, the bank provides technical and financial aid to private-sector companies for direct investments. It accomplishes this through two divisions:

- *The International Finance Corporation (IFC)*, which supports growth in the private sector of developing countries
- *The Multilateral Investment Guarantee Agency (MIGA)*, which provides guarantees against losses resulting from noncommercial risks for foreign investment projects in developing countries

---

[1]Paul Sweeny, "Sagging Performance at the World Bank," *Global Finance*, September 1993, p. 109.

International Finance Corporation

The International Finance Corporation (IFC) is the world's largest multilateral organization specifically structured to provide financial assistance in the form of loans and equity investments to private companies in developing countries. IFC's mandate is "to assist, in association with private investors, productive private enterprises that contribute to the development of its member countries."

The IFC has made worldwide investments that total in excess of US$11 billion to more than 1,000 businesses. Of this amount, more than US$7 billion went to Western Hemisphere projects. IFC assistance to private companies includes

- Identifying and structuring the formation and ownership of profitable projects
- Making direct equity investments and providing long-term loans without government guarantees
- Giving advice to encourage the growth of specific industries
- Funding domestic development finance companies
- Providing managerial and technical assistance.

In addition, the IFC helps prospective foreign investors find local joint venture partners and negotiate contracts with host-country government agencies.

The IFC provides capital for individual projects ranging from US$1 million to US$100 million. The average is approximately US$14 million. To qualify for IFC assistance, projects must satisfy two criteria:

- They must benefit the economy of the host country, and,
- They must be profitable for the company making the initial investment and any other external investors.

Applications for financial assistance can get quite complex, so it's a good idea to get instruction directly from the IFC at

International Finance Corporation
1818 H Street, N.W.
Washington, DC 20433
Telephone: (202) 477-1234
Fax: (202) 477-6391.

Multilateral Investment Guarantee Agency

The primary mission of the Multilateral Investment Guarantee Agency (MIGA) is to encourage foreign investment in developing countries by providing:

- Investment guarantees against the risks of currency transfer, expropriation, war and civil disturbance, and breach of contract by the host government
- Advisory services to the agency's member countries on means of attracting foreign investment.

According to MIGA's mission statement, the agency's participation in a project "enhances confidence that the investor's rights will be respected, an advantage inherent in the Agency's organization as a voluntary association of developing and developed countries."

MIGA offers the following types of insurance:

1. *Currency Transfer.* This protects against losses arising from the investor's inability to convert local currency returns in the form of profits, principal amounts of loans, invested capital, interest, and royalties into foreign exchange for transfer outside the host country. It also insures against excessive delays in acquiring foreign exchange caused by host-government action or failure to act, by adverse changes in exchange control laws or regulations, and by deteriorating conditions that govern the conversion and transfer of local currency. It specifically does *not* cover currency devaluation.

2. *Expropriation.* This protects against partial or total loss of investment as a result of acts by the host government. In addition to outright nationalization and confiscation, it covers "creeping" expropriation—a series of acts that, over a period of time, have an expropriatory effect.

3. *War and civil disobedience.* This protects against losses resulting from damage to or the destruction or disappearance of tangible assets caused by politically motivated acts of war or civil disturbances in the host country, including revolution, insurrection, coups d'état, sabotage, and terrorism. It also provides coverage if such events result in an interruption of project operations essential to overall financial viability for a period of one year.

4. *Breach of Contract.* This protects equity investments against losses arising from the host government's breach or repudiation of a contract with the investing company.

MIGA insures new investments from companies in any member country that are destined for any developing country. Such investments may involve expansion, modernization, or financial restructuring of existing projects, including the acquisition of privatized businesses. MIGA insurance covers the loss of equity invested in a project, stockholder loans, and loan guarantees issued by the equity holder.

The following entities are eligible for MIGA assistance:

- Companies from member countries other than the country in which the investment is to be made
- Companies incorporated in and with their principal place of business in a member country, or companies that are majority-owned by nationals of member countries
- State-owned businesses if operated on a commercial basis

Certain nonequity arrangements also qualify, such as technical and management contracts and franchising and licensing agreements.

MIGA insures up to 90 percent of the invested amount with a $50 million limit per project. Coverages run for terms of up to fifteen years, and in certain cases up to twenty years. Premium rates range from 0.3 to 1.5 percent per annum of the amount covered for each risk.

In addition to insuring against political risk, MIGA provides advisory services for projects aimed at improving the local economic environment in order to attract foreign investors, including the identification and qualification of joint venture partners for foreign firms.

Further information can be obtained from

Vice President, Guarantees
Multilateral Investment Guarantee Agency
1818 H Street, N.W.
Washington, DC 20433
Telephone: (202) 473-6168
Fax: (202) 477-9886

United Nations Development Program: Investment Feasibility Study Facility

Two special United Nations programs should be included as viable sources of technical and financial assistance. The first is the Investment Feasibility Study Facility of the United Nations Development Program (UNDP).

This facility provides short-term, low-cost financing for companies or public agencies that wish to undertake feasibility studies of potential investment projects in the poorest developing nations. It maintains a revolving $1 million capital base, and the amount of financing depends on the nature of the specific project. To date, funds of between $15,000 and $100,000 per project have been granted. Financing is channeled through local sponsoring financial institutions, which must reimburse UNDP when an investment results from the study. If the parties decide not to proceed with the project, UNDP absorbs the full cost of the study.

The borrower may be from any country seeking to make an investment in a low-income country. The general criterion used by the UNDP to define a low-income country is one with per capita income that does not exceed $750 (Haiti, for example). Applications will be considered on a case-by-case basis, and must originate from a sponsoring financial institution—national, regional, or multilateral. Once the project has been cleared, UNDP seeks concurrence from the appropriate host country agency. For further information, contact

Investment Development Office for Program Policy and Evaluation
United Nations Development Program
One U.S. Plaza
New York, NY 10017
Telephone: (212) 906-5060

Caribbean and Central America Business Advisory Service

U.S. companies considering investments in the Caribbean or Central America can get assistance in their capital search from the Business Advisory Service (BAS). This is another special program designed specifically to assist business development in Caribbean and Central American nations. It acts as a bridge between private enterprises in the Caribbean Basin and lenders and investors from around the world.

Although it is not a direct lender to or investor in private-sector projects, BAS helps companies structure and appraise new investments or expansion projects for presentation to prospective lenders and investors. Such assistance might include hiring technical and marketing consultants, advising on alternative sources of financing, and helping companies negotiate with financial institutions. The addition of BAS to a company's negotiating team goes a long way in assuring lenders that the project is economically sound and worthy of funding.

BAS charges "success fees" based on the amount of financing obtained. The 1992 fee structure was 2.5 percent of the first US$1 million, 1.75 percent of the next US$4 million, and 1.0 percent of the amount exceeding US$5 million. An up-front deposit is required based on the amount of financing sought; however, it will be refunded if BAS is unable to secure the necessary capital. Otherwise it is applied against the fee for the amount obtained.

Generally, BAS considers only projects exceeding $500,000, although a few have been for much less. Real estate development and trading operations are excluded. Guarantees or external security have not been required by lenders when BAS backs the project. Additional information can be obtained from

> Business Advisory Service
> 1818 H Street, N.W.
> Washington, DC 20433
> Telephone: (202) 473-0900
> Fax: (202) 334-8855

REGIONAL DEVELOPMENT BANKS

International development banks provide funds for building infrastructures and private businesses in less-developed countries. Even if a project doesn't meet appropriate criteria, development bank assistance is still available to help companies locate direct investment financing from other sources.

Many smaller development banks are privately owned by large multinational commercial banks or by local businesses and banks. Host country governments own part or all of others. The five regional "supernumerary" development banks are

- The Inter-American Development Bank (for Latin America)
- The Asian Development Bank (for Asia and the Pacific)
- The African Development Bank and Fund (for Africa)
- The European Bank for Reconstruction and Development (for Eastern Europe and the Commonwealth of Independent States)

- The European Investment Bank (for the funding of worldwide interests of the European Union).

These institutions are owned by the governments of many donor countries, both from the industrialized world and from developing regions, and serve mainly as central banks for local development banks. However, they also offer direct financing to private-sector businesses.

Each of the thousands of local development banks has somewhat different eligibility requirements and promotes various forms of financing assistance, depending on the country and the current economic climate. However, they are all similar. Host country attorneys, consultants, or local offices of international accounting firms are the best sources of information about possibilities for financing assistance.

Just as the World Bank has recently come under criticism for its lending policies, so have international development banks. The wasteful spending and bureaucratic knots that have come into being at the European Bank for Reconstruction and Development during Jacques Attali's reign are well documented. The other four banks have also come under increasing criticism.

The view of development banks as "fat-cat bureaucracies, far removed from the ideals behind their foundation" was crystallized by Elizabeth Morrissy, a partner in the Washington-based consulting firm Kleiman International: "They [international development banks] still suffer from political meddling and managerial abuses. A great deal more has to be done before they in any way reflect their charter objectives."[2]

Nevertheless, until something better comes along, these regional hybrid banks remain a viable source of funding for investments in developing countries.

Inter-American Investment Corporation

The Inter-American Development Bank (IDB) is the international development bank responsible for Latin American and Caribbean projects. Although the IDB expends considerable effort and resources supporting local development banks in the region, its merchant banking arm, the Inter-American Investment Corporation (IIC), offers the most help for companies interested in making direct investments in the region.

The IIC's exclusive mission is to assist private enterprise in the Latin/Caribbean region in two respects:

- By assisting foreign companies in the small and midsize range identify investment projects and potential joint venture partners
- By furnishing technical and financial assistance to develop the project.

The IIC works with member-country governments in designing programs to further economic development in the region. Funding passes through local devel-

[2] Richard Evans, "A Showdown at the Regional Development Banks," *Global Finance*, September 1993, p. 115).

opment banks directly to private enterprises. For small-scale projects, the IIC works through local financial intermediaries to set up investment and coinvestment funds and then to grant lines of credit. Larger-size projects are handled through syndicated loans and investments arranged directly by the IIC.

The IIC also offers nonfinancial assistance in such matters as

- Technical counseling for the preparation of preinvestment and feasibility studies
- Advisory services aimed at restoring the operating and financial capacity of companies requiring such assistance
- Advice on structuring privatization deals
- Helping companies identify investment projects
- Coordination with financial institutions for additional financing
- Assistance in starting up new companies.

To qualify for IIC financial aid, a project must meet at least one of the following criteria:

1. Use material and human resources from the host country (or other member country) and create new jobs in the region.
2. Create local management skills.
3. Encourage exports from the region.
4. Transfer technology.
5. Promote the saving and use of investment capital.
6. Generate and/or save foreign exchange.
7. Promote broad ownership structures.

For further information about IIC programs, contact:

Inter-American Investment Corporation
1300 New York Avenue, N.W.
Washington, DC 20577
Telephone: (202) 623-3900
Fax: (202) 623-2360

THE OVERSEAS PRIVATE INVESTMENT CORPORATION

Nearly every industrialized country has a government-owned or government-funded bilateral development-type financing institution. Various labels describe these institutions; development banks, finance funds, and investment corporations are the most common. Regardless of the label, they all provide financing of one form or another to further the economic expansion of the private sector in developing nations. The U.S. version is the Overseas Private Investment Corporation (OPIC).

OPIC is a self-sustaining U.S. government agency. Its primary mission is to assist smaller U.S. businesses to finance and insure long-term investments in foreign facilities and projects through four programs:

1. Direct loans or loan guarantees
2. Insurance against political risk: currency inconvertibility, expropriation, war, revolution, and civil strife
3. Investment missions stationed throughout the world
4. Investor information service.

OPIC continually reclassifies countries as eligible or not depending on the current status of development within the country and trade agreements. However, U.S. companies currently receive financial assistance for investment projects in approximately 100 developing countries.

OPIC insurance and finance programs are available for new foreign investments and for the expansion of existing overseas businesses. Both the project and the sponsoring company must be commercially and financially sound. The sponsoring U.S. company should have a minimum 60:40 debt-to-equity ratio.

To be eligible for OPIC funding or insurance, a project must meet two major criteria: (1) It must assist in the social and economic development of the host country, and (2) it must be consistent with the current economic and political interests of the United States.

To receive the full benefit of OPIC assistance, the project must be owned or controlled by U.S. companies that have a significant equity and management participation. If foreign parties own or control the project, OPIC will cover only that portion representing U.S. interests. The American company must also have a significant (25 percent or more) continuing financial stake in the enterprise.

Any company applying for OPIC assistance must have a proven record of competence and success in another business the same as or closely related to the one being financed. This precludes a company from starting up a foreign business in an industry different from the one in which it operates in the United States.

OPIC Financing Programs

OPIC finances three types of medium- and long-term projects:

1. Energy or energy-related projects (water systems, electric utilities, oil and gas drilling, businesses that produce products for local consumption, and the development of alternative energy sources)
2. Projects offering significant trade benefits or development of the infrastructure for the host country
3. In those countries where the per capita income is greater than $3,800 (the current measure of the stage of development of the country), only those projects that are sponsored by small businesses or co-ops.

Direct Loans

Only projects sponsored by or significantly involving the participation of a small business qualify for direct loans. Loan limits range from $200,000 to $4 million. Occasionally OPIC takes an equity position through some form of convertible debt instrument. It then sells these holdings to companies or citizens in the host country. Interest rates on direct loans match equivalent commercial rates for similar terms and risks.

All OPIC loans are nonrecourse, which means that OPIC must be assured of the economic and financial soundness of the project, including, but not limited to, the ability of the company to repay the loan. Once OPIC judges a venture to be financially sound and is assured that it will be run by competent management personnel, the company will not be required to pledge any additional collateral for the loan. Occasionally (but not very often), OPIC takes the role of secured creditor.

It is possible for a U.S. company to retain 100 percent ownership of the project, although OPIC prefers to see joint ventures or other participatory arrangements with local corporations or citizens. OPIC will not consider projects that are majority-owned by the host country government.

As a standard, OPIC finances up to 75 percent of the cost for expanding existing businesses and 50 percent for new projects. However, these ratios may vary depending on the country, political considerations, and current U.S. government policy.

Loan Guarantees

Most loan guarantees go to large projects or companies. They typically run from $1 million to $25 million, although they can reach $50 million or even more in some cases. Interest rates on guaranteed loans are similar to those on other U.S. government-guaranteed issues of comparable maturity.

OPIC charges a guarantee fee ranging from 1.5 to 3 percent of the loan balance, depending on a project's commercial and political risk. Repayment of both direct loans and guaranteed loans normally occurs in equal semiannual installments, although a suitable grace period is always permitted. Loan maturities range from five to twelve years.

One cautionary note: OPIC will not support foreign direct investment projects that result in the closing of an existing facility in the United States. Nor will it fund gambling facilities, distilleries, military projects, or any investment that poses a serious threat to the environment.

Feasibility Studies

For many smaller companies, the first step in considering a foreign direct investment is to conduct a feasibility study to determine whether the project makes economic sense. In industrialized nations where market information is readily accessible, determining a project's feasibility is relatively easy; in less-developed countries it may not be.

Recognizing the need to help smaller companies ascertain the viability of direct investments, OPIC provides funding assistance for feasibility studies. Funding takes the form of interest-free but reimbursable grants. Grants must be repaid over a two-year period if the U.S. company decides to move ahead with the project. If it does not, no repayment is required. The amount to be repaid can be reduced if the company insures or finances the project through OPIC.

OPIC feasibility study grants cannot exceed $100,000 and apply to only 60 percent of the costs incurred (50 percent if the study is undertaken by other than a small business). In addition to this outright grant, small businesses may apply for grants of up to $5,000 to cover travel and per diem costs for visiting a foreign country the first time.

Larger firms may also apply for feasibility funding, but it then takes the form of a two-year loan carrying an interest rate equal to two-thirds of the prevailing prime rate. The same repayment and loan-reducing provisions as for small business grants apply. The catch, however, is that the project must be in one of the poorest countries. Also, the feasibility study must be carried out by the U.S. company considering the project, not by a third party.

Special Projects and Grants

Many foreign projects require the training of local management and labor in new skills. OPIC offers grants and short-term loans of up to $50,000 per project to fund this training. The actual amounts and terms of the assistance depend entirely on the nature of the project, the type of training involved, and the perceived benefits of such training to the local economy.

These funds may be used to cover the travel and living expenses of U.S. experts sent abroad to provide training to local residents or to pay the expenses of bringing foreign residents to the United States for training. The U.S. company must contribute at least 25 percent of the cost in both situations, and OPIC picks up the difference (up to its maximum limit).

Nonprofit organizations can also benefit from this funding. Private volunteer organizations, foundations, or other nonprofit groups that assist in the transfer of technology to developing countries or that assist U.S. businesses in making investments can receive OPIC grants and low-cost loans. Funding is limited to $100,000 annually, but the project may extend for several years.

International Leasing

Over the years, leasing machinery and equipment (as opposed to outright purchases) for foreign facilities has not received much attention from U.S. companies. Recently, however, with the boom in foreign direct investments, leasing has gained favor. Rather than pass leasing profits to third-party lessors, several innovative U.S. companies have started their own offshore leasing subsidiaries. To guard against foreign expropriation, most foreign lessors turn to OPIC political-risk insurance.

Such policies must run for a minimum term of thirty-six months and cover four types of lease investment:

1. The lease transaction itself
2. A U.S. company's equity investment in and loans to an offshore leasing company
3. Consigned inventory being leased
4. Management and maintenance agreements for leasing firms.

Foreign joint ventures are a popular way to set up international leasing companies, since OPIC policies permit less than 100 percent ownership of the venture by U.S. partners. A U.S. company must, however, hold a significant interest in the joint venture.

OPIC also provides loan guarantees and direct loans for cross-border leasing projects. Guarantees to leasing companies run from $500,000 to $20 million for terms of four to seven years. The guarantee fees are the same as for standard OPIC financing programs. Foreign leasing companies with a significant U.S. small-business interest can get direct loans on the same terms and conditions as those applicable to other OPIC financing programs.

Small Contractor Guarantee Program

Small contractors may find that requirements for bank guarantees or surety bonds to warrant performance can be a major hurdle to bidding on lucrative off-shore projects. In many cases, they avoid such projects because performance bonds or guarantees are prohibitively priced or not available at any price. OPIC's Small Contractor Guarantee program attempts to fill that void.

OPIC provides performance guarantees that can be used by banks as collateral for standby letters of credit, which can then be used by contractors as performance bonds. OPIC guarantees are unconditional and cover all risks up to 75 percent of the credit. When coupled with an OPIC insurance policy under the contractors and exporters insurance program, this percentage may be raised to 90 percent, leaving a bank or surety company with only 10 percent of the risk.

Special Energy Programs

U.S. companies that make direct investments in oil and gas, oil shale, geothermal, mineral, solar, and other energy projects qualify for special OPIC insurance and financial aid programs. Companies investing in peripheral businesses may also qualify. The insurance program follows the same lines as other programs and includes coverage against currency inconvertibility, expropriation, civil strife, war, or insurrection, and any other type of interference with the project's operation.

OPIC's loan guarantees of up to $50 million cover 50 percent of the cost of a new project or 75 percent of the cost of expanding an existing one. Terms and maturities are similar to those for other programs. The one restriction, however, is that OPIC will not insure or finance projects in countries belonging to the Organization of Petroleum Exporting Countries (OPEC).

To get complete details about all OPIC programs, contact

> Overseas Private Investment Corporation
> 1615 M Street, N.W.
> Fourth Floor
> Washington, DC 20527
> Telephone: (202) 457-7010 or (800) 424-6742

When forming a foreign joint venture in a less-developed nation with a company from Canada or Western Europe, it may be possible to obtain at least partial funding from bilateral government-sponsored financing agencies located in one of those countries. The following Canadian and European bilateral programs are especially helpful for funding investments in Latin America and the Caribbean, but many stretch to other developing regions as well.

CANADIAN ASSISTANCE PROGRAMS

Two Canadian organizations can be particularly helpful in developing business contacts and marketing programs as well as financing investments in the Caribbean Basin: the Canadian-Caribbean Business Cooperation Office and the Canadian International Development Agency.

Canadian-Caribbean Business Cooperation Office

The Canadian-Caribbean Business Cooperation Office (CCBC) was created to help Canadian companies and entrepreneurs to conduct business in the Caribbean Basin. It is managed by the private-sector Canadian Exporters' Association and supported by the Canadian International Development Agency.

The principal objective of CCBC is to identify business opportunities in the Caribbean Basin that will benefit both Canada and Caribbean countries. It has been especially active in locating joint venture partners, negotiating joint venture contracts, and then assisting in business start-ups. It encourages applications from Canadian businesses and entrepreneurs interested in the Caribbean Basin for technology transfers, direct investments, franchising, licensing, training, and, most especially, manufacturing.

The organization also assists in the financing of qualified Caribbean Basin ventures. More information can be obtained by contacting

Canadian-Caribbean Business Cooperation Office
99 Bank Street, Suite 250
Ottawa, Ontario K1P 6B9
Telephone: (613) 238-8888
Fax: (613) 563-9218

Canadian International Development Agency

The Industrial Cooperation Program (INC) of the Canadian International Development Agency (CIDA) provides financing for Canadian companies wishing to establish joint ventures or other business arrangements for technology transfer to developing nations. INC programs fund the initial stages of such projects when financing assistance cannot be obtained from other financial institutions or international aid programs.

Canadian firms may receive loans and grants from the INC for preinvestment travel and other feasibility study costs as well as certain start-up costs associated with long-term business arrangements.

To become eligible under the INC program, Canadian companies must demonstrate that the proposed direct investment has mutual social, economic, and industrial benefits to the host country and to Canada. For further information, contact

Canadian International Development Agency
Industrial Development Program
Industrial Cooperation Division
200 Promenade du Portage
Hull, Quebec KIA OG4
Telephone: (819) 997-7901

EUROPEAN ASSISTANCE PROGRAMS

Several European countries support business development in Latin America and the Caribbean with technical, market, and financial assistance. Many are government-funded development-type financial institutions. They may be called development banks, finance funds, or investment corporations. Regardless of the label, they have one element in common: Each provides technical, market, or financing assistance (or a combination thereof) to foreign companies making direct investments that further the economic expansion of the private sector in the region.

Commonwealth Development Corporation

The Commonwealth Development Corporation (CDC) of Great Britain has been very active in the Caribbean for many years. Recently it expanded its activity to Central America. Its main thrust is to promote sustainable development by providing long-term funding, management expertise, and technical assistance to financially viable enterprises in both public and private sectors. CDC also trains local managers for senior management positions.

CDC provides financing assistance through long-term loans at fixed interest rates and equity investments. More than US$430 million in loans and equity contributions has been granted to foreign companies investing in the region. CDC ultimately sells its equity interest to local investors.

This organization is primarily interested in projects involving agriculture and aquaculture, telecommunications, and power and water projects, but it also participates in tourism, manufacturing, and financial services investments.

Normally, CDC will fund up to 50 percent of the project cost, and it likes to have a hand in management training until local managers become skilled. It also provides extensive engineering assistance when required.

The Caribbean Development Corporation can be contacted at any one of three locations:

East Caribbean Office
P.O. Box 1392
Culloden Office Complex, Ground Floor
Lower Collymore Rock
St. Michael, Barbados, West Indies
Telephone: (809) 436-9890
Fax: (809) 436-1504

West Caribbean Office
P.O. Box 23
17 Barbados Avenue
Kingston, Jamaica, West Indies
Telephone: (809) 926-1164
Fax: (809) 926-1166

Latin America Office
Apartado 721-1000
3er Piso, Edificio San Jorge
Calle 40, Paseo Colon
San Jose, Costa Rica
Telephone: 220969/220932
Fax: 220890

European Investment Bank

European Union member countries have funded the European Investment Bank (EIB) with capital of 28.8 billion ecus. The bank's mission is to provide long-term financing for productive direct investments in the Caribbean, Africa, and the Pacific regions. Countries participating in EIB programs must be signatories of the Lomé Convention or be included in the Overseas European Territories (OCTs) agreement.

EIB makes loans of $300,000 to $30 million. Guarantees from the host country or territory are normally required. The bank also makes equity contributions to both private and public enterprises for infrastructure projects.

In addition to these facilities, EIB offers credit lines to intermediary financial institutions in recipient countries for the purpose of financing small and medium-size companies.

Neither the status nor the nationality of the borrower has any bearing on the availability or terms of EIB financing. For further information, contact

European Investment Bank
100 Boulevard Konrad Adenauer
Luxembourg L-2950
Telephone: 352-43-791

German Finance Company for Investments in Developing Countries

The German Finance Company for Investments in Developing Countries (DEG) is wholly owned by the German government. Its aim is to provide long-term loans, equity contributions, and guarantees for private-sector projects in developing nations.

Most DEG financing supports joint venture arrangements. No maximum or minimum loan limits apply, although loans are usually denominated in deutsche marks. Recipient countries must be independent and not considered territories, departments, or other such dependencies of a home country. Actual borrowers must be private sector companies in developing nations, and DEG normally requires the equity involvement of a German or European Union partner in a joint venture, although exceptions can be made.

Contact

> German Finance Company for Investments in Developing Countries
> Belvederstrasse 40
> P.O. Box 45 03 40
> D5000 Cologne 41, Germany
> Telephone: (02 21) 49 86-1

Netherlands Development Finance Company

The Netherlands Development Finance Company (FMO) is jointly owned by the government of the Netherlands and Dutch private-sector businesses and industrial organizations. Its objective is to provide feasibility-study financing and technical assistance.

FMO has no requirement for Dutch participation in a project. Both equity and debt financing are available. Loan limits run from a minimum of 1 million guilders (approximately $480,000) to a maximum of 20 million guilders (approximately $9.6 million).

Contact

> Netherlands Development Finance Company
> 62 Bezuidenhoutseweg
> P.O. Box 93060
> 2509 AB The Hague, Netherlands
> Telephone: (31) (70) 419641

Industrialization Fund for Developing Countries

The Industrialization Fund for Developing Countries (IFU) is a wholly owned agency of the government of Denmark. IFU provides financing in the form of loans, guarantees, and equity capital for joint venture projects in developing countries. The fund also finances feasibility studies and technology transfer activities and offers training grants.

IFU prefers to finance joint ventures that include participation by a Danish private-sector partner, and it limits its participation to 25 percent of the total investment.

In special cases, IFU finances the transfer of Danish technology and commercial management know-how independent of a project investment. Finally, IFU finances training costs to support projects already receiving its funding assistance. For further information, contact

> Industrialization Fund for Developing Countries
> Bremerholm 4
> P.O. Box 2155
> DK-1069, Copenhagen, Denmark
> Telephone: 45-33-14 25 75

FOREIGN BANKS

Smaller companies can't count on U.S. banks to finance investments in overseas facilities other than as intermediaries, or in some cases as minor participants in a funding group. Constrained by archaic accounting practices and federal legislation enacted in the 1930s and hampered by a lack of international experience, U.S. banks remain locked in their traditional roles as depositaries and transfer agents.

Foreign banks, on the other hand, operate under a different set of rules and have actively participated in funding worldwide private investments for years. Uninhibited by stringent regulations, they offer off-balance sheet financing and a variety of creative loan and equity instruments. Both merchant and clearing banks eagerly participate in the financing of offshore investments by U.S. companies.

Clearing Banks

Clearing banks, the foreign counterpart of U.S. commercial banks, handle short-term working capital loans and other rapid turnover transactions. They also make smaller term loans. Branch offices in the United States are especially attracted to the needs of small and midsize companies that are trying to expand overseas. For a direct investment in the bank's home country, the local office can handle the transaction directly.

Merchant banks normally manage cross-border financing—that is, the funding of projects in a country other than the bank's home base. Many larger European banks are called *universal* banks and have both clearing and merchant banking capabilities. Universal banks engage in both local and cross-border financing.

Regardless of the country chosen, developing a relationship with a local clearing bank is mandatory. In addition to working capital loans, they manage overdrafts (a term used overseas for an open line of credit), performance guarantees, letters of credit, wire transfers, mortgage loans, and construction loans. They are usually the best source for loans of less than $1 million. Multinational banks and merchant banks won't touch smaller loans—unless, of course, a personal relationship with a decision-making bank officer can be established. Furthermore, local banks may be the only source of debt capital in certain countries.

Foreign banks also have less stringent collateral requirements than U.S. banks. Overdrafts are commonly used in place of actual working capital loans. Reputation and references carry more weight than the value of company assets. Customarily, compensating balances are required to extend overdraft balances; however, cross-collateral requirements are seldom employed.

Bank ownership can be a confusing but important issue in determining whether or not to use a specific bank. In less-developed countries, governments commonly own or control local banks. Using one of these requires a grasp of the importance and intricacies of unwritten agreements and understandings with appropriate government bureaucrats. It's usually safer to let an intermediary make the arrangements and act as a buffer in case provisions of the Foreign Corrupt Practices Act come into play.

Merchant Banks

Merchant banks provide a broader spectrum of financing choices than clearing banks. At the same time, they prefer larger, more profitable deals. Merchant banking is often referred to as the "granddaddy of cross-border financing," dating back several hundred years. Merchant banks were originally organized by groups of businesspeople—British, French, Dutch, Spanish—to handle credit needs and financing for merchant customers and suppliers around the world.

Eventually their business came to focus more on financing and investing and less on merchant trading. Further concentration on the money side became a natural evolution. Today merchant banking continues to be the cornerstone of global finance.

Merchant banks are an excellent source for larger amounts of long-term capital, either for starting new offshore companies or for buying going businesses. Although they provide both equity and debt capital for larger deals, they stick with debt capital for smaller transactions. Interest rates are higher than those of clearing banks, but because LIBOR is the base, they usually compare favorably with U.S. bank rates. Merchant banks play a major participatory role with international development banks, either as an equity partner or as a coordinating intermediary.

All British, Canadian, and Dutch banks seem to be easy to work with. French and Japanese banks are helpful in certain regions and for specific projects.

Part III
Offshore Marketing and Distribution

Chapter 12

Marketing and Distributing Exports

Once a company decides that its long-term strategic interests are best served by seeking out major new markets for its products, it has a limited number of choices. The company could decide to invest in the research and development of new product lines. It could go after the acquisition of a going business (perhaps a competitor) with product lines that complement its current lines. Or it could seek out new markets for its existing products. Some companies with sufficient resources tackle all three strategies simultaneously. In this book, however, we are only interested in the third option; developing new overseas markets for existing products—specifically markets that, in many cases, are far easier and less costly to develop than U.S. markets.

Global marketing strategies cannot be restricted to short-term returns. They must be focused on capturing long-term market share. Structuring a marketing organization and developing market leverage at key points around the world can be accomplished only with the long term in mind. General Electric, Campbell Soup, IBM, and Levi Strauss are good examples of companies that were willing to forsake short-term gains for long-term market position. That is exactly what smaller companies must do, even if it means incurring short-term losses during the development stage.

Once you have made the decision to tackle new overseas markets, the next hurdle is determining which markets have the greatest demand for your company's products. The starting point is to determine how your products are doing in domestic markets. Products that sell well in the United States will have an excellent chance of selling equally well in overseas markets with customer requirements similar to those in the United States, such as Western Europe, Canada, or Mexico.

A second possibility could be that domestic competition has increased to the point where cost-effective sales promotions, advertising, or other marketing techniques no longer produce increased market shares. Certain overseas markets may not have such intense competition because U.S. or foreign multinational companies have not, for one reason or another, chosen to sell there. Take jeans, for example. Levi Strauss, VF Corporation, and other large firms dominate the U.S. market. A midsize manufacturer might look at Finland, whose markets are generally too small for the Levi Strauss's and VF Corporations of the world, and decide that a substantial market exists for imported durable jeans.

Finally, U.S. market demand for a company's product lines may be declining. New technology, noncompetitive pricing by foreign suppliers, changing demographics, or restrictive environmental regulations could be destroying domestic markets. These same factors might not be present overseas, and with little or no change in product design—except for packaging—increased sales could be easily realized.

A case in point involved a midsize detergent manufacturer. It had done well for several years until consumer fears of contaminated water supplies attracted new, environmentally safe products from Procter & Gamble, Lever Bros., and other giants. Rather than spend considerable sums developing a competitive, environmentally safe detergent, the company found markets in South America, where consumers and governments were much less concerned about contaminating underground water supplies.

Two points should be noted. First, companies that cannot compete in domestic markets because of product obsolescence, high prices, delivery shortfalls, or other purely internal difficulties probably cannot compete overseas either. With very few exceptions, companies that have difficulty managing their business in domestic markets will also encounter difficulties overseas.

Second, exporting new products that have not been customer tested and accepted in domestic markets generally won't work. Companies face enough obstacles in offshore markets in coping with the product adjustments and modifications that are invariably necessary to meet local tastes and standards. Offshore markets are not the place to experiment.

Once you determine potential market demand, the next step is to decide how to market your products. Export marketing can be viewed in three segments:

1. Locating customers and implementing sales policies
2. Pricing export orders
3. Structuring export sales contracts.

In addition, since you may need assistance in identifying the best export markets to go after, the latter part of this chapter recaps a cross section of government and private sources of information and guidance.

It should be noted that the same selling skills required for success in U.S. markets are necessary in overseas markets. Foreign players may go by different names, time frames may be longer, and unfamiliar language and cultural barriers can cause confusion; but the skills needed to close orders are identical to those needed to make domestic sales.

There are four ways a company can sell exports, each of which affects overall export strategies differently. In order of complexity, the options are

Indirect Selling

1. To domestic buyers (U.S. purchasing agents of foreign buyers, export management companies, or export trading companies) who represent foreign end users
2. To export management companies and export trading companies who then export for their own account

Direct Selling

3. Through foreign sales agents, foreign trading companies, or foreign distributors
4. Directly to foreign customers, either with company sales personnel or through foreign joint ventures.

INDIRECT SELLING

A company's experience in international trade and its financial and management resources determine to a large extent whether direct or indirect selling makes the most sense. In nearly every case, companies that are just starting an export program find it easier and less expensive to go the indirect route, especially when serving unsettled markets, as in many Third World countries. Very small companies also go for indirect selling as a way to mitigate risks.

There is nothing magical about selling exports indirectly. Customer solicitation methods, terms and conditions of sale, packaging, shipping protocol, and credit and collection procedures are the same as when selling to domestic customers in Los Angeles, Dallas, Atlanta, or Boston.

Indirect selling does have two fundamental disadvantages:

- Exporters lose control over deliveries and customer service, and have to rely exclusively on the ability of the intermediary to sustain solid customer relationships.

- Margins are much lower than on direct sales, mainly because the intermediary's profit must come off the selling price.

Foreign Purchasing Agents

A growing number of foreign agents comb the United States for products or services for specific foreign buyers. In many cases, these agents represent foreign governments that need goods and services for infrastructure projects, for military arsenals, or to develop their business bases in manufacturing, retailing, or services (primarily financial services).

Independent purchasing agents also represent private-sector foreign buyers. They travel through U.S. markets seeking consumer products for foreign retail chains (e.g., European and Japanese department-store chains) or materials and components for foreign manufacturers. They are generally commissioned agents and function in the same way as American purchasing representatives in foreign lands.

Export Management Companies

Export management companies, or EMCs, are another indirect outlet for American-made goods. In some cases, export management companies function in a fashion similar to that of manufacturers' representatives, acting as the selling arm, or export department, for many manufacturers of noncompeting products. EMCs solicit orders and transact business in the name of the various producers they represent. They may be paid only salaries (retainers) or only commissions, or they may get a combination of retainers and commissions. In other cases, EMCs may operate independently, purchasing goods directly from manufacturers and then reselling them overseas for their own account. Some combine the two approaches.

The bigger EMCs should have sufficient resources to help small exporters arrange financing for their export orders. EMCs usually specialize either in product lines or in specific foreign markets (or both), giving them a sound background for searching out potential customers and determining competitive selling prices.

Nearly all large EMCs maintain their own sales representative networks to facilitate overseas selling and distribution. This puts them in a position to develop market strategies, arrange for shipping and customs documentation, purchase foreign risk and ocean shipping insurance coverage, and in some cases even arrange for supplier or buyer credit. Such immediate access to foreign markets could save your company significant expense and time that would be necessary if it were to develop its own foreign customer base.

Direct sales to EMCs are, in fact, domestic sales, not exports. No credit risks, shipping costs, overseas selling expenses, or customer service costs are incurred. You won't even know who the end-user customers are. Clearly, for manufacturers who are unwilling or unable to set up internal export marketing organizations, EMCs provide a method of increasing sales without adding risk.

The price for such a luxury, however, is steep. Since EMCs must earn their profits when they resell goods to overseas customers, they must buy the goods from manufacturers at prices significantly lower than market prices. Under the best of conditions, manufacturers recover product cost plus a small markup. EMCs that incur all the risks of selling, shipping, and collection make the most profit on export sales—not manufacturers.

Certain EMCs operate as commissioned sales agents, which also relieves exporters of the cost and effort of maintaining their own export departments. In this case, however, title to goods stays with producers until overseas customers accept shipments. Producers also bear all financing and credit risks. Furthermore, carrying charges and storage costs of inventory stocked at EMC distribution warehouses must be borne by manufacturers, reducing margins even further.

U.S. Export Trading Companies

More than a decade has passed since the U.S. Congress passed the Export Trading Company Act, permitting the formation of export trading companies (ETCs) by groups of competitors without fear of antitrust action. The avowed purpose of the legislation was to increase the competitiveness of U.S. companies by allowing them to market products jointly, as Dutch, Japanese, and British competitors have done for decades.

The Export Trading Company Act also permitted bank holding companies to form ETCs. The theory was that allowing banks to engage in commercial, non-banking transactions would encourage them to be more receptive to international trade finance requests, in turn encouraging more American companies to export. Within the Department of Commerce, the Office of Export Trading Company Affairs continues to oversee the activities of all ETCs.

After passage of the act, individuals, companies, trade associations, states, cities, and banks jumped in. Enticed by the presumed success of giant Japanese trading companies, Americans were eager to partake of the vast profits offered by global trade. Unfortunately, few took the time to understand what international trade was all about. ETCs failed as fast as they were formed. Though bank holding companies invested over $85 million in these new ventures, they had little impact in the world marketplace. Since they didn't know even the barest essentials of doing business in foreign markets, most of those who tried ETCs failed.

A perfect example of the stampede to obscurity by neophyte American traders occurred when an insurance salesman from Sioux Falls, South Dakota, abandoned his insurance business for the pot of gold. He incorporated himself as an ETC, packed his bag for a four-day stay, and took off for Hong Kong, expecting to land several orders for whatever anyone wanted to buy. On the flight over, his seat partner asked what product lines he represented. His response typified the naiveté of the new traders. "Any product you want. I'm going to get the order first and then source out a supplier back in the States."

Like EMCs, export trading companies either act as export departments of U.S. producers or take title to products and export them for the ETC's own account. Because of this similarity, the terms "export management company" and "export trading company" are often used interchangeably. However, there are some important differences. ETCs function as independent sales agents on a case-by-case basis. They do not maintain a retinue of client customers as EMCs do. Typically, an ETC performs a sourcing or wholesale function between buyer and seller and does not assume any responsibility to either party in the transaction.

In some instances, ETCs refuse to carry inventory in their own name or perform after-sale customer service activities. They operate as commissioned agents, charging the seller or the buyer a percentage of the export value. However, most export trading companies do just the opposite. They buy everything, from manufactured goods to raw materials, at 10 to 15 percent below wholesale price, then resell it for their own account.

Forming an Export Trading Company

It may be strategically beneficial to form your own export trading company. This can be done by one company, by a group of companies with similar (but noncompeting) product lines, or by companies in geographic proximity to one another. By owning part or all of an export trading company, you can avoid the loss in margin that occurs when you sell to independent ETCs.

Export trading company subsidiaries assume all risks associated with international trade by taking title to goods and handling subsequent export operations independent of the parent companies. Additional profits can be achieved if the ETC is allowed to export products for nonrelated producers. By passing all goods through an established network of overseas offices, shipping companies, insurance policies, and distribution centers, economies of scale can be realized that would be impossible for a single U.S. producer.

Export trading company subsidiaries may handle one product line or multiple lines, they may be regional or national in scope, and they can export to one country or trade worldwide. Furthermore, such trading company subsidiaries can be formed with banks, other manufacturers, state and city agencies, trade groups, or service organizations as partners Not infrequently, these passive partners provide working capital funds while the manufacturer who originates the ETC handles all management and administrative duties.

For those interested in exploring the possibilities of forming an export trading company, the federal Office of Export Trading Company Affairs lays out the requirements and advantages in a booklet entitled *The Export Trading Company Guidebook*. This office also sponsors seminars and regional conferences on various aspects of the Export Trading Company Act. You can order the booklet or get additional information from

> Office of Export Trading Affairs
> International Trade Administration
> U.S. Department of Commerce
> Room 5618, Herbert Hoover Building
> 14th and Constitution Avenue, N.W.
> Washington, DC 20230
> Telephone: (202) 377-5131

Pros and Cons

Many export intermediaries have evolved into combined export management and export trading companies. Others handle importing as well as exporting. Local chapters of export management or export trading associations (most major cities have them) can direct you to one that specializes in your specific product line.

Both export management companies and export trading companies offer a fast, low-cost way for small businesses to enter the global marketplace. The biggest disadvantages seem to be the following:

1. Company personnel do not learn the intricacies of global trade for future international expansion.
2. Companies lose control of marketing strategies.
3. Companies have no control over after-sale customer service or customer pricing.
4. Profit margins are meager (unless you form your own ETC).
5. Some foreign buyers are reluctant to deal through a third party.

It's important to remember, however, that indirect selling is generally not a viable long-term growth strategy. Trading companies are trading companies—that's all. Except in countertrade arrangements, relying exclusively on export management companies or an export trading companies merely emphasizes an "us" versus "them" or "home country" versus "foreign country" attitude. In and of itself, such an approach is the antithesis of a global view. A long-term stake in either domestic business or international trade cannot be delegated to an agent, whether that agent is a manufacturer's representative, an export management company, or an export trading company.

FOREIGN TRADING COMPANIES

Foreign trading companies are as different from U.S. export trading companies as night is from day. Exporters from Japan, Great Britain, the Netherlands, and several other traditional trading nations found long ago that wide-reaching trading companies could market and distribute products more efficiently than any single producer could. More recently, exporting companies from nontraditional trading nations, such as Germany, Argentina, and Brazil, have learned the same lesson. It's safe to say that in the 1990s, trading companies have become the principal form of marketing activity worldwide.

Trading companies are very active in foreign trade to and between Eastern European nations, the erstwhile Soviet Union, and China. U.S. companies that enter one of these markets, even through the back door with foreign subsidiaries, often find that trading companies offer the best way, and many times the only way, to sell and distribute goods.

A cross-section of foreign trading companies active in these regions includes Torimex for sales to Poland and Genex and Inex for sales to Croatia, Serbia, and the other provinces of the former Yugoslavia. The Russian center for trading with the United States is the Amtorg Trading Company out of New York. This is an umbrella organization for the representative offices of some fifty foreign trade organizations that specialize in various areas of CIS imports and exports.

The role of foreign trading companies in the sale of U.S. goods to Cuba, long isolated by the U.S. trade embargo, is an interesting example of how to tap markets closed to single companies. Beginning in 1975, the federal government permitted U.S. companies to sell goods to Cuba through their subsidiaries in third countries. Foreign trading companies, predominantly Japanese, were called upon to serve as intermediaries. Ford Argentina used foreign trading companies to sell trucks to the Cuban Tourism Ministry. Goodyear Canada used trading companies to sell tires to Transimport, a Cuban firm. In fact, subsidiaries of American companies located in more than twenty countries have used trading companies to sell Cuba a wide range of products—from hydraulic hoses to gelatin capsules for medicine.

However, this practice has now come to an abrupt halt. In 1993, the U.S. Congress passed legislation forbidding American subsidiaries from selling to Cuba, regardless of the country they may be located in.

The only similarity between foreign trading companies and U.S. export trading companies is the designation "trading company." Japanese trading companies such as Mitsui & Co., Mitsubishi, C. Itoh, and Sumitomo are huge conglomerates with marketing, financial, and distribution arms that permit a truly global reach.

Smaller trading companies that specialize in specific products for small or midsize companies dot the British landscape. Metallgesellschaft and Ruckhauser are examples of German trading companies. Bunge Trading Company is active in Argentina and Brazil. Some American corporations have formed joint venture trading companies with foreign partners, such as Lor-West out of Bermuda, which is 20 percent owned by Westinghouse and 80 percent owned by the Wraxall Group of Britain.

The fastest and easiest way to reach these and other foreign trading companies is through the respective country's consulate office in the United States. All are located in Washington. Many have branches in New York or Los Angeles.

DIRECT SELLING

To remain competitive, exporters sooner or later find that it's necessary to develop their own international marketing organizations, with either (1) key sales personnel who monitor foreign distributors out of U.S. offices or (2) a network of sales personnel (salaried or commissioned) stationed in key regional submarkets around the world.

It's a big mistake to dump exporting on your domestic marketing organization. Nine times out of ten, this won't work. The selling, distribution, and administrative activities related to direct export sales are so much more complex and time-consuming than domestic business that separating exporting from a domestic sales organization is the only way to go.

It's usually best to start with a small but separate export marketing group reporting to a top marketing executive. As export sales grow, along with the number of export sales personnel, reporting lines should shift to the president's office. Companies that have substantial export sales often find it convenient to centralize all direct and support functions in a separate international division. If your company exports two or more distinctly different product lines or plans to attack more than one major market, it might be advantageous to organize a separate export sales department for each product line or market right off the bat.

Although exceptions certainly occur, many companies that have been exporting successfully for a long time believe that their success has resulted more from the way they have organized their sales force and the methods they have used to sell and distribute their products than from unique product attributes. Once you have an export sales organization in place, the next step is to determine how to distribute your products overseas.

Sales Representatives

Foreign sales representation varies significantly from country to country, depending mostly on cultural and legal peculiarities. All countries, however, have agency laws substantially different from those of the United States. The peculiarities in Venezuelan laws are an example of the types of situations you can run into.

In Venezuela, actual market conditions and business protocol are seldom as advertised. Corrupt customs officials, obstreperous bureaucrats, at times unfathomable trade laws, and cagey hustlers held out as import agents can easily frustrate ill-prepared U.S. exporters.

One widely reported situation involved difficulties with sight draft payment transactions. Venezuelan buyers either delayed claiming or refused to claim merchandise from the receiving port. The products were then impounded by customs officials; U.S. shippers were subsequently charged large fines. The goods were then sold at auction; and to complete the circle, the original sales representative often purchased the goods at severely discounted prices. Venezuela is not unique in this regard; similar experiences have been reported in many other countries, especially less-developed ones.

But staying with our example of Venezuela: Venezuelan law does *not* require an importing company to pay its bank before obtaining the original documents in order to obtain the merchandise. Customs officials may release the goods merely upon presentation by the importer of a copy of the bill of lading and the posting of a bond for duties.

In Venezuela as elsewhere, trusted import agents or distributors can alleviate such problems. However, agents and/or distributors have been known to pull the same stunt as buyers. Therefore, prior to executing contracts with foreign sales representatives, it's important to get detailed references from other U.S. companies doing business in the country.

When Is an Agent an Agent

Companies unfamiliar with the peculiarities of Third World distribution channels frequently have trouble determining the identity of potential customers, mainly because distinctions between forms of representation are much murkier than in the United States, Canada, or Western Europe.

For example, a local company (or individual) can act as a manufacturer's representative, import distributor, dealer, wholesaler, and retailer—all at the same time. The company (or individual) may act as a sales agent who takes orders on commission, maintain inventory for distribution to other companies, and also have a retail store. Many retailers who import directly also order through agents and buy from exporters, jobbers, or dealers.

Returning to our Venezuela example for a moment, this country does not issue import licenses, nor does it publish a list of importers. This makes it very difficult to find out who is actually doing the importing. According to Venezuelan law, anyone can import. However, except for department stores, there are practically no general merchandise importers, and rarely do agents or distributors take on competing lines.

Once again, such loose definitions of sales representatives, distributors, and end users are not restricted to Venezuela. Each country has its own peculiar agency and contract laws. Virtually no two are alike. When exporting to any new market, but especially to less-developed countries, it only makes sense to clarify agency laws during a detailed country survey. Too many surprises can arise if you go in blind.

Confusing Laws

It's also important to grasp the key elements in a country's commercial code before executing an agency or distributorship agreement. Most countries require that to be valid, contracts must

- Be written in the host country language.
- Use metric measurements (with a few exceptions).
- State all monetary values in local currency.
- Be signed by an attorney.
- Be notarized.

Many less-developed nations have not yet enacted contract laws for agents or distributors. Therefore, when a contract is canceled, indemnification clauses cannot be enforced. Moreover, companies that choose to carry foreign agents or distributors on their payroll must abide by local labor laws, which frequently entitle employees to profit sharing, bonuses, social security, time of service, and separation allowances.

Laws that regulate sales to government agencies are another matter entirely. There is little or no uniformity, compliance requirements must be researched case by case. If you plan to sell to government agencies or state-owned businesses, be sure to (1) obtain all licenses and permits necessary to conduct business in the country and (2) register your company with appropriate government bureaus to get on the right bidders' lists—if any.

Distributors

As with agency laws, regulations affecting both the definition and the actions of distributors vary by country. Typically, a distributor is a merchant who purchases American-produced goods (often at substantial discounts) and resells them at a profit. Foreign distributors frequently provide after-sale customer service, offer product repair facilities, and stock spare parts inventories. It is not unusual for distributors to also carry noncompetitive but complementary product lines. It's only prudent to clearly set out in distributorship contracts those services to be performed by your distributor along with compensation arrangements.

In many countries, distributors provide valuable services that could not be provided, or could be provided only at great expense, by a U.S. exporter. For example, as residents of the host country, distributors should know the characteristics of local markets and advise U.S. exporters about customs regulations, pricing strategies, distribution mechanisms, and customer expectations. Competent distributors should also handle customer complaints and questions about technical product applications, both crucial elements for many exporters.

And finally, compliance with the federal Foreign Corrupt Practices Act, boycott regulations, and other legislation might preclude a U.S. company from being competitive if business were to be conducted by sales personnel on the U.S. company's payroll. Local distributors are not bound by these straitjacket restrictions and can therefore provide competitive parity with European and Japanese firms.

Some companies maintain training programs for their foreign distributors to be certain that they know the product. Others stock parts and materials at the distributor's warehouse for repair and maintenance work. Regardless of the specific relationship, it is crucial to negotiate the right contractual terms, in writing, to avoid future misunderstandings.

Monitoring Foreign Representatives

Just as when selling through domestic distributors, an exporter's personnel must monitor the performance of both distributors and sales agents. This can be done in many ways, although Rollster Ball Bearings (which has local distribution networks throughout Latin America) uses a very common tactic. Home office operations managers regularly visit distribution locations, not only to offer assistance and support when needed, but to monitor performance.

Valseon Corp. (computer accessories and supplies) follows the same tack. This company sells to South American, Central American, and Caribbean markets through local distributors. It also maintains company sales offices in Georgetown, Barbados; Rio de Janiero, Argentina; Quito, Ecuador; and Panama City, Panama. Regional marketing managers from these locations regularly travel to distributors' offices to provide technical, sales, customer service, and, when necessary, financing assistance. The Valseon marketing vice president has repeatedly claimed that face to face meetings are the only way to supervise distributors and sales reps. If a company is not willing to spend the resources to do this, it might as well forget about selling in international markets.

The Agent Distributor Service (ADS), an agency of the U.S. Department of Commerce, offers one of the most comprehensive sources anywhere of names, addresses, and specialties of foreign agents and distributors. ADS reports cost $90 per country or Canadian province, and can be obtained on request within sixty days. These reports contain information on up to six qualified representatives interested in handling your company's products. They also include brief comments about the suitability of each representative as a trade contact.

Salaried Sales Personnel

Some companies have their own employees sell direct to customers, bypassing both trading companies and distributors. Although it seems to be common for new-to-exporting companies going this route to expect international sales personnel to operate out of U.S. offices, this can be a big mistake.

First, international trade demands an inordinate amount of overseas travel, which tends to diminish the effectiveness of sales personnel. And second, with customers thousands of miles away, it's virtually impossible to provide quick answers to questions about pricing, contract terms, or technical product performance. Furthermore, operating out of U.S. offices creates a poor image when competitors station full-time sales personnel in the host country.

Despite the cost of maintaining overseas offices, it usually pays to have at least one or two sales personnel stationed in the region you are exporting to. (This is especially important in the highly developed markets of Western Europe and Japan.) Not only does a local presence improve customer relations, it enables face-to-face direct sales calls, the market testing of alternative bidding options, and the immediate negotiation of sales contracts. Moreover, with very few exceptions, these activities can be performed more efficiently by company sales personnel than by foreign sales representatives.

The sale of service contracts can also best be handled by in-country direct selling efforts. Each sale is different: It has its own time parameters, technical requirements, guarantees, financing scheme, and contract terms. In most cases, company personnel are the only ones technically qualified to deal with all these matters.

Even if a trading company or other sales agent solicits customer inquiries, building market share overseas should normally be the responsibility of company personnel. Although consultants and other intermediaries can pave the way, it's up to U.S. exporters to close sales contracts and negotiate terms and conditions. Here is a good example of a small U.S. contractor that tried to do it differently.

During the early stages of its venture into foreign markets, Morebe Contractors, Inc., tried to delegate sales contract responsibilities to an international consultant rather than using its own personnel. The following situation occurred when the company bid and won a hotel development job in St. Lucia.

The company's international consultant sourced the opportunity and assisted Morebe personnel in preparing the bid documents. So far so good. But when Morebe won the bid, instead of sending company executives to St. Lucia to negotiate and execute a sales contract, these tasks were turned over to the consultant (against his advice, I might add). Within four months, Morebe acknowledged that it could not comply with the contract terms and stopped work, blaming the consultant for executing an unmanageable sales contract.

JOINT VENTURES

The popularity of cooperative business structures has skyrocketed over the last two decades. High risks, unfamiliar business practices, language dissimilarities, and the need to establish political clout have contributed to the desirability of teaming up with one or more companies when entering a new foreign market. These cooperative structures carry various labels: cooperative alliances, cooperative ventures, and partnerships. In recent years, joint ventures have become the most popular version. In addition to enabling shared research, production, financing, and facilities costs and obligations, strategic alliances (especially joint ventures) serve a very real purpose in marketing strategy.

Marketing/Distribution Channels

One normally thinks of forming a joint venture as a convenient way to qualify a production facility for multilateral financing or to obtain local business licenses. In terms of sheer numbers, however, there are probably more marketing joint ventures than production ventures. And with good reason. Aside from any host country regulations that prohibit 100 percent foreign ownership of a business, local firms with established distribution and sales networks certainly provide better market coverage than could be achieved by U.S. companies going in alone.

A classic case of shared marketing know-how occurred during the 1980s when Glaxo, the British firm, wanted to distribute its newly-FDA approved Zantac product in America. Not having a marketing presence, Glaxo teamed up with Hoffman-La Roche, which already had a commanding sales network throughout the United States. The result? The successful introduction of Zantac in highly competitive markets.

Breaking Protective Trade Barriers

Some governments—notably those of Japan, Arab Middle East countries, and sub-Sahara African nations—have enacted stringent protective barriers against foreign imports, especially imports that compete with locally produced products. Strict laws prohibit foreigners from having a controlling interest in any local company, including sales or distribution organizations. Joining forces with a host country partner is the only possible way to enter these markets. But the advantages of a joint venture go beyond regulatory compliance.

In tightly regulated economies, political influence over pricing, distribution, customer service, and contractual arrangements makes it nearly impossible for an outsider to penetrate either consumer or capital goods markets. A well-established joint venture partner should have the connections to penetrate both formal and informal trade barriers.

Entering a Dominated Market

In some markets, a few large corporations—either local or multinational—dominate pricing, quality standards, and distribution channels to such an extent that new, smaller competitors are automatically locked out. High-capital-investment industries or those with significant ongoing research requirements (e.g., telecommunications, supercomputers, automobiles, trucks, and large gas turbines) are examples of industries dominated by a small number of large companies. Joining forces with a well-established local company is about the only way to gain entrance. (See Chapter 17 for a thorough discussion of the benefits, risks, and mechanics of setting up foreign joint ventures.)

PRICING

In U.S. markets, pricing is traditionally a function of

- Cost to produce, sell, distribute, service, and finance the product, including the cost of compliance with government regulations
- Market demand
- Competition for the same products, similar products, or substitution products.

Market demand and competition influence overseas pricing just as in domestic markets, although specific situations may require greater emphasis on one factor or another. A combination of high market demand and scant competition obviously yields the highest prices, and, of course, low market demand and intense competition force lower prices. Promotional sales, loss leaders, volume discounts, and new products or market entrants influence pricing in virtually any market for practically any product or service. Balancing these factors in overseas markets is not materially different from doing so in the United States. On the other hand, the relative influence of each factor could be significantly different.

Market demand may be greater or less. Competition will be different. Cost factors will certainly vary materially from U.S. costs. Although exported products are produced in the same facilities and with the same labor content as their domestic counterparts, the incremental costs of getting these products to foreign markets could increase total product costs significantly.

In offshore production facilities, foreign wage rates and legislated fringe benefits make labor costs either higher or lower than in the United States. The cost of materials and components sourced locally or imported will be substantially different from those of U.S. resources. Selling, distribution, and administrative costs may be higher or lower than those in the United States, but they will certainly be different. Taxes are generally higher, insurance lower.

It goes without saying that pricing strategies must reflect your company's market objectives. Are you looking for a way to get rid of excess inventory and make a quick killing, entering and leaving a market in short order? Then perhaps high prices supported by aggressive advertising campaigns are the answer. Are you looking for long-term growth in market share? If so, competitive forces will probably control pricing flexibility. If your objective is to dump products that have become obsolete in U.S. markets, fire-sale prices or large discounts might be in order.

This is not the place to elaborate on the theories of product pricing, nor will we worry about accounting aberrations that affect product-cost buildup. The only reason for mentioning pricing at all is to draw attention to those costs associated with both exporting and foreign production that may be unfamiliar to companies just getting started in foreign trade.

Several types of incremental costs apply the exporting process that never arise in domestic markets. Although not *all* the costs listed on the worksheet in Figure 12.1 are incurred for *all* export sales, most do apply.

Figure 12.1
Worksheet for Estimating Incremental Export Costs

Customer

1. Name _____

2. Address _____

3. Cable/Telex address _____

4. Telephone _____

Product

5. Product description _____

6. Quantity   _____

7. Gross and net weight of order   _____

8. Dimensions   _____

9. Cubic measure   _____

Product cost

10. Manufacturing cost per unit   _____

11. Number of units   _____

12. Total manufacturing cost of order   _____

13. Allocated selling, general and
     administrative costs for order   _____

14. Allocated interest expense   _____

15. Other allocated costs   _____

16. Total cost of order before export   _____

Export costs: Selling and administrative

17. New product packaging   _____

18. Promotional and sales literature   _____

19. Foreign trade exhibitions   _____

20. International travel expenses   _____

21. Credit search   _____

22. Risk insurance   _____

23. Financing costs   _____

24. Commissions and retainers   _____

25. Export license   _____

26. Certificate of origin licenses   _____

Shipping

27. Export packaging   _____

28. Freight forwarding charges   _____

29. Export documentation fees   _____

30. Cargo insurance   _____

31. Labeling and packing   _____

32. Inland freight   _____

33. Loading and unloading charges   _____

34. Customs duties _____

35. Total export costs _____

36. Total cost of order _____

37. Mark-on percent _____

38. Estimated selling price _____

It might be necessary to double or even triple domestic prices in order to cover all incremental costs and still yield acceptable profits. This, in and of itself, could make exporting noncompetitive and encourage the acquisition of a foreign production facility to produce products for local markets.

Foreign Pricing

Developing a cost estimate for products to be produced overseas, perhaps including the sourcing of materials or subassemblies from third countries, is a far more complex procedure—especially if the estimate is to be used to compare costs with U.S. product costs. For value-added materials, components, or subassemblies, be sure to include all costs of transporting the goods from one location to another. And don't forget the expenses of getting products to market.

Although these incremental costs are obviously different for each country, the worksheet in Figure 12.2 can serve as a guide for building cost estimates to be used either for project bids or for comparisons with other sales strategies.

Figure 12.2
Worksheet for Estimating Incremental Export Costs From a Non-U.S. Location

Customer

1. Name _____

2. Address _____

3. Cable/Telex address _____

4. Telephone _____

Product

5. Product description _____

6. Quantity _____

7. Gross and net weight of order _____

8. Dimensions _____

9. Cubic measure _____

Product cost

10. Final assembly cost per unit _____

11. Inter-facility price per unit _____

12. Total product cost per unit _____

13. Number of units _____

14. Total manufacturing cost of order _____

15. Allocated selling, general, and
    administrative costs for order _____

16. Allocated interest expense _____

17. Other allocated costs _____

18. Total cost of order before export _____

Export costs: selling and administrative

19. Promotional and sales literature _____

20. Foreign trade exhibitions _____

21. International travel expenses _____

22. Home office personnel travel expense _____

23. Credit search _____

24. Risk insurance _____

25. Buyer credit costs _____

26. Commissions and retainers _____

27. Export license _____

28. Certificate of origin licenses _____

29. Warranty and after-sale service _____

30. Value added tax (VAT) _____

31. Favors, gifts, and other promotion allowances _____

32. Field service training _____

33. Customer training _____

34. Legal and audit _____

35. Special in-country taxes _____

Shipping

36. Export packaging _____

37. Freight forwarding charges _____

38. Export documentation fees _____

39. Cargo insurance   _____

40. Labeling and packing   _____

41. Inland freight   _____

42. Loading and unloading charges   _____

43. Customs duties, export country and
      import country   _____

44. Total export costs   _____

45. Total cost of order   _____

46. Mark-on percent   _____

47. Estimated selling price   _____

Standard price sheets are seldom used outside the United States. Even if they are printed and distributed to sales personnel, they are seldom followed. Since prices for the same products sold to different classes of customers vary significantly, even without volume discounts, the basic principle in offshore pricing is that everything is negotiable.

Whether you are bidding on a construction project or selling capital equipment, computer chips, or ladies' gloves, expect to negotiate mutually agreeable prices. And expect these prices to be different, regardless of amounts calculated on cost estimate worksheets. The worksheet in Figure 12.2 should be used only as a starting point, not to determine final prices.

THE SALES CONTRACT

Sales contracts between buyer and seller are used for nearly all foreign sales transactions, including

- Exports from or imports to the United States
- Exports from or imports to a foreign facility
- Construction projects.

Since a sales contract serves as the basis for resolving conflicts between buyer and seller, it is vitally important to negotiate the contract with care. Both parties must agree that they can, and will, perform within its confines.

Obviously, both buyer and seller must have a clear understanding of all contract terms and conditions. If sales contracts are written under the laws of foreign countries, be sure to retain legal counsel from the host country to ensure equitable clauses.

Sales contracts may take a variety of forms and be either verbal or written. When written, they may be in the form of a letter, a Telex, a cable, or a formally drawn contract. Such documents form the legal basis under which agreement has been reached to sell and buy.

In addition to the name and address of both buyer and seller, minimum provisions in an international sales contract should include

- Description of goods or services, price, weight, quantity, and any special customer-defined specifications
- Shipping and delivery instructions, including all required documentation such as export/import licenses and permits
- Payment terms, conditions, and currency, including the designation of responsibility for paying customs duties, taxes, and other special fees.
- Designation of responsibility for providing goods-in-transit insurance coverage and for paying the premium.

Although a sales contract that includes the following provisions will be more difficult and time consuming to negotiate, it should save untold hours in resolving future disputes over long distances:

- Method of packaging and marking
- Inspections and tests by the buyer before goods are accepted
- Seller warranties
- Provisions for bid and performance bonds or guarantees
- Special financing provisions
- Provisions for patent and trademark protection
- Remedies allowed either party in the event of default
- Location and mediation service designated for arbitration
- Jurisdiction under which disputes will be resolved.

No contract is foolproof. Every sales transaction in each country is different. The list above merely indicates the types of items to be included. Specific clauses must be negotiated among buyer, seller, and competent legal counsel. Domestically, sales transactions occur daily without any reference to a sales contract and disputes are usually readily settled. In international trade, however, language disparities can often confuse the issue. Taking the time to negotiate a formal sales contract may prevent a profitable shipment or project from turning into a disaster.

ASSISTANCE IN IDENTIFYING MARKETS

With instantaneous media coverage, a steady stream of government pronouncements, and many foreign products becoming household brands, foreign trade has certainly invaded the American public consciousness. Any company wishing to avail itself of overseas opportunities has little difficulty in obtaining information about virtually any market. Detailed sources of information and guidance were described in Chapter 4. Here is a recap of the most helpful:

1. *International trade shows.* Trade shows of every type and size are frequently held throughout the United States and in many other regions of the world. By attending one of two of these trade shows, a company be-

ginning to export can probably glean enough information to determine the best approach, given its specific personnel and financial resources.

2. *Department of Commerce seminars.* These are presented throughout the country in every major city and many smaller ones. Subjects include everything from how to contact reputable agents and distributors, to arranging financing, to identifying potential markets.

3. *Export Management Association seminars.* These are also presented in major cities across the country. This trade association is primarily interested in attracting exporting companies, however, so don't look for much help here in identifying direct investment opportunities.

4. Other U.S. government agencies. Eximbank, the FCIA, the Departments of Agriculture and Transportation, the office of the U.S. trade representative, Department of State country desks, and many other agencies have reports, statistics, and information brochures by the truckload, covering everything imaginable about international markets. Most are free: some carry a small price. The Agency Distributor Service is probably the most helpful in locating qualified foreign agents and distributors. The *Foreign Trader Index,* another good resource, can provide customized lists of key foreign trade contacts, potential customers, and sources of additional information for overseas sales.

5. *Industry trade associations.* Many trade associations are eager to get on the global bandwagon. Brochures, trade statistics, marketing data, surveys, tax advice, invitations to seminars, and a variety of other assistance can be obtained. It is a good idea to check with your trade group before spending time on other sources.

6. *Cities and states.* Nearly every state and major city actively pursues foreign trade. Commerce bureaus and international departments have been set up to assist local producers to establish overseas contacts. Los Angeles, Chicago, Miami, Houston, New Orleans, and New York are especially active. The same holds true for the states of Illinois, California, Pennsylvania, New York, Massachusetts, Texas, Florida, and Hawaii.

7. *International development banks.* Regional development banks for Asia, Latin America, Africa, and Eastern Europe offer assistance in identifying countries and regions where specific products and services are needed. They also arrange contacts with distributors, international consultants, and even potential customers.

8. *Agency for International Development.* This federal agency actively pursues the economic development of Third World nations. Agency officials stationed throughout the world can put you in touch with local government officials who can identify products needed and potential customers. Call the Washington office of AID for a list of its continually changing foreign offices and projects.

9. *Journal of Commerce.* This daily paper publishes timely sales leads from overseas firms seeking to buy U.S. products or to represent U.S. firms.

10. *Commercial News USA.* This is a monthly magazine sent to all U.S. embassies and consulates, foreign American chambers of commerce offices, and Department of Commerce agencies. It accepts advertising and publicity announcements from companies wishing to promote their products or services overseas.

Chapter 13

Advertising and Sales Promotion

Doors to growing export markets are opened by (1) determining customer needs and wants, (2) fashioning displays and packaging to meet diverse market conditions, and (3) promoting products or services aggressively through advertising and sales promotions geared to achieving specific goals—the same keys that open doors to domestic markets. Discerning market demand is relatively straightforward. You may produce the best portable bread slicer ever conceived, and it may sell like hotcakes in U.S. markets. However, if Italians don't like sliced bread, or if Italian bakeries slice bread before delivering it to retail outlets, Italian markets are not likely to be receptive to imported bread slicers.

Selecting appropriate packaging shouldn't cause much of a problem either. If cardboard falls apart in the high humidity of central India, it does little good to package exports to Bangalore in cardboard containers instead of the heavy plastic packaging that "save the environment" pressures discourage in U.S. markets.

Focusing cost-effective advertising and sales promotions on specific goals, however, is not as straightforward.

One of the biggest mistakes that new-to-exporting companies make is to assume that advertising media, jargon, and sales promotion techniques used in U.S. markets will play successfully in foreign markets. Those that try this tack invariably end up withdrawing from exporting, blaming competition, bureaucratic interference, and other external conditions for their failure to penetrate new markets.

This chapter examines five aspects of overseas advertising and sales promotion:

1. Making the advertising and promotion fit the market
2. Evaluating the impact of advertising and promotion expenditures
3. Selecting appropriate U.S. and foreign advertising agencies
4. Designing and distributing appropriate catalogs and sales literature
5. Customizing displays and promotions for trade expositions.

MATCHING PROMOTIONS WITH MARKETS

A standard set of advertising guidelines that were equally effective in all world markets would certainly be desirable. Even regional standards would be welcome (e.g., standards applicable throughout Latin America). Unfortunately, extreme variations in consumer tastes, wide ranges of culturally acceptable advertising language, significant literacy differences, infrastructure peculiarities, and environmental factors make such standardization impossible. Although broad procedural guidelines can point the way, specific advertising and promotion campaigns must be uniquely designed for each market.

Take, for example, the matter of literacy. Universal schooling in the United States, Europe, and Japan has, over the years, brought adult literacy rates up to the 85 to 95 percent level. Most people can and do read newspapers and magazines, at least occasionally. Since advertising in these periodicals reaches broad markets, they are the best media in which to advertise various kinds of consumer products.

On the other hand, many of Brazil's 156 million people are scattered throughout the hinterlands, hundreds of miles from schools. No one knows for sure what the literacy rate may be for the entire population; however, adult literacy of 50 to 60 percent is a reasonable estimate for the approximately 100 million consumers that live in towns and cities. A similar lack of education exists in Guatemala, where 42 percent of the population is Indian (of Maya Quiche origin) and compulsory education ends with the sixth grade. Concentrated newspaper and magazine advertising in these cultures is wasted.

Infrastructure development, especially electric power and telecommunications, also has a major impact on the choice of advertising media. If television sets are a scarce commodity, advertising in this medium won't reach many consumers. On the other hand, radios are very common in nearly all nations except those in sub-Sahara Africa, the desert regions of the Middle East, and parts of central Asia. Radio advertising in less-developed countries usually reaches a broader market than television, newspapers, or magazines.

Throughout the world, the wide acceptance of movies as an entertainment medium makes cinema advertising highly attractive in otherwise unreachable markets. Throughout India, Pakistan, the Caribbean, and much of Eastern Europe, advertisements that immediately precede a feature movie will reach captive audiences that might not otherwise be receptive.

In many Third World countries, billboards with flashy pictures and mobile hawkers with high-amplification speakers are universally used to promote political candidates. Such media advertising works for politicians: it is also effective for promoting products.

Cultural Sensitivity

One word of caution for newcomers to foreign markets: Beware of intense national pride that tends to reject products that are "not made here." In the United States, Canada, Western Europe, Australia, and other developed markets, imported goods are often viewed as novel or even superior to locally produced products. Japanese marketers used this phenomenon to their advantage when first broaching American markets. U.S. firms like Avon, Radio Shack, and several fast-food chains have used the same psychology in exploiting new markets in Canada, Europe, Japan, Taiwan, and South Korea.

Notwithstanding the success of U.S. firms in industrialized nations, the not-made-here syndrome is still prevalent in most of the Third World, especially in those nations that have a large entrepreneurial business base (e.g., Colombia, the Czech Republic, Greece, and Mexico). Promoting products in these countries should downplay the fact that products are imported and slant advertising copy toward local pride.

A good example of how this can be accomplished occurred when Pleno Cosmetics first broached the Jamaican market with its Afro-American hair spray. Instead of exporting directly to Jamaican retailers or distributors, Pleno set up a local warehousing operation in a free trade zone. Local workers were hired to repackage the products and to add a small amount of an inert chemical, which was, in fact, merely a placebo. Advertising copy carefully accentuated the local additions, creating the image that these were locally made products. Although clearly deceptive, Pleno's initial advertising campaign was so successful that within a year it stopped adding the placebo and reverted to promoting its imported products in their pure form.

Culturally sensitive jargon must also be avoided. As American markets become more and more competitive, advertising agencies regularly invent new jargon to describe a product's features and benefits. Meaningless adjectives, misplaced nouns, double entendres, and clichés aim to attract the consumer's eye. You can turn on any television channel or pick up any newspaper or magazine and see this approach. Take, for example, four advertisements appearing in the October 1993 issue of *World Trade*:

- "Think of us as your travel agency for beans."—John V. Carr & Son, Inc.
- "The heart of Latin America beats in San Francisco . . . and in its port."—Port of San Francisco
- "Charting Your Course for Export Success?"—Reed Exhibition Companies
- "Cosco delivers reliable, responsible service that gives you time to putter around."—Cosco North America, Inc.

Would consumers in Poland have any idea what a "travel agency for beans" means? Would an Argentine shipper believe that Latin America has a "heart" or that it "beats" in San Francisco? To Indonesians, "charting your course" implies preparing a map for a boat trip. And what meaning could "putter around" have to buyers in Ghana? Before spending advertising dollars, it only makes sense to ensure that the copy can be understood in your targeted market.

Moreover, no one intentionally offends customers. Yet, many words or phrases commonly used in the United States have entirely different and often offensive meanings in foreign lands. Take "deodorant," for example. Italian consumers would be offended to see this in print or on television. "Raising a red flag" connotes a happy and pleasant occasion in certain East Asian cultures. The old cartoon and the now-discarded nickname for the Minnesota Vikings football team, "purple people-eaters," would bring dismay in Brazil and Mexico, where purple is the color of death.

A classic faux pas was committed by the Parker Pen company many years ago when it advertised its famous ballpoint pen as the "Jotter": in Latin markets, "jotter" translates as "jockstrap."

Advertising to Meet Specific Goals

Few marketing executives would argue with the statement that unfocused advertising wastes money and can do more harm than good. The trick is to develop programs that are both results-oriented and cost-effective—in other words, that attract the most sales for the least cost.

It's hard enough to know whether advertising expenditures are effective in U.S. markets; it's doubly difficult overseas. Nevertheless, as with domestic promotions, overseas advertising should be designed to open new markets, to capture customers from competitors, or to provide market intelligence. To be cost-effective, advertising campaigns must meet strategic marketing goals and achieve the greatest market impact at the lowest possible cost.

The most appropriate medium depends on the type of product, the size of the market, the degree and type of competitive advertising, and the special circumstances found in the host country. In focusing advertising on a select market niche, the identification of specific short- and long-term objectives is a crucial first step.

It's easy to become disillusioned and blame an advertising agency when incremental sales do not immediately materialize. Far too often, however, budget constraints force advertising cutbacks just when advertising is most needed. If export sales do not meet expectations or if competitors seem to be outdistancing us, our immediate reaction is to develop alternative advertising strategies—or to stop advertising entirely. A better approach may be to refocus out strategies on specific marketing objectives whose achievement can be accurately measured.

Why Advertising Campaigns Fail

Most overseas advertising campaigns fail to deliver because

1. The expected results were ill defined.
2. The time frame within which results could be expected was too short.
3. Advertisements were inappropriately presented.
4. The wrong media were used.

It seems obvious that spending advertising dollars without clearly defined objectives makes little sense. Furthermore, expected results must be quantified. How much should a specific advertising campaign increase sales? How big an increase in market share should be expected? What type of market intelligence should be forthcoming?

Increased sales volume or market share cannot be achieved in the short run, regardless of how well the advertising campaign is structured and managed. One week, one month, even six months may be too short a period in which to realize concrete benefits. Sustainable growth strategies take time to jell, and advertising aimed at short-term results does little to meet such objectives.

Gaining Market Share

Although a relationship between advertising expenditures and increases in sales or market share may hold for certain U.S. markets, this is rarely the case overseas. Over the long pull, advertising cannot by itself create brand loyalty. Customers must realize continued, long-term benefits from switching brands or products. If they don't, any increase in market share will be short-lived. Permanent market share should be viewed as a long-term investment.

Of course, if product life cycles are short (as with designer clothes) or if your objective is to dump surplus inventory, "permanent" may mean one season or one buying cycle. In any event, to achieve cost-effectiveness, specific advertising programs must correlate with strategic objectives.

Controlling Advertising Expenditures

It's also important to control advertising expenditures. Once you have developed specific objectives for a given market, pinpoint advertising to achieve those objectives—no more. One of the costliest mistakes exporters make in overseas advertising is to use an expensive advertising campaign to build a public image. Other, less costly means should be used to introduce the company's name and reputation to the market, such as trade shows (either in the United States or overseas) and free publicity coverage in local news media. In other words, focus advertising dollars on building product acceptance; use public relations publicity to establish brand recognition and your company's reputation.

The guidelines in Figure 13.1 should provide a helpful reference for keeping advertising expenditures under control.

Figure 13.1
Guidelines for Cost-Effective Advertising

1. Use advertising for specific purposes (e.g., test new markets, increase a specific market share, gather intelligence about new markets), not to create or sustain a public image.

2. Define precise, quantifiable objectives for each advertising campaign, such as the anticipated sales increases or the expected number of new customers.

3. Design advertising programs to target specific, focused marketing goals, such as raising prices by 5 percent, increasing sales volume by 10 percent, improving market share by 2 percent, or getting a foothold in a new market niche.

4. If you use an advertising agency, retain control over expenditures, format design, and responses.

---

5. Define the targeted recipients (e.g., types of customers, geographic coverage, specific competitors) before starting the advertising campaign.
6. If your objective is to win business from competition, know your competition and compare your products or brand names with those of competitors.
7. Define the time frame within which results can be expected.
8. Segregate short-term expectations from long-term objectives and use different advertising techniques for each.
9. Establish a schedule for the advertising agency to follow, including progress milestones that can be measured.
10. Devise a follow-up procedure to monitor the agency against these milestones.

MEASURING MARKET IMPACT

Although media cost is important, defining the target audience is crucial. If you are trying to sell in England, advertising in American telephone directories won't help, but newspaper announcements in the London *Times* might work well. One-on-one sales promotions may help sell industrial cleaners to manufacturing plants in Buenos Aires, but it will never work for increasing sales of household detergent to several hundred thousand consumers in Stuttgart, Germany. Although TV advertising might work well for selling automobile tires in Tel Aviv, it won't help the sale of aircraft spare parts to the Israeli Air Force.

To identify the market impact of any advertising campaign, especially one whose benefits may be realized over the long term, a monitoring system should be set up. It doesn't have to be complicated to be effective. In fact, the simpler the better. Although no prescribed format fits every situation, experience has shown that successful measuring systems have two features in common: quantifiable results and milestone events.

Quantifiable Results

The monitoring system must be able to measure quantifiable results against original expectations. In other words, if a direct mail campaign is expected to produce a 10 percent sales increase, you must be able to monitor where the new customers come from. In some situations this is fairly easy. Asking British customers what motivated them to buy your products should help you measure the impact of advertising efforts.

In other cases, however, a broader approach must be used, especially to monitor long-term results. Historical records should identify the approximate changes in sales that result from industry or national business cycles. Also, if competitors leave the market, sales increases from the absorption of latent demand are normally a fairly obvious result. On the other hand, if sales increase and uncontrollable factors such as these cannot be identified, then it is reasonable to assume that the advertising campaign was the main cause.

Milestones

To effectively monitor advertising results over the long term, some type of milestone measurement must be used. For example, suppose the objective is to increase market share by 6 percent over the next three years. It would be reasonable to assume that an advertising campaign today will have little effect 2½ years from now; however, indirectly it may have a material effect. New customers attracted in the short term may provide repeat business, with a secondary effect of drawing additional new customers later on.

Advertising should bring a big jump for the first six months, with the increase tapering off over the next four or five periods. If an increase does not occur during the first six months, chances are good that your campaign failed to achieve its objective.

SELECTING THE RIGHT ADVERTISING AGENCY

It is often difficult to judge how much to spend on advertising and what type of media to use in a foreign market. More often than not, it pays new exporters to follow the advice of an advertising agency that knows specific market characteristics and unique cultural norms. Also, be aware that some countries tax advertising expenditures. Others restrict the amount that can be spent. Many countries have inferior printing and other production facilities. And long lead times in several European countries may make your advertisement out of date before the public sees it.

Before spending the first advertising dollar, it's crucial to check out each of these potential trouble spots. Understanding the basic characteristics of a foreign market makes the selection of an appropriate advertising agency faster and less costly.

Some new-to-exporting companies try to handle foreign advertising with their own personnel. This nearly always results in high expenditures that bring few results. Difficult as it may be to conduct an advertising campaign in the United States without an advertising agency, it's virtually impossible to do so overseas. Cultural tastes, language peculiarities (even in English-speaking countries), media availability, local postal systems, and infrastructure development (e.g., electricity, telephones, etc.) make the assistance of local agencies a must.

It's fairly easy to get leads to local agencies—and, at times, recommendations—from the local American Chamber of Commerce office. It's usually a good idea to interview two or three referrals before signing a contract to be certain that agency personnel are capable of communicating the various aspects and results of the campaign to your U.S. office. In certain cases, foreign agencies do not fully comprehend the objectives of U.S. exporting clients and therefore are unable to communicate effectively. It's far better to take the time to interview a sufficient number of agencies than to be sorry later on—after advertising expenditures have been made.

Several U.S. agencies have gone international, with branch offices in key markets around the world. Although these agencies can usually perform as well as local firms, don't be surprised if they charge significantly more. The industry trade magazine *Advertising Age* is a good place to begin a search for U.S. firms that have offices in your export markets.

Cooperative Advertising

Cooperative advertising has become a popular way for smaller exporters to cut expenses. Two of the best ways to arrange for cooperative advertising are (1) through a group advertising program sponsored by your trade association (especially for trade shows) and (2) through shared advertising programs sponsored by your local chamber of commerce and other regional business groups.

The major advantages in cooperative advertising are that it

1. Costs less per individual member.
2. Generates a better response from U.S. advertising agencies (with foreign branches, of course) because of its larger budget.
3. Reduces the time and effort of doing your own market research on specific overseas markets.

Shared advertising also has glaring weaknesses:

1. It results in a loss of control over advertisement substance and media choice.
2. Making sure that each member contributes the right proportionate share of advertising expenditures is difficult.
3. It makes developing customer (or foreign sales representative) loyalty virtually impossible.

Cooperative advertising is an alternative, however, that under certain circumstances can be very productive. For example, noncompeting companies with products that are similar but that cannot be substituted one for the other may combine advertising budgets to get bigger or farther-reaching campaigns than any of them could afford individually. Furthermore, increased sales of complementary products may, in fact, boost your sales as well.

The toy industry in the United States has used this approach for years. Small manufacturers of wooden pull toys, plastic and rubber dolls, and miniature metal cars all sold to major department stores. Since none of them could afford to compete with the advertising budgets of industry giants, they decided to combine resources and send joint flyers, posters, and other circulars to major retailers. They also combined their booths at the annual New York toy show. Such efforts may not be as effective as individual programs, but reports indicate that participants believe that the results are more cost-effective than sharing advertising programs promoted by the trade association.

PUBLIC IMAGING

The second leg of effective overseas promotions should focus on introducing the U.S. exporting company to its new market. This involves creating a public image that portrays quality, competitive pricing, outstanding customer service, and longevity.

Public imaging—that is, the creation of a favorable company image in the public eye—can usually best be achieved through a professionally managed public relations program. It is not uncommon to find that in foreign markets, market reputation can make or break service companies as readily as it can those that sell consumer goods or commercial products.

When you attack a new foreign market, the chances are good that neither sales representatives nor customers know much, if anything, about your company. Since many foreign markets regard new imported products—or services—with skepticism, it's essential to create a favorable, recognizable identity as soon as possible. Moreover, one of the biggest complains from foreign buyers is that new U.S. exporters tend to be "here today, gone tomorrow." This attitude makes it all the more important to establish your reputation as a company that has the staying power to remain competitive over the long haul and will be available to serve its customers and stand behind its products for many years to come.

Unfortunately, while advertising results may be difficult to measure, identifying specific benefits from a public relations program is virtually impossible. Most companies rely on the reputation of established public relations firms to present and maintain a good client profile over the long term, without attempting to quantify benefits.

Implementing a Public Relations Program

Professional public relations firms run the gamut from one-person businesses to multinational companies with offices throughout the world. The choice of one over another should be based on

- Experience in the particular foreign market you are exporting to
- Reputation in that market as an honest, reputable, highly confidential firm—usually confirmed by an extensive reference check
- Fee structure.

Also, it's important to ensure a good rapport between the representative of the public relations firm and your company's liaison officer.

A public relations contract may be structured either for a single, time-limited project or on a continuing basis. Regardless of the choice, however, it's important to rely on the firm's professional judgment as to what types of promotions will and will not work in a given foreign market. After all, it doesn't make much sense to ignore expertise when you're paying for it.

A qualified public relations firm should design an appropriate image-building program and make all arrangements for its implementation, including media coverage. It is not unusual to find that public relations projects overlap with advertising programs. So much the better. For example, a television commercial in Germany might be followed by interviews with the company's key executives responsible for European markets. Or a magazine advertisement could combine the virtues of your products with evidence of your company's reputation in American markets.

The two biggest advantages of using host-country professional public relations firms are that (1) they know specifically who to contact to arrange promotions in any local medium and (2) they handle all selling and administrative details, which can be very time-consuming.

Here are a few examples of publicity campaigns that have worked well for small U.S. exporters:

1. Invite a local newspaper to write an article on some unique aspect of the company.
2. Invite television reporters to cover a special event sponsored by the company (e.g., a fund-raising drive, an athletic event, the introduction of ecologically safe new products).
3. Start a company school for employees' children.
4. Sponsor a young people's athletic team.
5. Sponsor an entrant in a local parade.
6. Donate materials, space, or services to community theater groups.
7. Get behind a social cause (e.g., homes for the homeless, food and clothing drives for the poor, clothing and activity donations for mental hospitals).
8. Donate used computers, office equipment, and so on to local schools, hospitals, or welfare agencies.

The main idea in a public relations program is to create a favorable public image. Companies that sell products in markets deemed environmentally or socially harmful have an especially difficult time sustaining a favorable image. One of the best ways to overcome this stigma is to project a sense of caring about and participation in the community, town, or region you are trying to penetrate. Obviously, this won't buy much in broad markets; however, in selected local markets, parlaying community involvement into national recognition often enables exporting companies to open new markets well beyond the immediate locale.

Well-conceived and conscientiously managed advertising and public relations programs are important tools for implementing long-term export growth strategies. Businesses of all sizes and in virtually any industry need to seriously consider either an advertising campaign or a public relations program, or both, in the markets they are attempting to enter or expand in. Unfortunately, many smaller companies tend to shy away from both advertising and public relations, assuming that the expense is too great for tight budgets. Too often, a lack of advertising or public relations effort defeats an otherwise effective exporting strategy.

Since advertising and public relations are so important in developing overseas markets, it makes good sense for even the smallest business to find a cost-effective way to use these tools. With a little effort and creativity, nearly any type of program can be designed and managed at minimum expense while still getting good results.

SALES LITERATURE AND TRADE EXPOSITIONS

Companies that have tried to use the same sales literature and/or catalogs in overseas markets as in the United States nearly always find the effort a waste of time and money—even when the documents are translated into the local language. Cultural responses to color, message, idioms, and pricing are different in each country. No two markets will assess your written sales promotions in the same light.

In many Eastern countries, white is a color of mourning, red one of joy. Scantily clad models can be used effectively in U.S. sales brochures, but would be scandalous if used for selling attire or toiletries in Islamic countries—or, for that matter, in any less-developed country. Quantity discounts, open returned goods policies, and "one-day sales" will be a waste of money in Bolivia.

Furthermore, distributing sales literature and/or catalogs through the mail is totally ineffective outside the United States. No country in the world has as extensive a postal service as the United States, and in most Third World countries, reliable mail service is virtually nonexistent.

To avoid costly errors in the design and distribution of any written sales promotion, using a local advertising agency or sales promotion bureau is imperative. Spell out what details you want covered in the literature, then turn design, layout, and copy responsibility over to local experts. Define the customers you wish to attract and let a local agency worry about distributing your promotions.

A good example of the harm that can result from conveying the wrong message in industrial sales literature occurred when a midsize American company designed its own brochures to sell mining equipment in Gabon. The company forgot to use the metric system in its product specification sheets, showed Caucasian models using the equipment, and quoted prices in sterling (Gabon is a former French colony whose foreign currency is the French franc). The literature cost more than $200,000 and was in the field for three months (without a sale) before a conscientious Gabonese distributor notified the U.S. exporter of its errors.

Designing displays and promotions at trade fairs should also be handled with care. If you hope to sell anything through an exposition, you will need to customize your booth and literature to suit local customs without losing the unique identity of your company and its products. The experience of a first-time U.S. exporter who had a booth at a recent trade show in Caracas, Venezuela, illustrates the point.

A Caribbean hotel developer had an oversized booth replete with models, a variety of pass-out sales literature, miniature bottles of rum, and a constantly playing video. It attracted potential customers, suppliers, and curiosity seekers like flies. Next door was a booth draped with U.S. flags, with a pile of six sales brochures, manned part-time by one salesman in a wool suit, button-down shirt, and tie. The name of the company appeared in six-inch letters in the upper corner of the booth. A description of its products was nowhere to be seen. Over a three-day period, the "Ivy-leaguer" collected a total of three business cards.

Clearly, if either a trade-show booth or sales literature plays a role in your marketing strategies, it makes sense to get advice from experts. And as with any type of advertising or sales promotion, those experts should be intimately familiar with the design, message, and promotion gimmicks necessary to attract customers in that country.

MEDIA CHOICES IN THIRD WORLD MARKETS

There are many direct marketing choices available in the United States and most of Western Europe. Companies may choose any or all of the following media, depending on market breadth, types of products, and advertising budgets:

1. Direct mail
2. Telemarketing
3. Television or radio
4. Cinema
5. Closed-circuit video
6. Newspaper announcements
7. Popular magazine and trade journal ads
8. Billboards or posters—roadside or indoor (e.g., in sports arenas)
9. Commercial envelope flyleaves
10. Matchbooks
11. Holiday greeting cards
12. Pencils and pens
13. Calendars
14. Newsletters
15. Telephone Yellow Pages.

However, in most Third World countries, demographics, infrastructure, and local customs significantly reduce the number of choices. Take Latin America and the Caribbean, for example. In these widely dispersed markets, direct marketing is still in its infancy. Unreliable (or nonexistent) mail service, low telephone penetration, and inefficient transportation systems severely limit exposure.

In addition, lists of potential customers, either by address or by telephone number, are virtually nonexistent. Those that are available tend to be of poor quality or closely controlled by preparers. This makes it impossible to know the buying characteristics of mail or telephone recipients. Sparse use of credit cards presents additional challenges. And accessibility to potential customers varies significantly between rural and urban markets.

If you decide to use potential customer lists of any type, it pays to take the time to build your own database—even if that means beginning with a very small one. One way to begin building a database (at least for the direct marketing of business-to-business products) is to collect names and addresses through advertisements in trade journals and participation in trade shows and conferences.

Consumer product companies often find that flyers left in stores, beauty parlors, lobbies of movie theaters, and ticket offices of sporting events bring good results. Properly designed brochures left in such locations can also help build a database. Bus posters reach a fairly large audience, as do roadside billboards.

Although many Third World countries have a high penetration of television sets (especially in Latin America and the Caribbean), nearly everyone has access to radios. Moreover, cinema attendance is usually very high. Print media such as magazines and newspapers have caught on in several Third World countries where literacy rates are climbing. Be aware, however, that in many countries experiencing high inflation rates, such as Brazil, the purchase price of newspapers and magazines is well beyond the means of the majority of consumers.

Toll-free numbers are catching on in a few more developed countries and can be an effective way to reach industrial and commercial customers. It should be recognized, however, that telemarketing through 800 numbers is still very much in the beginning stages in many countries—and nonexistent in the most severely underdeveloped nations.

Looking to the future, many countries currently classified as Third World have shifted from state-controlled to market economies. As income distribution improves and infrastructures (primarily postal systems) are developed, many current deficiencies will be eliminated. Also, the extensive privatization of telephone companies should, over the long term, vastly improve telemarketing potential.

Chapter 14

Shipping and Transportation

Although the *principles* involved in transporting goods overseas are the same as those for shipping within in the United States, the *mechanics* are entirely different and the complexities are greater. Packing, labeling, documentation, and insurance must be differently managed, and every country has special regulations for the inland transport of goods. Although the shipping and transportation practices described in this chapter generally apply worldwide, it's important to recognize that modifications will be necessary to comply with importing regulations and practices unique to a given country.

Practically all foreign shipments involve special features that differ from U.S. domestic freight practices. They can be summarized under the headings

- Packing and labeling
- Shipping documentation
- Collection documents
- Cargo insurance.

Moreover, when exporters are responsible for transporting the goods from the port of debarkation to customer locations within a foreign country, arrangements must be made with local carriers. To ensure that carriers fulfill their contractual obligations, it is as important to monitor the cargo's progress during inland transport as it is to monitor ocean shipments.

The following discussions assume that readers already have experience in the preparation of invoices, bills of lading, packing lists, and so on, for domestic shipments. Therefore, elementary samples of these documents are omitted. Those unfamiliar with them can get samples from any freight forwarder.

FREIGHT FORWARDERS

Although experienced export shipping personnel could certainly handle the preparation and submission of export documentation themselves, nearly all companies find that freight forwarders can perform the tasks at less cost and more efficiently. Freight forwarders are shipping and transport agencies of exporting companies. They serve as primary coordinators among exporting companies, shippers, bankers, customs officials, and a variety of other parties.

Freight forwarders prepare all documentation necessary for shipping goods, insuring cargo, and collecting from a customer. They also provide information for bid packages. All licensed international freight forwarders are familiar with international letters of credit (L/Cs). As soon as the L/C is prepared, a copy of it and any special shipping instructions should go directly to the forwarder, who then advises the exporter about special packing, labeling, and export/import licensing that may be required. All ocean forwarders are licensed by the Nonvessel Operating Common Carriers; air forwarders are licensed by the International Air Transportation Association. Most freight forwarders handle both ocean and air freight.

Although a complete compilation of services performed by freight forwarders would comprise many pages, here are the major ones:

Freight forwarders

1. Research tariff rates and determine the most economical method of transport.
2. Offer advice about current conditions in the buyer's country relative to dockage and airport facilities.
3. Arrange to obtain licenses, permits, certificates, consular invoices, legalizations, and other regulatory documents, both to satisfy U.S. laws and to comply with the laws of the country of destination.
4. Make appropriate arrangements for inland transport in the United States to the port of embarkation and in the destination country to the customer's location.
5. Consolidate shipments, including containerization, and transport goods to the appropriate carrier.
6. Arrange for special crating, packing, loading, and unloading equipment.
7. Receive a clean bill of lading or waybill consistent with L/C or shipping instructions.
8. Prepare export declarations, customs clearance documentation, bank documents for L/C drawdowns, and claims against airlines or ocean carriers.
9. Arrange for cargo insurance.
10. Track the shipment to its destination.
11. Provide communications and courier service during the entire transportation period.

Such services are not only valuable but absolutely necessary for companies without a full complement of experienced export shipping and transportation personnel. In certain situations, exporters may elect to retain control over collections from customers. In that case, the forwarder sends all documents to the company's office for verification before presentation to a bank. The exporter should then be prepared to track its own shipments on vessels leaving and arriving in various ports around the world. This can easily be done by following announcements of arrivals and departures in the *Pacific Shipper*, the *Journal of Commerce*, and, for the East coast, the *Shipper's Digest*.

The best way to locate an appropriate freight forwarder is to ask other companies in your area or industry that have been in the export business for a while. Forwarders that don't measure up can easily be weeded out.

Figure 14.1 sets out important criteria for choosing the right freight forwarder.

Figure 14.1
Guidelines for Choosing a Freight Forwarder

A freight forwarder should

1. Be large enough to have clout with major shipping lines, but small enough to give personal service. Those that handle major corporations' business are often too busy to care about small accounts.
2. Have a location near the U.S. port you plan to ship from.
3. Be willing and able to prepare all license applications, declarations, collection documentation, and customs forms.
4. Maintain listings of import restrictions from foreign countries worldwide.
5. Have a good reputation with your international bank.
6. Offer consolidation services.
7. Be willing to come to your office rather than meeting at its location.
8. Furnish references from other customers.
9. Allow you to check these references.
10. Permit bank references to be checked.

GETTING PRODUCTS READY FOR SHIPMENT

Exporters must retain responsibility for

- Protecting the cargo against losses from moisture, breakage, or pilferage, and minimizing the cargo weight
- Choosing among unitizing, palletizing, and containerization
- Determining the appropriate exterior identification of the cargo.

Proper packing ensures the first; the size of the product and the quantity of parcels controls the second; and the degree of product hazard determines the third.

Packing

A variety of packing methods and materials are available to protect goods against moisture and breakage. Their suitability in any given situation depends on the nature of the product. Fiberboard boxes continue to be the most popular type of exterior container for hard goods. They are relatively inexpensive, strong, and light in weight. Proper support by tension straps, water-resistant glue and tape, and staples normally prevents breakage in cartons of a test strength of at least 275 pounds per square inch. Impregnated multiwall fiberboard boxes are usually impervious to moisture, unless they are submerged for extended periods. Moreover, fiberboard is one of the lightest-weight materials available.

Inserting fiberboard cartons into a nailed wooden box provides added security and strength. The box won't keep out the moisture, but it will protect against breakage. Weight is an important factor in overseas shipping, however, and wooden boxes are heavy.

Wirebound boxes and crates, cleated plywood boxes, and drums and kegs—either steel, fiber, or wooden—are good packing containers for heavy loads or granular, liquid, or gelatinous products. These containers all add significantly to shipping weight, however. Multiwall shipping sacks and bales are used primarily for agricultural, powdered, or granular products, especially dry chemicals. Both bales and sacks are subject to moisture damage, pilferage, and breakage by lift hooks and should be containerized.

Fragile or brittle goods must be cushioned against shock and vibration. The type of material chosen depends on the size, weight, surface finish, and built-in shock resistance of the goods. Any freight forwarder can advise the best form and material for a specific shipment.

Unitizing, Palletizing, and Containerization

Whenever possible, it's a good idea to use either unitizing, palletizing, or containerization to facilitate moving the goods and to protect the cargo during stowage. In shipping parlance, *unitizing* means the assembly of one or more items into a tightly compacted load, secured with cleating or skids for ease of handling. *Palletizing* refers to the assembly of one or more containers on a pallet base and securely fastened to the pallet. Most overseas shipments of hard goods are either unitized or palletized. Both systems offer several advantages:

1. Manual handling damage is eliminated. Forklifts, cranes, and other mechanical devices must be used to move the load.
2. Since the load is handled as a unit, individual packages are further protected from handling damage.
3. Theft is reduced.
4. Loading and unloading from the vessel is faster.
5. Physical inventory counts are facilitated.
6. Waterproof coverings are more easily attached.

To further protect against moisture, breakage, and pilferage it's a good idea to use shipboard *containerization*. Shipboard containers are large, metal, free-standing enclosures that contain several unit loads or pallets. They can be stacked, thus saving space aboard ship. They are easily loaded and unloaded by cranes. They may reside dockside for long periods waiting for a ship or inland transport without damage to the enclosed goods.

Nearly all ocean freight vessels accumulate loads for containerization. Ideally, a single exporter will fill one or more containers with its own merchandise. But this isn't necessary. Partial loads can be combined, at the option of the vessel's captain, to save space and secure the loads. When goods from two or more shippers are consolidated in a container, the shippers share loading and unloading costs. Freight forwarders normally arrange for shared containers.

Exterior Identification—Labeling

Usually a buyer specifies what type of labeling should be affixed to the exterior of the cartons, crates, or other shipping containers. These markings may be in pictorial form or in words, and may be stenciled or imposed using any other indelible ink process. Labels should be at least two inches high and appear on the top of the package and at least one side. Sacks should be marked on both sides; drums should be marked on both top and side. The reasons for accurate labeling are probably obvious, but it can't hurt to review the major ones. Markings and labels must identify the following:

1. Shipper, consignee, reference number, and contract or purchase order number
2. Country of origin
3. Weight in both pounds and kilograms
4. The number of packages, if there is more than one in the shipment
5. Handling instructions: "fragile," "this side up," "store in heated place," and so on
6. Final destination and port of entry (Guatemala City via Livingston)
7. Whether the package contains hazardous material.

All labels and markings should be in both English and the language of the country of destination. It's extremely important to label shipments according to the laws of the host country. Freight forwarders keep track of these changing laws for every port in the world.

SHIPPING DOCUMENTS

In international trade, shipping documents serve a far broader purpose than merely authorizing shipment and providing a record of the transaction. All kinds of harmful results can occur if exporters do not pay close enough attention to shipping documents. Without proper documentation, payment may not be received on time—or at all. The shipment may not clear customs at the destination port, resulting in charges, fines, and penalties. The goods may be returned to the exporter, thereby incurring additional freight charges and customs fees. In some ports, goods without proper documentation will certainly be seized by customs officials.

There are three broad types of shipping documents:

- General export licenses
- Validated licenses
- Export declarations.

Some licensing activities are controlled by the federal Bureau of Export Administration (BXA) in close association with the Departments of Defense and State. Others are controlled by a sixteen-nation committee called the Coordinating Committee for Multilateral Export Controls (COCOM). COCOM coordinates regulations for shipments to Communist nations. Current members of COCOM are Belgium, Denmark, Germany, France, Greece, Italy, the Netherlands, Japan, the United States, the United Kingdom, Luxembourg, Norway, Portugal, Spain, and Canada.

The primary purpose of licensing exports is to enforce export trade barriers. With a few exceptions, the United States maintains the most restrictive and rigid barriers to export trade of any nation. Perhaps the recent culmination of the Uruguay Round of the GATT negotiations will alleviate this condition. However, intense lobbying by several U.S. special interest groups makes it likely that many restraints will remain in effect for some time—at least until certain political conditions are ameliorated (e.g., relations with Cuba, North Korea, Vietnam, Myanmar, etc.).

General License

The general license is obtained from the BXA and acts as a blanket permit to allow exports of different types of goods to a variety of countries. Any freight forwarder can file the application for you. It's a good idea to do it before you finalize a sales contract, however. That way you can be certain that the goods to be shipped are not defined as strategic commodities. It's also necessary to determine that the buyer's country does not have a "sensitive" designation. A general license takes about two weeks to wend its way through the approval cycle. Information about its status can be obtained from the Office of Export Licensing, (202) 377-4811 or (714) 660-0144.

Validated License

A validated license authorizes the sale of particular goods to specific countries. It must be obtained for the export of strategic goods that the government wants to control for any reason. It also permits export to a country on the government's restricted list. This license requires a lengthy and costly application and review process. The Departments of Defense and State get in the approval loop, and it's possible that COCOM will want to approve the transaction as well.

The normal time for processing an application through the entire approval chain is 120 days; although partial approvals can be obtained in less time. Continuing shifts in world political institutions and U.S. trade policies, however, lead to changes in both the strategic product list and restrictive country classifications, creating wide variations in these time estimates. When you are ready to submit an application, call the Export Licensing office for the current status.

Special Licenses

Special licenses may apply in specific situations. For example, project licenses cover the export of all goods requiring validated licenses for certain large scale operations, such as construction or development projects. One year distribution licenses are granted for exports to consignees in countries that maintain good relations with the United States. A service supply license is required to provide service on equipment exported from the United States or produced abroad with parts imported from the United States.

Foreign Export Licensing

Each country has its own export trade barriers with it own definitions of strategic goods and restrictions. Few developed nations are as paranoid as the U.S. government, however, about what can and can't be done. Traditional trading nations such as the United Kingdom and Japan realize that the well-being of the country depends on an active domestic export program. Exporting from these nations, or even from less-developed nations, usually involves substantially less paperwork than exporting from the United States. Caribbean nations that come under the Caribbean Initiative Program have relatively open export policies, especially for shipments to the United States.

Wherever your export facility may be located, however, some type of licensing will probably be required. Contact your local trade or commerce office for details.

Shipper's Export Declaration

A shipper's export declaration must be completed for all shipments valued in excess of $1,000 for which a validated license is required. An export declaration identifies the license under which the export is being shipped. It verifies that the shipment complies with authorization regulations. And it shows appropriate U.S. government product codes, quantities shipped, value of the shipment, and destination. The Census Department requires this data for statistical reports published monthly.

COLLECTION DOCUMENTS

Collection documents must be submitted to the importer, the importer's bank, or the shipper's bank before payment can be made. These documents vary from country to country, from importer to importer, and from bank to bank. Although a specific transaction will probably never require all of the following documents, various classes of shipments to different destinations may require one or more.

1. *Commercial invoice.* As with domestic sales, a commercial invoice follows every export shipment. Some countries require special certification to be incorporated in the invoice, often in the language of the host country. The Department of Commerce keeps a list of requirements from each country.

2. *Consular invoice.* In addition to a commercial invoice, most Latin American and other developing nations require a consular invoice prepared on forms supplied by their respective consulates. These invoices

must be prepared in the language of the host country. They are visaed by the resident consul, who certifies the authenticity and correctness of the documents.

3. *Bill of lading.* Of the two types of bills of lading, straight (nonnegotiable), and shipper's order (negotiable), the latter is used for sight draft or L/C shipments. According to the rules of international trade as specified in the *Guide to Incoterms,* 1980 edition (issued by the International Chamber of Commerce), a bill of lading acceptable for credit purposes must be marked "clean on board." This means that the carrier has not taken any exception to the condition of the cargo or packing, and that the goods have actually been loaded aboard the carrying vessel. A bill of lading is the most important document accompanying a foreign shipment. It serves as

- A contract between the carrier and the shipper
- A verification of the receipt of goods
- An identification of the right of title to the goods.

A signed copy of a negotiable bill of lading is sufficient evidence of ownership to take possession of the goods.

4. *Packing list.* A packing list is even more important overseas than for domestic shipments. Very often customs officials at both the port of embarkation and the port of debarkation use the packing list to verify the type and quantity of goods in the shipment. The list should include a complete description of the goods being shipped.

5. *Certificate of origin.* Some countries require a separate certificate stating the origin of the goods. This certificate is normally countersigned by a chamber of commerce member and visaed by the country's resident consul at the port of embarkation.

6. *Inspection certificate.* Many buyers request an affidavit, called an inspection certificate, from the shipper or an independent agent, certifying that the quality, quantity, and description of the goods conforms to the original order.

7. *Dock receipts, warehouse receipts, etc.* When a shipper's responsibility is limited to moving the goods to a warehouse or dock at the port of embarkation, buyers often request receipts from the storage company that the goods have been received and await further disposition.

8. *Certificate of manufacture.* The manufacturing cycle for certain goods can be quite long. If a buyer intends to make a down payment or an advance payment before the goods are shipped, the manufacturer prepares a certificate of manufacture, which serves as evidence that the goods have been produced in accordance with the order and have been set aside awaiting shipping orders. As soon as payment and shipping orders are received, the goods are shipped.

9. *Insurance certificate.* In cases where sellers provide cargo insurance, an insurance certificate must be furnished, indicating the type and amount of coverage.

For a small charge, freight forwarders will prepare all documents required by a customer's order. Even large exporters rely on forwarders to take care of this voluminous paperwork; and smaller exporters should do the same. Although the form of these documents varies among countries, the content remains approximately constant. Since international freight forwarders know both the special requirements of the U.S. Customs Service and the regulations of foreign countries, it only makes good sense to let them handle all paperwork chores.

OCEAN MARINE CARGO INSURANCE

Coordinating payments, following the proper shipping procedures, and reducing the amount of risk in a transaction are all essential ingredients of international trade. Regardless of the country of origin, a company must manage all three elements efficiently to remain competitive. Insuring marine cargo may seem of minor importance relative to getting paid and reducing political risk, but companies that slight this area more often than not live to regret their inaction. Any number of mishaps can occur during an ocean voyage, and it is only prudent business to safeguard against the damage or loss of goods by purchasing adequate insurance.

Although an increasing amount of merchandise is shipped overseas by air, the high cost and the weight and size restrictions imposed by air carriers make ocean shipping the predominant mode of transport for most products. Ocean shipments are exposed to several unique hazards. Damage or loss of cargo from fire, stranding, moisture, collision, rolling of the ship, or theft is a real possibility.

Because of the dangerous nature of ocean shipping, the Carriage of Goods by Sea Act of 1936 strictly limits the liability of carriers to $500 per package. Therefore, practically all ocean shipments should be independently insured against damage or loss. In fact, marine cargo insurance is required by all financing sources—banks, joint venture partners, private financing organizations, and government agencies. Either importer or exporter may arrange for such insurance, depending on terms in the sales contract.

Types of Policies

There are two types of marine cargo insurance:

- Specific or special policies written for each individual shipment
- Open policies covering all shipments by the insured as long as the policy is in effect.

The first is used mainly by infrequent exporters, the latter by everyone else.

With an open policy, the shipper must inform the underwriter of each shipment made, including all the particulars. Premiums are billed each month depending on the number of shipments reported. An insurance certificate issued by the underwriter evidences effective coverage for a specific shipment.

It is difficult to get an open policy directly from an underwriter until you have established a record of continuous and fairly substantial shipments. Therefore, most smaller exporters purchase their insurance through a broker. Brokers know which underwriters currently handle your shipment size to your customer's destination. Furthermore, since underwriters, not exporters, are responsible for the payment of brokerage fees, it won't cost your company a penny to use one.

Cost

Premiums for marine cargo insurance vary all over the lot based on

- Type of coverage desired
- Shipping routes
- Types of conveyances
- Nature of goods shipped
- Duration of the voyage.

The best type of coverage for most smaller exporters is the *all-risk* policy. Such a policy covers loss of or damage to cargo for any reason. It's also a good idea to insure against losses *warehouse to warehouse*. This means that coverage begins when the goods leave the company's shipping dock and remains in effect until the goods arrive at the customer's receiving location. Policies cover both marine and inland transport.

Shipments made by aircraft and connecting conveyances can also be included under all-risk policies. Generally, premiums for air freight coverage alone are substantially less than charges for ocean shipments because the risks of loss are lower, the time duration is shorter, and there is less chance of pilferage.

Limitations

All-risk policies generally exclude war risks, but do cover losses resulting from strikes, riots, and civil commotion. The exception, of course, would be for those countries or parts of the world where the likelihood of such losses is high. Premiums can then become exorbitant.

Additional limitations on cargo insurance include

1. Losses due to the inherent nature of the goods being shipped—for example, losses incurred because the goods deteriorated on the journey (perishable goods) or because of improper packaging or normal wear and tear.
2. Loss of market due to delays en route.
3. A shipment that is itself illegal when the shipper fails to provide this information to the underwriter. By definition, a shipment is legal if it complies with the laws of the export country and any international agreements in effect at the time of shipment.

Cost, inconvenience, and complexities notwithstanding, beginning exporters are generally penny wise and pound foolish to ignore or underestimate the importance of door-to-door cargo insurance. This lesson was painfully learned by a client who exported for the first time to Guatemala.

This small international contractor was installing a replacement turbine for a power station in the hills of Guatemala. Ignoring my advice to purchase an all-risk insurance policy covering door-to-door transport, the contractor decided to insure only the ocean part of the voyage. The equipment reached the dock at Puerto Barrio all right. It was then unloaded onto several trucks for the long overland haul to northwestern Guatemala. When the trucks finally arrived at the job site two weeks later and the equipment was offloaded, substantial damage had occurred to several pieces.

A claim was first filed with the ocean carrier. The carrier turned it down flat, claiming that the damage occurred during inland transport. Efforts to obtain reimbursement from the Guatemalan trucking company were totally frustrated when the trucking company claimed that the damage occurred on board ship. In the end, no amounts were recovered and my client stood the cost of replacing the damaged equipment—for $162,000!

There are many reputable marine insurance companies to choose from. CIGNA, for example, offers a complete package. There are many others, however. Your freight forwarder can make helpful recommendations, an insurance broker can find one, or you can select one yourself. Regardless of who does the selection, the guidelines in Figure 14.2 can be of assistance in qualifying a carrier.

Figure 14.2
Guidelines for Choosing a Cargo Insurance Carrier

The marine insurance underwriter should
1. Have an office in close proximity to your shipping location.
2. Be willing to meet in your office.
3. Offer a comprehensive package of marine, air, and land cargo insurance, including all-risk.
4. Encourage the all-risk option.
5. Not push for third-party joint beneficiary.
6. Offer competitive rate comparisons.
7. Provide a claim procedure you can understand.
8. Have representatives and adjusters stationed throughout the world.
9. Provide financial statements and bank references.
10. Encourage checking references with other customers.

INTERMODAL SHIPPING

One of the most interesting developments in the international freight handling business is the concept of intermodal shipping. Intermodal shipping refers to one carrier assuming the responsibility for moving merchandise door to door, whether that involves ocean, air, truck, or rail transport—or a combination.

Currently used extensively in East Asia, intermodal shipping is gradually coming to America. Large international carriers such as American President Companies and CSX Corp. are actively marketing this concept to American exporters and importers. From a shipper's perspective, door-to-door transport solves the huge problem of determining where the loss occurred when filing an insurance claim (the problem my contractor client ran into in Guatemala). An intermodal carrier assumes full responsibility regardless of which carrier does the actual transporting.

Unfortunately, such an integrated transportation concept continues to run into obstacles in the United States, partly because of the structured transportation departments within large shipping organizations and partly because of a lack of cooperation among American ocean, rail, air, and truck carriers. Nevertheless, the favorable economics of integrated transportation, including less shipping time, single insurance coverage, and simplified rate tariff charges, makes the concept viable.

Several trade organizations continue to actively sell the idea. These advocates have also encouraged carriers to restructure internally to handle intermodal shipping. The Intermodal Marketing Association, the National Railroad Intermodal Association, and the Intermodal Transportation Association are all working diligently to find the right answers.

Third parties that don't own any transport assets are also entering the intermodal fray. Bay State Shippers, Inc., for example, has no carrier assets. As a transport packager, Bay State puts together the best freight package available for door-to-door shipments. Ocean shipping, air freight, rail, and truck lines can be used in whatever combination gives customers the best service and lowest cost.

Intermodal transport companies are well accepted overseas. Any U.S. company that exports from a foreign country, especially from an Asian facility, should seriously consider using either a broker-packager such as Bay State or an intermodal steamship line to carry its products.

AIR FREIGHT

Although ocean shipping remains the predominant form of transport for large cargo, it has some definite drawbacks. High cargo insurance costs and risk of damaged goods are two of the worst. The amount of time it takes to move merchandise across the high seas can lead to disgruntled customers or market changes by the time the merchandise arrives. Multiple handling at loading and unloading stages and lengthy dock storage increase the likelihood of damage or pilferage. For smaller exporters, it may not be possible to fill an entire shipboard container, and sharing one with another shipper can mix up the merchandise and delay receipt at the buyer's destination.

To overcome these hazards, many companies are increasingly turning to air freight. As more Third World countries improve airport facilities and encourage multiple carrier service, the old problem of finding an airline willing to carry freight to remote locations has all but vanished.

Mergers and combinations of worldwide delivery services have further enhanced air freight as a viable alternative. For example, air carriers such as Federal

Express actively encourage shippers to consider intermodal shipping. With its vast worldwide stable of inland transport contacts (added to by the company's acquisition of Flying Tiger), Federal Express offers door-to-door service to most areas of the world.

Some analysts believe that air cargo companies offering intermodal service could shake up the entire industry by jeopardizing the role of freight forwarders. It's entirely possible that Federal Express has the potential to shape the international shipping market as it did the domestic market. This prediction seems to be coming true in the competitive arrangements now being offered by other large worldwide couriers such as DHL and UPS.

Even with the rapid, reliable service offered by many air freight carriers, this mode of transport continues to be applicable to a limited number of shippers. Shipping containers must be small enough to fit into a 747 plane—the largest commercial aircraft in use today. The goods must be relatively insensitive to low pressure and wide variations in temperature. The value of the products must be high enough to justify the significantly greater freight cost.

Because of a lack of capacity, air freight continues to be a seller's market, which tends to keep rates high. Regardless of the drawbacks, however, for certain types of goods, air freight can't be beaten, especially when short delivery time is important.

Most reliable freight forwarders handle air freight as well as ocean shipments. When choosing an air carrier, the same reliability criteria applied to ocean shippers should be used, and the same shipping and collection documentation is required.

Chapter 15

Technology Licensing, Leasing, and Tax Havens

Two issues stand out as the biggest hurdles to emerging market economies:

- How and where to get new technologies to produce the cornucopia of goods demanded by consumers and commercial enterprises
- How and where to get the management know-how to turn inefficient, nonproductive private-sector and state-owned businesses into competitive entities that can produce new technology products for in-country markets and exports.

It's safe to say that virtually all less-developed countries hunger for American technology and state-of-the-art management know-how. U.S. companies, both large and small, have an excellent opportunity to meet this demand by licensing technology (either directly or through franchises) and by teaching American management techniques in jointly owned production facilities. Chapter 17 covers joint ventures in detail. This chapter reviews the major benefits, risks, and techniques of licensing technology and management know-how. In addition, the latter part of this chapter suggests strategies for locating offshore subsidiaries in tax-haven countries as a means of maximizing foreign income from royalties, leases, and other transactions.

A technology license is a contractual agreement that spells out the amount of compensation (known as royalties) a buyer (called a licensee) will pay an owner for the use of a patent, trademark, service mark, copyright, or know-how. The amount of such compensation is agreed upon in advance of the buyer's using the asset.

For many smaller companies, technology licensing (often referred to as technology transfer) offers the most inexpensive, lowest risk, and fastest way to expand into international markets. Experienced export departments are not needed. Shipping problems disappear. And trade finance headaches can be completely avoided. Furthermore, the management, financing, and customs difficulties associated with establishing an overseas presence do not enter the picture. And by licensing their technology, U.S. companies can avoid both tariff and nontariff trade barriers that frequently interfere with the competitive pricing of exports.

The term "technology licensing" also applies to the acquisition of technology developed by a foreign producer. This is done through cross-licensing agreements or grantback clauses in a contractual agreement that grant the original licenser rights to any improvements in its technology developed by the licensee.

FRANCHISING

Franchising is one form of technology licensing. In this case, the franchiser permits the franchisee to use its trademark or service mark in a contractually specified manner for the marketing of goods and services. In addition, the franchiser may transfer management know-how by assisting the franchisee in advertising and promotion, accounting and administrative systems, training, signage, financing of equipment, purchasing of supplies and materials, and many other related activities.

Compared with the exporting of products, however, technology licensing does have several disadvantages. The major ones are as follows:

- Control over the use of technology is severely diminished when nonaffiliated companies are allowed to use it in their business.
- Profits are generally lower because preagreed royalty rates do not take into account variations in competitive pricing, nor are improved manufacturing efficiencies passed back to the licenser.
- Many foreign countries tax royalty payments at significantly higher rates than profits.
- In certain countries, the definition of royalties is very murky, opening the door to fallacious accounting of amounts due the licenser.
- Technology in the hands of foreign producers can easily be copied.

During the last few years, the increased emphasis on trade with Latin America, especially trade with Mexico under NAFTA, has caused a mini-boom in U.S. franchising. By early 1994, there were more than 3,500 franchises operating in Mexico—not only in metropolitan areas, but in suburbs and small towns—representing all major U.S. franchise chains. Moreover, room for growth seems to be unlimited, according to the September/October 1993 issue of *Sales and Marketing Strategies & News*.

As another example, in 1991 Brazil reported total revenues of about $600 million from approximately 3,900 service franchises. Furthermore, expectations were that this sector alone would grow 40 to 60 percent through 1995.

Franchises that offer services that support and facilitate business are in high demand throughout Latin America, as are consumer service franchises. Sir Speedy, Inc. (the quick-print-shop franchiser) is one example of a U.S. company moving rapidly to take advantage of these openings. The company opened its first Latin American franchise in Buenos Aires in 1992 and projects 250 international printing centers throughout Latin America and Europe within five years.

The best advice to potential U.S. franchisers, regardless of the selected foreign market, is

- Set up the business properly.
- Don't overlook the importance of market research.
- Determine market size, competition, and investor potential.
- Establish connections with a knowledgeable host-country intermediary.

PROTECTING INTELLECTUAL PROPERTY RIGHTS

The unauthorized copying of products is by far the greatest risk in transferring technology. Not only do patent-, trademark-, or copyright-holding companies lose royalties, they also must compete directly with these inexpensively made copies in both foreign and U.S. markets.

Although such piracy exists in Japan and European countries, it is most pronounced in less-developed nations. Companies in Taiwan, Hong Kong, South Korea, Malaysia, Thailand, Indonesia, and China are notorious for copying U.S. products. However, East Asia does not have a monopoly on this nefarious practice. Latin American companies do the same thing.

U.S. computer software developers have railed for years against piracy losses in Mexico, Brazil, and other Latin American countries, claiming that in total they have sacrificed more than $4 billion in sales to copied products. Music and film producers and distributors, authors and publishers, and biotechnology and pharmaceutical companies have suffered similar losses.

In 1993, four major U.S. pharmaceutical companies closed their production facilities in Chile, choosing instead to serve this market through exporting. Their reason was that too many Chilean companies were copying their products. Although laws to prevent such piracy were on the books, they were seldom enforced.

The problem of enforcing laws protecting intellectual property rights is common in all less-developed nations. A good example occurred during the 1993 free-trade debates, when the ineffective enforcement of Mexico's relatively strict intellectual property laws nearly blocked NAFTA's passage.

One enforcement tool available to U.S. trade officials is the "Special 301" section of the Omnibus Trade and Competitiveness Act of 1988, which requires the U.S. trade representative to annually produce a "priority watch list" and "watch list" of countries known or suspected of intellectual property rights piracy. Unfortunately, as in so many other cases involving political considerations, rigid enforcement is a rarity.

In reality, U.S. companies have little recourse when local laws are not enforced. Occasionally, lawsuits may forestall the production of so-called knock-off or copied products; however, if local laws are not enforced, it's nearly impossible to prove your case in court. Also, most courts in less-developed countries treat local producers with more leniency than foreign producers when it comes to interpreting what is and what is not a direct copy. Since U.S. patent, trademark, and copyright laws do not extend to foreign countries, nothing can be done in U.S. courts.

The successful conclusion of the Uruguay Round of GATT negotiations offers a ray of hope, since the protection of intellectual property rights was one of the mutually agreed-upon provisions. However, the fact remains that regardless of the laws on a country's books, their lack of enforcement probably means that we are doomed to having to find other solutions for many years to come.

Several possible solutions come to mind. As a first step, register your patent, trademark, or copyright in the host country. If infringement laws do exist, at least you have a possibility of recourse. Of course, this means retaining local counsel either to bring suit in a host-country court or to pressure the pirates to stop. If possible, try to get both host-country and U.S. government officials to exert political pressure. This sounds like a reasonable expectation, but it frequently isn't.

Second, file your patent under the Patent Cooperation Treaty, to which forty countries are parties. This can be difficult and expensive, however. The fees are substantial and all claims and documents must be translated into other languages. Nevertheless, if piracy is a real problem and your property rights are crucial to the survival of your company, it may be worth the cost and effort.

Pragmatically, however, the best way to beat infringements on intellectual property rights is to continually update your technology so that copied products are always last year's model. This is exactly the tack taken by U.S. jeans manufacturers Levi Strauss and VF Corp.

Because of the complexities of technology licensing, it is vitally important to seek legal advice before entering into a contractual agreement. Legal counsel should not only be familiar with U.S. laws relating to intellectual property rights and the commensurate recourse available in the event of breach of contract, but also have direct access to legal advice about the host country's laws and potential recourse actions.

Information about protecting intellectual property can be obtained from any of the following:

1. Office of the Trade Representative, telephone: (202) 395-7320;
2. Patent and Trademark Office, telephone: (703) 557-3065;
3. U.S. and Foreign Commercial Service, telephone: (202) 377-8300;
4. Department of State, Bureau of Economic and Business Affairs, telephone: (202) 647-7971.

LEASING

Leasing has become an increasingly popular way to finance exports of large capital equipment. In many cases, buyers demand much longer terms (as much as fifteen years) than the relatively short payback periods provided by traditional trade finance or Eximbank guarantees. This calls for alternative financing strategies, and leasing often fills the bill.

Since leases frequently require secondary collateral guarantees from suppliers, export leasing works best when the foreign buyer is a large company, a government agency, or a state-owned business.

Using Leasing to Finance Expansion

It is also possible to expand offshore production or distribution facilities through leasing. However, cross-border leasing—that is, leasing equipment or facilities located in France, for example, from a leasing company located in the United States—does become quite complex. It gets even more complicated when facilities located in France, for example, are leased by an American company from a lessor located in Japan.

Customs and contractual peculiarities, collateral rights, foreign tax structures, creditor/debtor rights, government expropriation risks, and a variety of other matters unique to each country add a level of administrative complexity that someone must pay for. Since the leasing company isn't going to absorb the extra costs, the lessee usually does, through relatively high monthly rent payments.

A host-country leasing company is usually more satisfactory than a U.S. one. Local lessors know host-country rules. They are structured to take advantage of local tax regulations. And—by far the most important consideration—they can source their own funds locally to purchase the asset. This reduces both the risk and the cost of capital built into rental payments.

Using Leasing to Finance Exports

If your company plans to finance exports through leases, it should be fairly easy to interest either a large commercial bank or a foreign merchant bank with an international leasing department. Multinational investment banks also have divisions to manage international leasing. The quickest way to start the ball rolling is with one of the major Japanese, French, British, Dutch, or German merchant banks that has offices in the United States. Regional or money center American banks can also produce good leads to appropriate contacts, even if they won't handle the deal.

If all else fails, try the following:

- The American Association of Equipment Lessors (AAEL). This trade organization's membership roster lists the most active equipment leasing companies based in the United States; both domestic lessors and those that handle international leases.
- Foreign leasing companies can be identified through the *World Leasing Yearbook*, published by Hawkins Publishers, Ltd, London. This book includes leasing industry descriptions from more than forty countries and listings by name and address of leasing companies operating in over sixty countries.

Some U.S. exporters have found leasing so profitable that they have started their own leasing subsidiaries. This could be a viable strategy for companies with sufficient financial savvy to handle the complexities. If such a strategy fits your marketing plans, at least consider setting up a leasing subsidiary in an offshore tax-haven location. It should be noted that similar offshore subsidiaries can be used to shelter royalty payments and other foreign-source income from U.S. taxes.

OFFSHORE SUBSIDIARIES TO REDUCE TAXES

As everyone knows, careful tax planning is a viable tool for reducing or deferring taxes on domestic-source income. In many cases, offshore transactions are even more susceptible to creative tax planning because of the broader base of business structures and local laws. And more room to navigate means greater flexibility. While some flexibility can be achieved with multiple business entities (foreign corporations, limited partnerships, S corporations, offshore trusts, or combinations of two or more), companies that judiciously make use of tax haven locations reap even greater benefits.

Subsidiaries set up in tax-haven locations are most useful for recycling foreign earnings into new overseas investments. In many cases the prudent use of tax-haven corporations, partnerships, or trusts to receive and reinvest foreign-source income can save taxes and simultaneously provide secure, confidential custody of cash and cash equivalent assets. It should be noted in passing that tax haven holding companies can also be used effectively to manage captive insurance companies (discussed later in this chapter) and to raise capital in foreign markets.

Tax-Haven Countries

Not too many years ago, the use of tax-haven countries as depositaries for foreign-source income was a popular way for entrepreneurs, and others, to build retirement nest eggs. The IRS did not, and does not now, have agreements with tax haven countries to reveal reciprocal tax information (Chapter 3 describes these Tax Information Exchange Agreements, or TIEAs). These 50-plus, mostly tiny countries prospered, secure in the knowledge that American and foreign taxpayers would never have to worry about a bank or government agency revealing business transactions or monetary holdings to any taxing authority, including the IRS.

Eventually, however, several federal agencies were able to penetrate the bank secrecy laws of many tax haven countries. So far, U.S. enforcement agencies have been successful in destroying tax haven business for Bermuda, the Bahamas, Switzerland, Luxembourg, the Netherlands Antilles, and several less-important countries. Although these countries still do not tax foreign-source income, since knuckling under to U.S. enforcement authorities, they no longer offer secure asset custody.

But don't dismay! As long as business entities are properly structured to meet IRS regulations and income is generated from legitimate (not criminal) overseas transactions, several tax haven countries scattered throughout the world remain viable locations for reducing or deferring U.S. taxes. The use of foreign tax-haven countries by American taxpayers is entirely legal, but it does involve careful planning, cash expenditures to set up and maintain tax haven entities, and some loss of control over investment portfolios.

What Tax Havens Do

Tax havens are countries, territories, colonies, or other governmental jurisdictions that have chosen by law to grant foreign companies and individuals the use of their banks and other financial institutions as depositaries for offshore earnings without imposing any tax or imposing very low taxes. The Organization for Economic Cooperation and Development (OECD) defines a tax haven as a "jurisdiction actively making itself available for the avoidance of tax which would otherwise be paid in relatively high tax countries."

The primary function of tax havens is to provide a means for taxpayers of high-tax countries (such as the United States) to avoid current and possibly future taxes from their home country and to avoid annoying exchange controls when repatriating or exchanging foreign currencies.

The operative word is "avoid." Tax havens permit foreign taxpayers to avoid taxes, not evade them. Tax avoidance is completely legal under the IRS code; which accounts for the myriad deductions and credits permitted against earned or passive income. On the other hand, tax evasion is always illegal and is grounds for severe fines or even jail.

Many times permanent tax avoidance is impractical. In those cases, tax havens can be used to postpone the imposition of taxes to future periods, thereby permitting the more rapid accumulation of assets.

A third use of tax havens, just as important as avoiding or deferring taxes or bypassing exchange controls, is as a safe haven for business and personal assets. The laws of many tax havens, although certainly not all, provide absolute confidentiality and security for money or securities held in their banks or other financial institutions. Only in the case of suspected criminal activities will anyone from the IRS, the U.S. Justice Department, or any other organization be permitted access to a depositor's transaction records, money, or other assets.

Foreign-source income from both lease payments and royalties can be maximized by offshore reinvestment, either in interest-bearing bank instruments or in additional securities, properties, or currencies. By holding foreign assets that generate such income in tax-haven entities and depositing reinvested earnings in tax-haven accounts, either to earn interest or to be held in temporary custody while awaiting new opportunities, all U.S. taxes can be avoided or, at a minimum, deferred. Once earnings are repatriated to the United States, of course, they become fully taxable.

With those clarifications and brief definitions, we can proceed to look at the pros and cons of using tax havens. The balance of this chapter looks at

1. Several tax-haven locations around the world that provide varying benefits for American investors
2. How tax havens differ from offshore financial centers
3. Ground rules for selecting the right tax haven
4. Criteria for maximizing tax haven benefits.

Different Types of Tax Havens

Broadly speaking, tax havens come in three forms:

1. Countries that grant special tax privileges to certain types of investors, companies, or operating businesses. The Isle of Man, the Channel Islands, Luxembourg, Monaco, and Liechtenstein fall into this class.

2. Jurisdictions that impose taxes on income generated within that country, but do not impose taxes or impose them at very low rates on foreign-source income. Hong Kong, Malta, Panama, the Netherlands Antilles, Cyprus, and the British Virgin Islands meet this criterion.

3. Locations that do not impose any relevant tax on any type of income. The Bahamas, the Cayman Islands, the Cook Islands, and Vanuatu are probably the best known.

In addition, countries like the Seychelles, Gibraltar, and Singapore impose a modest tax only on repatriated income.

How Tax Havens Differ from Offshore Financial Centers

One final distinction must be made. Tax havens are often equated with off-shore financial centers. This interpretation is dead wrong and can lead to useless or potentially harmful strategies for companies that need the services of an off-shore bank. Efficient offshore banks can generally be found only in offshore financial centers, not in tax havens that do not have fully developed offshore banking capabilities.

An offshore financial center comprises one or more banks and other financial institutions that take deposits, dispense loans, and sell bank instruments in currencies other than that of the resident country, thereby remaining outside the jurisdiction of the bank's home country banking regulations and reserve requirements. Some tax havens, such as the Cayman Islands, are also offshore financial centers; others, such as the Marshall Islands, definitely are not.

SELECTING THE RIGHT TAX HAVEN

The first question to address is how to choose the right tax-haven country. To provide maximum benefits to U.S. companies, tax havens should have the following characteristics:

- No taxes or very low taxes
- Absence of exchange controls
- Free repatriation of earnings and principal
- Political stability
- Stable and secure banking system
- Modern communications facilities
- Physical accessibility
- Proximity to investment assets
- Legal accessibility
- Investor-friendly amenities
- Competent support personnel.

Tax Structure and Exchange Controls

By definition, a country's tax structure is the primary determinant of its acceptability as a tax haven. Does the country tax foreign-source income? If so, it is clearly not a tax haven. Does it tax locally generated income? Many tax havens do and, unless other considerations outweigh this disadvantage, should be avoided.

Several other questions also need answers:

- What taxes apply to corporations, trusts, and joint ventures with local partners?
- Are taxes levied against interest or dividend income from foreign bank deposits?
- Is there a remittance tax? A withholding tax?
- Does the country have tax treaties or a TIEA with the United States?
- Does the government tax foreign-owned property resident in the country?

Clearly, a location without any of these taxes or treaties is the most desirable. The more taxes a country imposes, the less valuable it is as a tax haven.

Exchange controls and repatriation regulations go right along with tax structures as crucial considerations. Such tax havens as the Cayman Islands have no exchange controls. Virtually any foreign currency may be freely converted to any other. And any foreign company can repatriate earnings without restraints. Conversely, Cyprus taxes remittances, and several depositaries in the Channel Islands accept deposits and make disbursements only in British sterling.

Political Stability

The political stability of a tax haven country is second in importance only to jurisdictional tax and exchange control laws. Companies and individual investors who for years used Panama as the ideal, convenient tax haven were aghast when Antonio Noriega tainted the banking system with transactions from the Medellin cartel and the American invasion turned the nation into an inferno. Bahrain and Dubai are tax-free oases, but periodic Middle East conflicts keep off all but the most determined foreign companies.

By far the most acceptable tax havens are those countries that depend entirely on imports to meet the needs of their citizens and on foreign investors to provide hard currency for the purchase of imported goods and services. Since the chances for long-term political stability increase geometrically with the level of dependence on foreign investments, the best locations are those that have no sustainable industry other than offshore financial services and perhaps tourism. The Cayman Islands and the Turks and Caicos Islands are two prime examples.

Certain political changes known well in advance of their happening tend to steer U.S. companies away from certain popular tax havens. A prime example is the uncertainty about the safety of Hong Kong's banking system after the colony's takeover by China in 1997. A potential merger of Taiwan with mainland China also brings cold shivers to corporate treasurers.

Banking System

The stability of a country's banking system and the regulations governing bank secrecy play major roles in the desirability of a tax haven. It's impossible to conceive of anyone deliberately depositing principal or earnings in a bank that is likely to fail. Placing money in a bank subject to government manipulations is equally unimaginable. In some cases, however, privately owned banks can be more dangerous than state-owned. A good example was the collapse of several privately owned Panamanian banks during Noriega's rule, creating sizable losses for depositors. State-owned Costa Rican banks, on the other hand, benefit from forty years of a stable, American-friendly government, and these banks rank very high as secure depositaries.

Bank secrecy laws are equally important. When we must rely on the veracity of fiduciaries, we want to be dead certain that neither the records of the transactions nor the money itself fall into unfriendly hands. Yet, when bank secrecy laws are broached, that's exactly what can happen. Prime examples are Bermuda and the Bahamas when the IRS and the U.S. Justice Department fractured bank secrecy laws. Switzerland is another case where secrecy laws have been abrogated.

Companies that want to tap foreign capital markets will need a tax haven that also has offshore financial center capabilities and can provide ready access to major international banks and securities houses. Some countries, such as Singapore, began as tax havens but, because of the large influx of international banking and securities firms, evolved primarily into offshore financial centers.

The Malaysian government has opened a new offshore center on the island of Labuan, off the coast of north Borneo, to attract international companies. Already a tax haven, intense efforts by the Malaysian government to bring international banks to the island may yet turn it into a viable offshore financial center competing with Singapore.

Communications

The efficient use of offshore banking facilities requires reliable, state-of-the-art communications systems. International telephone service, fax capabilities, and computer-reliable data transfer systems with access to satellite networks, and preferably fiber-optic transmission, are needed. Without world-class communications facilities, it's impossible to manage business assets or move capital.

Accessibility, Proximity, and Investor Amenities

Even when excellent communications are supplemented with such support personnel as trust officers, attorneys, bankers, public accountants, and consultants, relatively frequent on-site visits by company personnel are mandatory to maintain control. This, in turn, means that the jurisdiction must be physically accessible for making relatively short, convenient trips.

As a corollary, the tax haven should be relatively close to a company's foreign facilities. It doesn't make much sense to use the Caymans if income flows from Southeast Asia; or Hong Kong to manage transactions originating in South America. Some oases—the Maldive Islands, the Seychelles, and Pitcairn, for example—are tax-free but, for most Americans, totally inaccessible.

Amenities for foreigners go hand in hand with physical accessibility. If we have to travel, we might as well choose a location that has comfortable living accommodations, good restaurants, and facilities for leisure activities. Most of us find that our only real vacation time comes when we make periodic business trips to interesting locations.

Legal accessibility is also important. Vatican City, although a tax haven, has strict laws to keep foreigners out. British citizens benefit from tax advantages on the Isle of Man that are denied to Americans. Cuba is a tax-friendly location for citizens of certain European countries, but not for U.S. citizens.

Other factors also come into play. Must foreign visitors go through a complex procedure for obtaining visas every time they visit? Is a passport necessary for entrance? Are foreign visitors harassed by local customs officials on entering or leaving the country? All add to the aggravation of international travel.

Support Services

Finally, acceptable tax havens must have competent, reliable support personnel resident in the jurisdiction. This means a full cadre of corporate and trust lawyers, trust and fund managers, bankers, investment bankers and brokers, tax and accounting advisers, and insurance personnel. And for Americans, English must be the common business language.

No tax haven meets all criteria. Some have zero taxes but require a three-day plane trip to get there. Others have excellent offshore banking facilities, but bank secrecy laws have been fractured; or they impose taxes on remittances, or tax domestic earnings, or have turbulent politics or failing infrastructures, or don't like Americans. We would be fortunate indeed to find a tax haven that met even most of the criteria; 100 percent is unrealistic. Nevertheless, some offer more advantages to American companies than others, and those are the ones to concentrate on.

The best tax havens for U.S. companies are the Cayman Islands, the Turks and Caicos Islands, and Panama in the Caribbean Basin; Liechtenstein (for individuals only) and the Channel Islands in Europe; and Vanuatu, Palau, the Marshall Islands, the Federated States of Micronesia, Naura, and the Cook Islands in the Pacific.

STRATEGIES FOR MAXIMIZING TAX-HAVEN BENEFITS

Although any type of business may operate from or through a tax-haven country, most U.S. companies reap the greatest benefits by using a tax-haven entity

- As a conduit for the repatriation of earnings from foreign subsidiaries
- For collecting rental or royalty income from foreign technology licensing and franchises
- To handle part or all of a company's insurance needs
- To set up and manage offshore real estate or property-based businesses
- To manage an offshore securities portfolio
- For operating a captive bank.

Specific procedures for using tax havens vary somewhat from country to country and depend to some extent on the source of foreign income; however, similar techniques apply in all locations.

Most Fortune 500 companies have funneled offshore transactions through tax havens for years, as have the majority of serious international investors. And they do it within the constraints of the U.S. tax code. No one asserts that tax havens are a sure-fire way to shelter all foreign income. But they can be beneficial to any company with foreign income, and their use is perfectly legal, provided IRS guidelines are followed.

To make tax havens work effectively, specific criteria must be met. Figure 15.1 summarizes the most important conditions.

Figure 15.1
Criteria for the Use of Offshore Tax Havens

1. A separate corporation must be set up in the tax haven to own offshore assets.
2. Ownership of the corporation must be held by an offshore trust in the same tax-haven country, not by U.S. taxpayers.
3. Beneficiaries of the trust should not be U.S. taxpayers.
4. Income earned by the offshore corporation should not be repatriated to the United States. It should be reinvested offshore.
5. Funding of the offshore entity should be through loans rather than gifts or capital contributions.
6. Companies with operating subsidiaries overseas should establish a trading company in a tax-haven country to absorb most of the profit.
7. If possible, these foreign operating subsidiaries should be located in countries without TIEAs.
8. Careful planning and structuring is required to avoid classification as a controlled foreign corporation or a foreign personal holding company.

Structuring a Tax Haven Business Entity

Corporations, partnerships, limited partnerships, and personal trusts (for individual investors) are all frequently used as tax-haven vehicles. Closely owned companies that have physical assets located in foreign countries or that raise debt or equity capital on foreign exchanges frequently use a tiered organization structure, with a trust at the apex holding the controlling interest in an offshore corporation or limited partnership. The offshore corporation or limited partnership, in turn, holds the stock of offshore operating subsidiaries.

The structure of a tax-haven company has a direct bearing on its success or failure as a mechanism for maximizing returns from offshore assets. Since the

IRS taxes American taxpayers on worldwide income, regardless of its source and whether or not it is remitted to the United States, companies must be extraordinarily careful to avoid direct or indirect ownership of the tax haven entity. Indirect ownership includes ownership by a U.S. parent company or by entities in an affiliated group. In the case of privately held companies, spouses and other U.S. family members would be considered indirect owners.

The extent to which trusts, corporations, or limited partnerships make sense depends on the type of offshore assets or business. Securities investments can be managed as well with a pure trust as with a tiered structure. A limited partnership with a trust as the general partner meets the needs of property-based businesses. Trust ownership of a corporation is the most flexible structure for managing offshore income from foreign operating businesses or collecting royalties and rental income. In addition, companies with multiple offshore holdings achieve better control if they set up a trust/partnership/corporation tier in more than one tax haven, often with interlocking ownership.

As an example of how a trust/corporation vehicle could work, assume that an American company owns 51 percent of a hotel in Mexico, is a general partner in a California factory, and raises capital on European and Latin American exchanges. The company's tax and legal advisers suggest setting up the following tax-haven configuration in Grand Cayman:

1. Fortrust, an irrevocable foreign trust set up in Grand Cayman, owns 100 percent of a Caymanian corporation, Holdall.

2. Fortrust's beneficiaries are the teenage children of the majority shareholders in the U.S. closely held parent corporation. They cannot receive trust income until they reach age thirty five.

3. A Georgetown attorney acts as the Fortrust trustee.

4. The initial deposit in a Holdall Cayman bank account is made with after-tax dollars loaned to the corporation by the U.S. parent. Additional cash can be lent as needed.

5. As trustee of the only shareholder of Holdall, the Cayman attorney (the trustee could also be a local investment adviser, banker, or any other Caymanian resident named by the company) invests this capital in foreign stocks and bonds, depositing gains, dividends, and interest income tax-free in the Holdall bank account. The trustee also collects rental income for Holdall from offshore property investments and Holdall management fees from the Mexican hotel. As occasions warrant, Holdall might own shares in an Argentine company that could float bond and stock issues on the Buenos Aires Exchange.

6. Since the U.S. parent has no ownership interest in Holdall and no legal control over its policies, controlled foreign corporation and foreign personal holding company laws are avoided.

7. Even though the trust is irrevocable and the U.S. parent has no legal control over it, pragmatically, Cayman trustees take investment/management orders from the trust grantors.

8. As tax-free income builds in Holdall, dividends are paid to Fortrust. Eventually the U.S. company could use this income to purchase a villa on the Grand Cayman beach, which the officers could then use as living accommodations when visiting the island, as a vacation retreat, or as a retirement home.

This is only one way to structure a tax haven company and modifications recommended by U.S. tax counsel may be needed. There are as many other ways to do it as one can imagine. But all methods have two common elements: (1) the ownership of the company and the beneficiary of foreign-source income must be segregated from any U.S. citizen or resident, and (2) all U.S. domestic assets and transactions must be excluded. It goes without saying that any U.S. company intending to structure a tax-haven company should verify current U.S. tax laws with a competent adviser before proceeding.

Using Tax-Haven Countries with Other Foreign Subsidiaries

U.S. operating companies that make direct investments in offshore manufacturing companies (either direct acquisitions or joint ventures) might consider a slightly different approach to maximizing combined income. Although the specific procedures vary somewhat depending upon the country within which the foreign income originates, a similar approach can be used for all. The following example applies only to products exported from the country in which the foreign subsidiary is located, not to products sold within that country. Here's how to set up the chain of transactions:

1. Set up a trading company in a tax haven country.

2. Record foreign subsidiary customer orders on the books of the trading company. The trading company also receives a sales commission from the foreign subsidiary as compensation for marketing services rendered.

3. The trading company then places orders on the foreign manufacturing subsidiary for products to be drop-shipped direct to the end customer.

4. When the subsidiary ships the products, it invoices the trading company at cost, plus a small profit.

5. The trading company then invoices the customer directly, with instructions to remit to the trading company's lock box in the tax-haven country.

6. The trading company pays the manufacturing subsidiary for the goods shipped at the invoiced price.

7. The trading company records the bulk of the profit on the sale. Since it is located in a tax haven country, of course there is no tax to pay there.

Under this arrangement, the foreign manufacturing subsidiary records a small profit on the sale and a commission expense to the trading company. To the extent that there is taxable income, a tax must be paid in the manufacturer's country of origin (perhaps qualifying for a foreign tax credit or deduction against U.S. taxes of the parent).

To make this arrangement comply with the U.S. tax code, certain organizational steps must be taken:

1. The trading company should be owned by a trust, set up in the tax-haven country and administered by an appointed agent. The trust must be irrevocable; the foreign subsidiary, the U.S. parent company or shareholders cannot be beneficiaries.

2. Although superficially managed by the trustee, the trading company can have employees, managers, and sales personnel on its payroll.

3. Commissions to the trading company should not be paid in cash, but offset against the amounts owed by the trading company for products shipped.

4. Cash earnings of the trading company cannot be repatriated to the United States without incurring a tax liability. Therefore, these earnings should be reinvested offshore (or in the tax haven) so that income from the investment will also flow to the tax-haven country.

5. Under this scheme, the U.S. parent company must be careful to avoid constructive receipt of earnings, either in the foreign subsidiary's country or in the United States. Of course, the trading company cannot be a controlled foreign corporation or a foreign personal holding company, as defined by the IRS.

Although this procedure seems complex, it is similar to that used by most Fortune 500 companies with manufacturing subsidiaries. Provided the trading company is devoid of U.S. ownership and its earnings are not repatriated, the IRS cannot object.

Just a word about repatriating earnings to the United States. Although some tax havens impose a tax or fee on repatriated earnings, the best ones (e.g., the Caymans) do not, nor do they enforce any restrictions on the amount or timing of remittances. Under the U.S. tax code, however, such repatriation results in taxable income to the U.S. recipient, whether a corporation, partnership, or individual.

Another interesting use of tax havens is as the home base for captive insurance subsidiaries.

CAPTIVE INSURANCE COMPANIES

Wholly owned insurance subsidiaries, or "captives," are the self-insurance wave of the future. With insurance premiums skyrocketing and large competitors able to charge lower product prices by self-insuring, smaller companies have no choice but to self-insure. Captives are usually set up to self-insure part or all of property loss; comprehensive product liability; workers' compensation; medical, legal, and other professional malpractice; marine; and virtually any other coverage, including, in some instances, health and life insurance.

In their simplest form, here are the steps for using captives:

1. Establish a wholly owned insurance subsidiary in a tax-haven country.
2. Pay insurance premiums to the captive and structure a program to invest these premiums from the tax-haven subsidiary.
3. Designate the captive as fully responsible for the covered risks.

One or both of two variations have become favorite ploys for offshore investors. The first, "fronting," is used to comply with some state requirements that insurance be placed with a domestic insurer. A deal is negotiated with a domestic insurer to reinsure all or part of the risk of the captive. This, of course, requires the payment of reinsurance premiums, which are normally much less than charges from a primary insurer.

In the second variation, a captive agrees to take back a portion of the normal coverage from the primary insurer, perhaps assuming the first US$250,000 of annual losses. The full coverage stays with the primary insurer, but upping the deductible means that premiums drop. The savings could then be invested by the captive until needed to pay for losses. Rather than paying high premiums to outsiders for predictable, noncatastrophic losses, the company keeps the cash inhouse and earns income on it.

Although many tax havens do not have sufficient stability to warrant the risk associated with captives, the Cayman Islands does. Insurance regulations are well structured, and since the islands provide a reputable environment for insurance companies, reinsurance premiums are very low. In addition, many local management companies and a solid international banking system make absentee management very viable.

To obtain and retain an insurer's license in the Caymans, the company must have net worth of (1) CI$100,000 if no long-term insurance business (as defined) is written, or (2) CI$200,000 for only long-term business. Most captives fall into the first category. The nature of the business must be disclosed and an annual fee of CI$1,000 paid, according to regulations, for the "principal insurance representative per representation."

In addition to the Caymans, several other nearby tax havens, including Bermuda, Panama, the Turks and Caicos Islands, the Bahamas, and Puerto Rico, offer excellent captive insurance environments. In all cases, income earned by captive investments is tax-free.

Companies that haven't experimented with captive insurance companies are missing the boat. As premiums continue to escalate for virtually all types of insurance and an increasing number of carriers either go out of business or decline new coverage, it only makes sense to protect assets with the cheapest and most secure insurance possible. And what could be less expensive and more secure than your own insurance company?

OTHER STRATEGIC USES OF TAX HAVENS

Variations in tax-haven strategies are virtually unlimited. One of the most common and easiest to administer is a tax-haven trust that serves as a holding company for rental income from offshore properties. The greatest benefits are achieved by purchasing the property (equipment or real estate) with reinvested funds from a tax-haven trust. Any connection with a U.S. taxpayer is avoided, and both rental income and any gain on the eventual sale of the asset remain tax-free.

In a similar manner, offshore trusts or corporations can hold title to stocks, bonds, bank instruments, and other securities. Interest income and dividends received by the tax-haven entity are tax-free, as are capital gains realized upon the sale of securities.

Royalties from patents, copyrights, trademarks, or franchise fees can also be funneled into a tax haven. It's important to transfer asset title to the tax-haven entity, but once that has been accomplished, royalty or licensing income remains tax-free.

One cautionary note: Do not try to use tax haven locations for income derived from U.S sources. That won't work. Tax havens are viable only for foreign-source income, and preferably income derived from countries that have not executed TIEAs—although that is not always possible.

Part IV
Foreign Sourcing and Production

Chapter 16

Importing

Importing materials and products from foreign suppliers has been a way of life in many industries for decades. Most U.S. companies import because they can buy products, materials, or components at less cost from foreign suppliers, because the goods are of higher quality than similar goods produced in the United States, or because materials and components needed in their production processes are not available from U.S. companies. Companies import products for direct resale, for use in a manufacturing process, or for transshipment to foreign destinations. Virtually all consumer and industrial products sold in the United States carry some foreign material or labor. Automobiles, building materials, clothing, food-stuffs, athletic equipment, home appliances, farm implements, airplanes, ma-chine tools, electronics, and military hardware are only a few examples.

Global value-added production has become a way of life, not only for U.S. companies but for foreign competitors as well. Moving materials, components, and subassemblies from one country to another through various stages of assem-bly offers companies an ever-expanding panorama of combinations that can give them a competitive advantage. Moreover, free-trade zones provide a cost-effec-tive way to transship goods duty-free throughout the world. To remain competi-tive, companies must source the lowest-cost and highest-quality products, materials, and services, regardless of whether suppliers are physically located in the United States or overseas.

However, cross-border sourcing has become increasingly complex, with each country maintaining its own trade restrictions and quotas and its own unique conditions for moving and storing goods. Since a thorough discussion of import-ing procedures in every trading country of the world would be impossible, this chapter deals only with importing to the United States. Although U.S. import re-quirements and procedures should provide a sufficient base for judging situations in other countries, it only makes sense for companies that require imports for for-eign branches in Europe, Latin America, the Pacific Basin, or other areas to fur-ther investigate the importing regulations applicable in countries within which they have facilities.

American importers must be concerned with a variety of commercial, gov-ernment, and legal matters regardless of the use made of imported goods. It should be noted, however, that except for financing (in which letters of credit, banker's acceptances, and other trade finance instruments used for importing are identical to those used in exporting), the topics discussed in this chapter are unique to importing and have no bearing on U.S. companies engaged solely in exporting.

The first set of circumstances affecting importers is those necessary to monitor incoming shipments.

MONITORING THE MOVEMENT OF GOODS

Whether imported goods are to be transshipped, resold domestically, or used in production, their movement must be monitored from the point of embarkation to delivery on a company's receiving dock. Someone in the receiving organization must be responsible for this monitoring from start to finish. More often than not, purchasing and receiving personnel who are inexperienced in importing expect goods to flow naturally from the foreign shipper to their door on schedule. This never happens. The importing process is so complex that relying on shippers, carriers, or others outside the organization to complete the transaction invariably leads to lost or damaged goods or, at best, late deliveries. The responsibility for monitoring and controlling the movement of imported goods must rest solely with the management of the importing company.

Ocean or air freight companies, brokers, terminal operators, U.S. customs officials, and domestic freight carriers all get involved in moving foreign shipments to the United States, as indicated in the following summary:

1. *Ocean or air freight company.* Notifies consignee two days before the arrival of goods at the port of entry. Provides freight release to terminal operator.

2. *Customs broker.* Responsible for obtaining customs releases and necessary clearances at the port of entry. Checks bills of lading and delivery orders for completeness. Forwards originals of these documents to motor carrier for pickup.

3. *U.S. Customs officials.* Verify compliance with customs regulations and collect duty.

4. *Terminal operator.* Arranges with domestic carrier for pickup. Makes arrangements for payment of demurrage, if any. Verifies the accuracy of the delivery order and loads the merchandise onto the domestic carrier.

5. *Domestic freight carrier.* Receives the merchandise at the port of entry. Verifies clearance documents and delivery order. Delivers to importer's receiving dock.

With so many companies and people involved, something is bound to go wrong. Therefore, once the shipping company has notified the importing company of the shipment's arrival date, it's always a good idea to station a company representative at the port of entry. This person not only coordinates the activities of each party but is available to eliminate bottlenecks as they occur. Company representatives should also be prepared to arrange payment of customs duties, demurrage, and any other clearance fees required. The following case demonstrates how important this assignment is.

The president of a $7 million chemical processor readily admits to literally missing the boat the first time around. Taking on a new line of industrial filter compounds, the purchasing agent for ZE-RITE Corporation successfully located an Egyptian source for one of the compounds used in the mixture. The company arranged to purchase a full container of the compound and waited patiently for its delivery. After sixty days passed and nothing arrived, the ZE-RITE president became concerned and asked the company's controller to trace the shipment.

Three weeks later, it was discovered that the steamship company had forgotten to unload the container in Philadelphia. Since no one from ZE-RITE was at the port to coordinate receipt of the shipment, the container remained on board for the next port of call, Buenos Aires.

Maintaining close surveillance of ocean shipping may seem inconsequential, but in the long run it's safer to spend the money and take the time to be sure. Don't rely solely on customs brokers, foreign suppliers, or carriers. Do it yourself. No one wants to chase a shipment to Argentina!

U.S. CUSTOMS

Once cargo reaches a U.S. port of entry, customs officials take over. All goods with a value of more than $1,000 arriving at U.S. ports must go through a formal entry process. This process consists of four steps:

1. The filing of appropriate entry documents
2. Inspection and classification of the goods
3. Preliminary declaration of value
4. Final determination of duty and payment.

In most cases, the processing of foreign imports at a port of entry requires about five days. Once the amount of duty has been established and the importer has been notified, the broker receives instructions to make payment and obtain release of the goods. If merchandise is not moved out within five days, customs officials transfer the goods to a warehouse and the importer gets charged for storage. If the goods remain in custody for one year, the government has the right to auction them for storage fees.

Entry Documents

Of the twenty two different types of customs entries, six are the most common:

1. The *consumption entry* is the most common type. It is used for goods intended for domestic resale and brought directly into the importer's stock.
2. An *immediate transportation entry* allows merchandise to be forwarded directly from the port of entry to an inland destination for customs clearance.
3. A *warehouse entry* is used to store goods in a Customs-bonded warehouse for up to five years.

4. When goods are ultimately withdrawn from a bonded warehouse, a *warehouse withdrawal for consumption entry* applies.

5. An *immediate exportation entry* is used when goods are to be trans-shipped to a foreign country.

6. U.S. citizens returning from a trip abroad file a *baggage declaration and entry* form.

Before goods are allowed out of the U.S. Customs area, certain documents must be made available to customs agents, specifically

- A commercial invoice from the exporter
- A bill of lading from the exporter or freight forwarder
- One of the above entry forms completed by the importer or its broker.

Each of these entry forms must contain a valuation of the shipment, its description, and the amount of duty to be paid. Goods may be removed from the customs area by paying this duty immediately or by posting a bond guaranteeing payment at a later date. The bond may be in the form of a single-transaction bond that applies to entry through one port or a continuous bond that covers all U.S. ports of entry. Either brokers or importers may arrange for such a surety bond.

Types of Duty

Whether an item is dutiable or free from duty frequently influences the decision to import. Import duties are classified into three types:

1. Specific duties assessed against a unit of the goods, such as 5 percent per pound.

2. Ad valorum duties assessed as a flat percentage of the total value of the import transaction, such as 10 percent of the total imputed value of the goods.

3. A compound duty combining specific duties and ad valorum duties, such as $5 per pound of a commodity *plus* a percentage of the value of the transaction. Certain types of agricultural commodities are assessed in this manner.

All duties assessed by the U.S. Customs Service are included in a voluminous document called the Tariff Schedules of the United States. It resembles freight tariff schedules for rail and trucking lines. An official ruling from the head office of the port of entry determines the type of duty and the applicable rate for specific goods that for one reason or another are excluded from tariff schedules.

In addition to assessing commodity duties, the U.S. Customs Service enforces statutory duties. These apply to imports of any goods, either directly or indirectly, from countries the federal government deems unfriendly. Obviously this list keeps changing with foreign policy shifts.

For purposes of valuation, currency exchange rates from the exporting country are determined by the daily buying rate for foreign currency established by the Federal Reserve Bank of New York.

Duty-Free Items

The U.S. Customs Service defines certain types of imported items as duty-free. A bond must be posted with the Service when these items are imported to guarantee that they will be either exported or destroyed. Though slight variations occur periodically, Figure 16.1 lists current duty-free items. In addition, foreign residents may import personal items (cars, films, boats, etc.) for use while temporarily in the United States.

Figure 16.1
Items Imported Duty-Free*

1. Materials or goods imported specifically to be repaired, modified, or processed in the United States, with the intent of shipping the final product offshore. The product may also be totally destroyed while in bond rather than exported. The end product cannot contain perfume, alcohol, or wheat. A complete accounting of the articles must be made and any scrap or waste turned over to Customs.
2. Women's clothing to be used strictly for modeling in a U.S. garment maker's establishment.
3. Samples used solely to attract sales.
4. Motion picture advertising films.
5. Items intended solely for review, testing, or experimentation, such as drawings, plans, or photos.
6. Containers for handling or transporting items.
7. Items used solely in the preparation of illustrations for catalogs, pamphlets, or advertising.
8. Professional equipment, trade tools, repair components for these tools and equipment, and articles of special design for temporary use in the manufacture or design of items for export.
9. Props, scenery, and apparel for temporary use in theatrical performances.

* As of 1990.

In all cases, if the articles imported or modified while in the United States are not exported or destroyed within a year, the bond will be forfeited and the goods seized.

DRAWBACKS

The term "drawback" as used in U.S. Customs Service regulations refers to refunds of duties previously paid on imported goods. Normally drawbacks on imported goods are not allowed if the goods are exported after they are released from the customs area. However, as with other government regulations, there are exceptions:

1. A total of 99 percent of duties paid are refundable if the goods are used in the manufacture or production of final products in the United States. and these final products are exported.

2. If the importer rejects the goods as not meeting order specifications, they may be returned to the U.S. Customs Service for supervised shipment back to the exporter. A 99 percent drawback is allowed.

3. The same 99 percent drawback is allowed if the imported goods are returned to the exporter within three years in the same condition as they were received.

4. Goods found to be banned from import by U.S. government decree must be returned to the exporter or destroyed by customs officials. All duties paid are included in a drawback.

5. Total refunds are also granted if goods are exported from a Customs-bonded warehouse or if the goods are withdrawn from the warehouse for repair, supply, or maintenance of vessels and aircraft (under certain conditions).

Preparing the paperwork for drawbacks is a complicated exercise. Most companies that import and then export hire customs brokers who specialize in drawback management. Comstock & Theakston, Inc., of Oradell, New Jersey, a drawback specialist, defines companies that qualify for drawbacks as "importers who export their products or exporters of articles manufactured with imports." If your company falls into one of these two slots, contact a drawback specialist to be certain of receiving full refunds.

A drawback specialist handles the entire drawback process, including the preparation of all paperwork and the processing of all claims. A competent drawback broker can also design in-house procedures to help companies identify drawback items. Most import/export companies find that drawback specialists more than pay for themselves in cost savings and actual cash recoveries.

U.S. IMPORT RESTRICTIONS AND QUOTAS

Governments of nearly every country enforce import restrictions and quotas of one type or another, just as they control the export of goods. There are four classes of U.S. import trade barriers:

1. Goods that the government deems detrimental to the well-being of its citizens as a whole or to special interest groups of citizens

2. Quantities or quotas of specific goods

3. Anti-dumping regulations to protect certain U.S. industries from foreign competition

4. "Preference" regulations that apply to favored nations.

Goods Detrimental to U.S. Citizens

For a variety of reasons, including pressure from special interest groups, the federal government has declared specific products harmful to U.S. citizens. Consequently, trade barriers either prohibit or severely restrict the importing of these goods. The most severe restrictions call for the seizure of such goods by the U.S. Customs Service. Less severe barriers include limiting entry of the goods to certain ports; restricting the routing, storage, or use of the goods; or requiring special labeling or processing before the goods can be released to the market.

These restrictions apply to all imported goods, whether or not they pass through U.S. foreign trade zones (discussed later in this chapter). The list of items falling under these restrictions is voluminous and constantly changing. Although U.S. Customs Service offices retain complete, up-to-date listings, here are the better known items considered to be detrimental to U.S. citizens:

1. Alcoholic beverages
2. Arms, explosives, ammunition, and implements of war
3. Automobiles and accessories
4. Coins, stamps, currencies, and other monetary instruments
5. Eggs and egg products
6. Fruits, vegetables, plants, and insects
7. Milk and cream
8. Electronic products
9. Food, drugs, and cosmetics
10. Animals
11. Wild animals and endangered species
12. Wool, fur, textile and fabric products
13. Livestock and meat
14. Pesticides and toxic substances
15. Viruses and serums
16. Rags and brushes
17. Narcotics
18. All products from "Communist" countries.

Quotas of Specific Goods

Most import quotas are administered by the District Director of Customs. Other government agencies handle special products. For example, quotas for dairy products are established by the Import Branch, Foreign Agricultural Service (a section of the Department of Agriculture). Quotas for imported fuel and oil products are set by the Director of Oil Imports at the Federal Energy Administration. Watch and watch movement quotas are controlled by the Special Import Programs Division of the Department of Commerce.

There are two types of import quotas: (1) tariff-rate and (2) absolute. The federal government uses tariff-rate quotas to control the pricing of domestic products (thereby inhibiting free-market movement). If consumer prices are higher than the government wants, it sets tariff-rate quotas that allow the importing of specific products at very favorable duty rates for a specific period of time. Tariff-rate quotas are frequently used to keep the price of agricultural products down when, for example, bad weather causes free market prices to rise. A few of the current products subject to tariff-rate quotas are milk, fish, tuna, and potatoes. Quotas also apply to whisk brooms and large motorcycles!

Absolute quotas have nothing to do with favorable duty-rate adjustments. They are established solely to control the quantity of specific goods that may be imported during any given period of time. Examples of imports restricted by absolute quotas are peanuts, ice cream, steel bars and rod, cotton, sugar, and condensed milk. Because all quotas are for specific periods of time, it is impossible to predict with any certainty in advance of shipment whether or not a given import transaction will be restricted by quotas when the goods arrive at a U.S. port of entry. If your shipment arrives after quotas have been filled, an over-quota duty applies, which could make the pricing of imported products noncompetitive.

Antidumping Regulations

Antidumping laws are another tool used by the federal government to shore up inefficient American producers. These laws restrict the importing of goods that, according to the federal government, create an "unfair competitive environment" for U.S. producers. The determination is made solely on a comparison of the price of the imported goods with prices of similar domestic goods. Production or purchasing inefficiencies are not taken into consideration.

The dumping test is very straightforward. If the selling price is less than that of similar goods produced in the United States, imported goods are assume to be dumped on U.S. markets. For goods that cannot be so tested because they are not sufficiently similar to U.S.-produced goods, the rules call for a constructed-value test. Constructed value is the foreign manufacturer's total of

- Materials and labor costs
- Factory and administrative overhead
- Packing and shipping expenses
- Reasonable profit.

If a product falls under the anti-dumping provisions, additional duties will be assessed. Theoretically, these additional duties make the prices of imported items sold in U.S. markets competitive with those of U.S.-produced goods.

Preferential Trade Partners

There are two classes of preferential trade partners:

1. Designated developing nations or territories
2. Canada, Mexico, certain Caribbean Basin countries, Andean Pact nations (excluding Venezuela), and Israel.

Currently, more than 140 developing nations or territories qualify for preferential treatment; but the list changes frequently. Items deemed to be preferential fall within the General System of Preferences (GSP). Over 2,700 products in the Tariff Schedules of the United States are so classified. For specific information on current GSP coverage, contact

> Trade Policy Staff Committee
> Office of the Special Representative for Trade Negotiations
> 1800 G Street
> Washington, DC 20506

Canada

The 1988 U.S.-Canada Free Trade Agreement (FTA) removes nearly all trade barriers between the two countries in gradual steps over the next ten years. When specific tariffs and quotas are to be removed depends on the product. Some have already been removed, others fall in five-year increments, and still others will be removed at the end of the ten-year period.

The FTA affects American importers in a major way. As trade barriers fall, the prices of Canadian goods will, theoretically, become competitive with the prices of those manufactured in the United States, opening markets on both sides of the border.

Mexico

The passage of the North American Free Trade Agreement (NAFTA) in 1993 was a historic event for trade among the United States, Canada, and Mexico. In addition to a wide range of provisions affecting special situations and industries, NAFTA calls for the abolition of tariffs on most products shipped between the signatories. A lengthy schedule of stepped tariff reductions will take effect over the next fifteen years.

The special Mexican free-trade zones called *maquiladora* zones were unaffected by NAFTA. Since 1965, the following special arrangement have applied to *maquiladora* manufacturing facilities:

1. A U.S. company ships materials and components to its 100 percent owned manufacturing plant located in a *maquila* free trade zone.
2. These materials and components are then processed into finished or semifinished products.
3. When these products are shipped back to the United States, U.S. customs duties are paid only on the value-added labor.

In addition to 100 percent ownership of *maquiladora* facilities, U.S. firms benefit from

1. Duty-free entry of machinery and equipment to be used in the production of these goods
2. No restrictions on the type of goods produced for export
3. Authorization to lease land and facilities within these coastal and border zones under a thirty-year beneficial trust arrangement.

More than 3,000 American plants currently operate in Mexican *maquiladora* zones.

Caribbean Basin Initiative

The initial purpose of the Caribbean Basin Initiative (CBI) was to encourage exports from CBI nations to the United States by removing most barriers. In addition, special financing schemes were enacted to assist U.S. companies in establishing production facilities in CBI countries. U.S. technical teams provide CBI nations (and CBI-based companies) assistance in everything from growing sugar cane to assembling watches. With low labor costs and ready access to certain raw materials, CBI nations offer American importers an excellent opportunity to acquire parts, materials, subassemblies, and a variety of other goods and services at prices substantially below U.S. standards. The Department of Commerce publishes an excellent recap of the CBI program entitled *Guidebook to the Caribbean Basin Initiative*.

Andean Trade Preference Act

The Andean Trade Preference Act applies to trade between the United States and Colombia, Bolivia, Ecuador, and Peru. Guidelines for duty-free imports from these countries are essentially the same as those established under the Caribbean Basin Initiative. Accordingly, benefits to U.S. importers are also similar. Those interested in sourcing goods from these countries should obtain a copy of the *Guidebook to the Andean Trade Preference Act* from the Department of Commerce.

Israel

In 1985, the United States and Israel enacted a free-trade agreement. The agreement calls for all customs duties and most nontariff barriers to be abolished on both sides, with reductions becoming effective in increments through 1995. When the agreement went into effect, such products as metalworking equipment, machine tools, and many electronic components immediately became duty-free. Provisions of the agreement can be found in the Israeli Government Investment and Export Authority's booklet entitled *Guide to the Israel-U.S. Free Trade Area Agreement*.

FREE-TRADE ZONES

Nearly every trading country in the world has one or more free-trade zones that enable companies to ship goods into the country and then export them duty-free. In the United States, such zones are called foreign-trade zones. U.S. foreign-trade zones, or FTZs, provide a convenient way to import products; repack, modify, or otherwise finish them; and then ship them offshore to the ultimate customer, exempt from all customs duties and other import restrictions.

A foreign-trade zone is defined by regulations as an "isolated, enclosed, policed area, operating as a public utility." Although FTZs are located within the boundaries of the United States, they are treated as if they were outside U.S. Customs Service territory. Currently, 141 FTZs operate in the United States. Only South Dakota, West Virginia, and Idaho do not have at least one. Texas has sixteen FTZs.

FTZs may be used for a variety of purposes, including storage, distribution, assembly, light manufacturing, modification of products, or transshipping. Goods in an FTZ may also be sold, exhibited, broken up, repacked, repackaged, graded, cleaned, and mixed with other foreign or domestic merchandise. One of the most interesting applications of FTZs, in the context of saving costs for a company producing goods overseas, is as an intermediate stop for adding value to the product on its way from the overseas manufacturing location to the ultimate offshore customer.

For example, assume that you have a plant in Italy assembling washing machines. You want to ship the machines to a customer in Trinidad. The most direct route would be to ship from Italy to Trinidad. However, ocean freight might be substantially less if you shipped only the components, and perhaps some subassemblies, part way, say to a Jacksonville or Miami FTZ. There they could be assembled, tested, and packed, and the final product shipped to Trinidad.

Ordinarily, U.S. duties would apply, as would insurance, taxes, and the completion of myriad forms to ship the products to Trinidad. With an FTZ, however, no import duties apply. There is no tax liability, and no additional insurance coverage is required. In other words, an FTZ is treated as a foreign port, affording substantial savings to U.S. importers. Using an FTZ also permits a parent company to use American workers to complete and test final products.

One unusual and at times very helpful feature of FTZs is that importers may exhibit their wares to potential customers. Companies may maintain their own showrooms in the zone and may display merchandise for an indefinite period of time. Since goods may also be stored and processed in the zone, companies can stock merchandise in a display room and sell wholesale quantities directly from the zone without incurring any duty.

IMPORTING WITH COUNTERTRADE

Countertrade has become a convenient and often necessary way to finance exports to, or investments in, soft-currency countries. Countertrade arrangements also conserve cash for U.S. importers. For example, you could provide exports to a CBI country in exchange for imports from that country. The experience of a small toy manufacturer is a good example of how this works.

UltraSafe, Inc., produced dolls, stuffed animals, and other "soft" products for handicapped preschool children. Several product lines required hand sewing. Other lines used a stuffing material treated with nonflammable chemicals. As sales tapered off and competition from foreign producers intensified, it became apparent that UltraSafe would have to find ways to cut costs if it was to survive in its niche markets. Concurrently, the company saw new markets opening in Argentina and Brazil.

UltraSafe developed a strategy to take advantage of lower wage rates by setting up sewing shops in Guatemala. It purchased stuffing material from Malaysia. The final safety testing had to be performed in the United States by certified inspectors. The final products could then be sold domestically as well as in Argentina and Brazil. Countertrade deals were structured as follows:

1. A major producer-distributor in Buenos Aires agreed to a three-year contract to purchase and distribute three lines of dolls and animals. In exchange, UltraSafe agreed to purchase processed beef from Buenos Aires.
2. The Argentine beef was shipped directly to a producer in Kuala Lumpur. In exchange, UltraSafe imported Malaysian stuffing direct to its foreign trade zone plant in Los Angeles.
3. UltraSafe formed a joint venture with a Guatemalan company to perform the in-process sewing operations. These subassemblies were then imported to the Los Angeles plant.
4. The stuffing was added in Los Angeles and final assembly sewing was completed. The products were then safety tested. Some lines were shipped to the distributor in Buenos Aires, and the balance were sold domestically.

This countertrade arrangement enabled UltraSafe to resume its commanding position in its niche markets. Its president attributed the company's entire recovery to the extra profitability provided by the unusual countertrade deals. (See Chapter 10 for a full discussion of countertrade.)

A New Twist for Imports and Exports

The Dominican Republic has long been a favorite location for U.S. companies investing in offshore production facilities. Low labor costs, a pro-American political climate, close proximity, and beneficial CBI subsidies have enabled the Dominican Republic to become a principal exporter to the United States. In addition, the inclusion of the Dominican Republic in the European equivalent of the Caribbean Basin Initiative, dubbed the Lomé IV Convention, gives Dominican producers duty-free access to the entire European Union (EU, formerly the European Community or EC).

The Lomé IV Convention is a trade agreement between a sixty eight-member group of African, Caribbean, and pacific nations and the European Union. Lomé IV, a successor to three previous five-year agreements, provided for a continuation of duty-free provisions through the year 2000.

Locating a facility in the Dominican Republic now has a double-barreled advantage for U.S. manufacturers: They can ship duty-free to both the United States and Western Europe. Conceivably, establishing a facility here could give U.S. companies a competitive advantage over both foreign and domestic firms.

In addition to an abundance of skilled and semiskilled labor and low wages, industrial free zones in the Dominican Republic offer substantial tax, tariff, and regulatory incentives. Such incentives include freedom from foreign currency holding and exchange restrictions and unrestricted repatriation of profits.

Furthermore, the Dominican Republic's pro-business climate offers significant growth opportunities, as evidenced by a three-year increase in the number of U.S. businesses located in free zones from 160 to 280.

THE CUSTOMS AUDIT

By importing, a company automatically consents to keep certain records and make them available for examination by the U.S. Customs Service. No one is exempt. All companies, regardless of company size, classification of products, or the value or frequency of imports, are subject to customs audits. And, as with IRS audits, the chances of discrepancies are high.

In the past, the U.S. Customs Service has limited its investigations to large corporations that import fairly large quantities. But times have changed. The computer age has hit the Customs Service. As the federal government increases its computerized data banks, the U.S. Customs Service leads the way in the automation of the entire import documentation paper flow.

National Entry Processing, also know as DABA, Paired Ports, and Triangular Processing, comprises a totally electronic environment for automated importers, including paperless entry and summary, electronic invoices, electronic payment of duties, preclassification of merchandise, and binding rulings attached to a company's specific style or part number. This information appears on an electronic invoice, which is then used to obtain an electronic release and entry summary to calculate the duty charges. Finally, the U.S. Customs Service automatically debits an importer's bank account.

The Customs Service is quick to point out that electronic processing permits importers more rapid access to their imported goods. And that is true. What the Service does not reveal, however, is the price importers must pay for this more timely access. The biggest cost of any government audit, exclusive of discrepancy findings, is the substantial amount of nonproductive time spent by company personnel in arranging records for audit and answering auditors' questions. In addition, recordkeeping, which in the past could be somewhat haphazard, now must be formalized—and that costs money.

Recordkeeping for import transactions must be maintained in a manner that allows "rapid access to transactions in an orderly and systematic fashion." Owners and managers of importing companies must have more than a passing knowledge of transactions. And a company should be sure to have competent personnel managing the importing activity.

Customs regulation 19 CFR Part 162 is quite specific about which records must be made available for examination, as well as about those records that must be maintained by third parties (such as custom brokers) and how they will be accessed by customs auditors apart from a broker's internal records. Invoicing requirements are also clearly delineated in 19 CFR Part 141.

The Customs Service holds importers responsible for all aspects of invoices relating to import transactions. To be certain that the invoice properly reflects all required information, management personnel must be intimately involved in the detailed preparation of the purchase order. Importing companies must also insist that exporting suppliers copy this data in total. (This appears to be a rather silly requirement, since importers have absolutely no control over the actions of suppliers; however, that is what Customs regulations require.) Information about terms, inclusions or exclusions from the price, shipping instructions, dangerous markings, insurance, and so forth, must be spelled out in detail.

In addition to verifying hard data, customs auditors determine whether importers have taken "reasonable and prudent actions" in the transactions. This means that companies must place qualified personnel in import management roles. One way to assure compliance is to hire an international consultant to conduct an in-house audit of your international transactions prior to any customs audit. Corrective measures resulting from such an audit go a long way toward satisfying customs auditors that reasonable and prudent management actions have been taken.

The importance of maintaining good internal controls, adequate accounting records, and qualified management personnel cannot be overemphasized. It's too late to try to put things together once you are notified that an audit is imminent. Regardless of audit requirements, however, companies that enjoy success in either exporting or importing know that good recordkeeping and sound management practices are essential to remaining competitive.

QUALITY CONTROL

Most U.S. companies now realize that global competitiveness requires quality products. They spend billions on quality assurance programs, testing procedures, and in-line inspection criteria. They station quality assurance auditors at major suppliers to ensure that purchased materials, parts, and components meet their quality specifications.

Unfortunately, the same degree of quality control is not exercised over imported materials, parts, and components. The reason seems obvious: It is much more difficult to ensure that foreign producers live up to U.S. quality standards, especially for goods imported from less-developed countries. It is difficult and costly to ascertain that suppliers in Jakarta, Guayaquil, Port of Spain, or Tel Aviv maintain the same rigid quality standards as their American counterparts. Yet, to remain competitive, companies must make the effort.

The best way to avoid lengthy negotiations and perhaps litigation of import quality problems is to avoid or at least mitigate them in the first place. This can be achieved by following the few simple guidelines shown in Figure 16.2.

Figure 16.2
Guidelines for Quality Assurance of Imported Goods

1. Know your foreign supplier. Check references from other American firms it supplies. Verify its litigation record.

2. Understand the quality control standards in place in your supplier's plant. Visit the location. Talk to quality assurance managers. Obtain a copy of the testing and inspection procedure manual, if possible.

3. Make sure your supplier understands how important high quality standards are to you. The more dogmatic and obsessive you are about quality, the better. If possible, use a second or third source occasionally to impress upon a supplier your insistence on quality products. Competition often does what mere words or contracts will not.

4. Be sure your product specifications include quality testing and inspection procedures. Make sure that the supplier understands the specifications thoroughly.

5. For large orders of critical parts, spend the money to station your own quality inspector at the supplier's location. Aerospace and military hardware manufacturers do this continually. Many times it's the only way to be sure of what you are getting.

6. When quality problems arise, communicate with the supplier immediately. Find out what caused the failure. Be sure it is corrected before more products are shipped.

7. Make certain the purchase order/contract spells out litigation and arbitration procedures, including what laws apply in the event of dispute.

8. Use letters of credit for payment. Include in the documentation receiving inspection procedures that must be satisfied prior to acceptance and payment.

9. Maintain close personal contact with your supplier's sales representative. Visit your supplier's facility; invite the sales representative to visit yours. Stay in constant contact by telephone, telex, and fax.

Although these guidelines won't ensure the quality of imported products, they are a good start. Once shipments reach your U.S. plant, it may be too late to take action to correct materials or products that won't work, that wear out, or that otherwise do not meet your specifications. And recovering from a foreign supplier is very difficult—if not impossible.

Chapter 17

Foreign Joint Ventures

Exporting will always be a dominant force in international trade. However, it is becoming increasingly clear that exporting alone falls short as a means for gaining increased shares of foreign markets. To sell and distribute exported products and then to service customers after the sale, some form of foreign marketing/distribution presence is necessary. To meet local market requirements for delivery and quality, components or finished products must be produced within a host country. To ensure the continued availability of parts and materials, it is frequently necessary to hold equity interests in foreign suppliers. And finally, many foreign governments insist that local residents hold equity interests (either majority or minority) in any local business owned partially by foreign companies.

To take advantage of foreign market and resource opportunities and to meet host-country legal requirements, companies of all sizes must of necessity seriously consider joining forces with local businesses. And this has led to the widespread use of strategic alliances with other American companies, local residents (individuals or companies), or businesses domiciled in third countries.

DuPont, IBM, Ford, American Home Products, Ernst & Young, and Chase Manhattan are examples of well-known U.S.-based companies in diverse industries that have included foreign strategic alliances in their long-term marketing strategies. Over the last ten years, midsize companies like Loctite Corporation, SnyderGeneral Corp., and Connor Peripherals, Inc. have adopted the same foreign-partnership policies. More recently, small firms with less than 500 employees, such as EZ4 Electronics, Inc., Washclor Systems Corp., and MortorSound Electric Fasteners, have utilized foreign strategic alliances to boost their exporting business.

Many benefits accrue from such alliances. For smaller U.S. companies, the major benefits are

- Direct ties to local bureaucrats
- Close relationships with key suppliers
- Resolution of customs logjams
- Access to trade finance through host-country government agencies
- More efficient management of countertrade transactions.

There are many different forms of strategic alliances, each specifically structured to meet the needs of U.S. companies on one hand and the requirements of local markets, suppliers, and government regulations on the other. For smaller U.S. businesses, joint ventures, licensing, and franchises are by far the most popular forms of alliances. Of the three, a joint venture tends to be the easiest to monitor and generally yields the highest returns.

JOINT VENTURE BENEFITS

By definition, a joint venture involves the formation of a new operating entity (typically either a corporation or a partnership) that is independent of the joint venture partners. The equity contributed by each partner may take the form of money, facilities, technology, inventory, management know-how, or marketing expertise.

Although many problems can and generally do arise with joint ventures, a carefully structured contractual arrangement that spells out the responsibilities of and contributions from each party usually minimizes the severity of future disputes. Despite the fear of losing valuable assets by sharing closely guarded patents and proprietary know-how with a partner, companies of all sizes have found foreign joint ventures an acceptable way to market and finance foreign trade.

Joint Ventures as a Marketing Strategy

Most new-to-exporting companies prefer to join forces with a partner that sells complementary products through an established in-country marketing network. The partner may be either a U.S. company already doing business in the host country or a host-country national. For example, assume that your company makes short-wave radios and you want to open new consumer markets in Jamaica. ElectroTime Corp. has been selling its line of electric clocks in Jamaica for several years. Your company and ElectroTime form a Jamaican joint venture specifically to sell and distribute clocks and radios. Your company contributes working capital; ElectroTime contributes its sales/distribution network.

Another common reason for forming joint ventures is to break protective trade barriers. Many Third World countries, as well as the European Union and Japan, enforce stringent trade barriers against the importing and distribution of American-made products. A host-country joint venture partner with access to import licenses is frequently the only feasible way to enter these markets.

Moreover, despite all the hoopla about state-controlled economies converting to market economies, many governments continue to interfere in pricing policies and distribution channels. This makes it virtually impossible for U.S. exporters to penetrate these markets without an inside track to powerful bureaucrats. Someone in your partner's company should be responsible for "greasing the skids" to obtain preferential treatment. Such an individual should know who to contact, when to negotiate, and how to satisfy government officials who might otherwise block the import or distribution of your products.

Foreign joint ventures are also a convenient way to enter dominated foreign markets. Nearly every country has certain industries that government regulations protect from competition. In the United States, electric and water utilities certainly fall into this category. Most Third World (and many industrialized) countries protect their telecommunications, airline, power utility, and computer industries, causing markets to be dominated by one or two large companies, either public-sector or private. Pragmatically, to sell in these markets, U.S. exporters must join forces with resident partners that already have government approvals and an established track record in dealing with these dominant companies.

Joint Ventures as a Financing Mechanism

In addition to forming an integral part of a company's marketing strategies, foreign joint ventures can be a handy way to finance local production or distribution facilities or to finance reexports to third countries.

Many countries prohibit foreign companies from raising capital through local banks or capital markets. If you need to finance trade or expansion within the host country, the only way to do it is through a joint venture with a local partner. This national then has a legal right to raise varying amounts of local capital as the occasion warrants. A joint venture with a cash-rich foreign company (American, Western European, or East Asian) is especially beneficial when entering a depressed economy, such as Eastern Europe or the Commonwealth of Independent States.

In the Caribbean, Mexico, and Central America, potential joint venture partners are frequently small local manufacturers or distributors, just like your company. In this case, financing can usually be arranged through a combination of U.S. government and multilateral aid, host-country government agencies, development banks, and multinational foreign banks. Although exceptions certainly arise, each of these capital providers tends to favor joint ventures in which a U.S. partner brings jobs and management know-how to local companies. Not infrequently, a U.S. parent can participate in a foreign venture without incurring any debt on its books and without using any of its own funds.

Studies by the Department of Commerce and several export trade organizations point to three prominent ways U.S. companies benefit from financing foreign trade and direct investments through foreign joint ventures. Such alliances enable them to

- Qualify for local export trade credit
- Source local capital markets
- Limit initial capital investment, and therefore risk, by tapping multilateral and bilateral aid programs.

Local Export Credit Assistance

Qualifying for government export credit in such countries as Japan, South Korea, Taiwan, Britain, Germany, or France is reason enough to form local joint ventures. These countries (and many others) support lucrative export/import trade credit facilities that are easier to use and have much broader coverage than those available from Eximbank. However, most government trade credit programs require that local companies participate in the transaction. East Asian programs tend to be more liberal about financing foreign-owned companies, but even here, a local partner can be invaluable as a qualifier and arranger.

Sourcing Local Capital Markets

More than sixty countries support over 175 active stock, commodity, and financial futures and options exchanges; however, listing on most of them is restricted to national companies. Even though new trading instruments such as global depositary receipts are finding their way into world exchanges, most stock exchanges in less-developed countries continue to require local licensing and incorporation. A host-country corporation formed with a local partner is one of the easiest ways around this obstacle.

Tapping Multilateral and Bilateral Aid Programs

Chapter 11 describes in detail how multilateral and bilateral aid programs can be used to raise long-term capital for foreign direct investment. Nearly all of these programs require equity participation by host-country companies. To ignore such lucrative avenues because of ownership constraints makes little sense, especially when a joint venture could open the doors.

Discussions later in this chapter cover additional joint venture financing possibilities.

JOINT VENTURE STRUCTURES

Joint venture partners may share equally or unequally in the ownership of the new company and/or in the responsibility for carrying on its business. They may also share the profits and losses of the venture proportionately or disproportionately to their ownership holdings.

Some joint ventures are not intended to produce independent profits or losses but merely to generate longer term gains for each of the partners, as in arrangements to share technology and market intelligence. In most cases, however, a joint venture is a separate operating entity. Partners may hold equal or unequal ownership in the entity. Profits and losses are usually shared in proportion to each partner's equity interest.

The care taken in drafting a joint venture contract often determines whether the arrangement will be beneficial or detrimental to one or both parties. Since the parties to the contract might be from different countries, accustomed to significantly different negotiating techniques, contract language, and local interpretation of contract phrases, the most beneficial contracts are normally negotiated and drafted by intermediaries from both sides. Intermediaries may be management consultants, investment bankers, attorneys, government bureaucrats, or a combination thereof.

Since no two joint venture contracts are alike, any attempt to demonstrate universal contract language or format would be futile. However, a few standards seem to apply in most cases. Adherence to the following standards won't guarantee a successful marriage but ignoring them will certainly strengthen the possibility of a near-term divorce:

1. *Multilingual.* The contract must be both in English and in the language of the foreign partner. Even if personnel from both companies are conversant in each other's language, legal contract terminology tends to have different meanings in different countries. It's crucial to reach mutual agreement on the interpretation of all contract clauses under each party's local laws and customs.

2. *Objective of joint venture.* The objective of the joint venture should be clearly stated in the contract, whether it is to market specific products, to build a manufacturing plant, to manage the operations of a facility, to export, to transfer technology and know-how, or to provide financing for a project.

3. *Expiration date.* All joint venture contracts should have a definite expiration date, regardless of how far into the future that may be. Along with a defined life for the joint venture, the contract should spell out specifically how the venture's assets and liabilities—including inventory, receivables, plant and equipment, trade liabilities, and unpaid loans or other indebtedness—will be distributed upon dissolution.

4. *Specific activities.* The joint venture's activities may require that specific functions be performed by one or both of the partners, such as managing the operation, arranging financing, marketing, engineering, or liaison with government officials. Regardless of the number of duties assumed by each partner, each should be thoroughly described. The contract should also include specific responsibilities for settling claims, lawsuits, and any other legal or contingent matter that may arise during the operation of the joint venture as well as for paying all taxes, license fees, permit fees, and so on.

5. *Sharing profits and losses.* The contract must contain definitive language that spells out how the profits and losses of the joint venture will be allocated to each partner. It should also describe how, when, and to whom cash will be distributed, and how compensation to the parties will be determined.

6. *Board of directors.* A board of directors or other policy-making body must be defined. Veto rights, withdrawal rights, new or additional equity contributions from partners, eventual transfer of ownership interests at the liquidation date, and other policy matters should be defined.

7. *Escape clause.* In the event that one or both partners wish to withdraw from the venture, contractual provisions must spell out their right to do so, under what circumstances withdrawal will be permitted, what forfeiture or compensatory allowances will be paid, and any other items germane to the agreement.

Although joint ventures agreements have many provisions similar to those in standard partnership agreements, they take on an added level of complexity. Now the parties must agree on such arcane issues as

- The relationship between the newly formed joint venture entity and its participating owners
- Initial and ongoing capital contributions
- Control of the venture
- Conflict resolution procedures
- Termination provisions.

Relationship with Participating Owners

Contract provisions should describe the amount and form of each partner's contribution to the new entity, whether it be capital, technology, machinery, processes, facilities, distribution network, management know-how, or other tangible or intangible assets. When each partner contributes only corporate assets, the downward relationship from parents to the joint venture entity may be quite simple. However, relationships get significantly more complex when partners share management responsibilities (i.e., when one partner provides accounting services for the venture and the other partner is responsible for venture personnel recruitment and evaluation, or when one partner manages legal matters and the other handles insurance coverage).

The transfer of assets, capital, or technology from the venture back to the parent companies can also be convoluted. For example, a manufacturing venture might sell products or components to one or both parents. Or perhaps develop a technology that will be used by one or both partners. Or supply a marketing or distribution network to handle the sale of products from one or both. Or receive royalties from patents belonging to one partner or another. Such relationships must be clearly spelled out in the joint venture agreement to avoid future disputes.

Capital Contributions

The form and amount of capital contributions must also be clearly defined in the agreement. Three areas need to be covered:

- How much capital each party will ontribute to fund the initial start-up.
- Which party will provide working capital, as needed.
- Which party will arrange necessary financing from government agencies, local development banks, foreign banks, and/or local capital markets.

For joint ventures between large and small companies, it might appear that responsibility for initial capital and ongoing funding should rest with the larger of the two; however, this may not always be desirable. A case in point arose when a small U.S. manufacturer, Horkel Products, Inc., formed a joint venture with a large British telecommunications company to establish an assembly facility in Barbados.

The British company agreed to provide initial capital of $5 million and to fund ongoing working capital needs. However, to take advantage of certain provisions in the U.S. government's Caribbean Basin Initiative, Horkel arranged bank guarantees from Eximbank and trade credit with U.S. banks for exports back to the United States. The British partner managed export credit needs for shipments to Europe.

Control of the Venture

Disagreements over management control of a newly formed company have caused more than one joint venture to bend, if not break. If such control followed ownership percentages, there would probably be much less difficulty, but in joint ventures this seldom happens. When a large corporation brings capital to the table and a smaller company brings management or technical expertise, ownership control generally rests entirely with the large company and management control with the smaller company.

Most companies experienced with joint ventures would probably agree that 50-50 partnerships rarely work. Each partner has its own venue, its own strategies, and its own operating style. To expect agreement on all decisions is asking too much. One party or the other must be responsible for daily operations, and these responsibilities must be provided for in the contractual agreement.

On the other hand, regardless of which partner has management control, the other party will certainly want a say in major decisions. This is especially true when management control rests with the minority shareholder, that is, the smaller company that did not contribute initial capital. This problem can easily be resolved by granting the majority partner contractual rights to block major decisions affecting the newly formed company. Typically, such decisions include

- The sale or disposal of venture assets
- Changes in the venture agreement
- The hiring and firing of key management personnel
- The acquisition of capital equipment
- Corporate finance matters such as the acquisition of new debt or equity capital and the concurrent pledging of venture assets
- Major tax strategies
- Distribution of profits.

Conflict Resolution

Disagreements are bound to arise in any joint venture. The contractual agreement must clearly spell out how conflicts that cannot be negotiated quietly and quickly between the partners will be resolved. Mutual approval of major decisions certainly helps, but additional provisions may also be required.

Ventures conceived between two companies of approximately equal size (and that make similar equity contributions) often provide for a separate committee made up of senior members from both companies to act as a medium for dispute settlement. Such a committee should be divorced from the joint venture's board of directors, with no authority over the operations of the venture. Its sole purpose is to meet periodically to resolve those major conflicts between the partners or between venture managers and one or both parent companies that the board of directors cannot resolve.

Arbitration is another possibility. Every joint venture agreement should specify conditions that could lead to arbitration, how an arbitrator will be appointed, and the finality of an arbitrator's decision. When agreement cannot be reached through normal channels, the agreement may stipulate the buyout of one partner by the other, similar to provisions in a standard partnership buyout agreement.

Termination

Contract clauses must spell out the joint venture's life span; that is, when and under what circumstances it will be terminated. Provisions that permit the extension of the venture's life upon mutual agreement of all partners may also be included. However, if extension options are not exercised by the termination date or when specified conditions that give rise to a termination occur, then the joint venture dies. Specific provisions in the agreement should identify how the venture's business will be wound down, how assets will be distributed (including cash balances), and what liability each partner will assume for future claims that may arise against the venture once it is disbanded.

Occasionally, the agreement provides for an independent third-party overseer (perhaps an attorney or a major accounting firm) to supervise liquidation proceedings. In some instances it may be desirable to transfer the assets of the venture to a trust and let the trustee liquidate the business and distribute assets. Regardless of the mechanism used, provision must be made to end the joint venture.

CRITERIA FOR JOINT VENTURE FACILITIES

You're not alone if you shudder at the thought of setting up a foreign facility when all you really want to do is export. No one would argue with the statement that pure exporting is a lot simpler and less costly than foreign joint ventures. Still, as we have seen, host-country import barriers and competitive forces may make it necessary to include joint ventures of one form or another in long-term marketing or sales finance strategies.

Joint ventures are clearly not for everyone. In fact, to make joint ventures worthwhile, a company should meet four criteria:

- It must be of sufficient size to warrant an overseas facility. Very small companies just don't have the resources.

- It should be well established in its domestic markets. A foreign location is not the place to experiment with new products or with products that won't sell in the United States

- It should face serious foreign distribution obstacles. Distributors, sales agents, trade barriers, or local cartels may inhibit the distribution of imported products.

- Competitive pricing structures should restrict the inclusion of shipping, packing, customs fees, and other exporting expenses in product selling prices. If you mark up your prices to cover these expenses, your prices may not be competitive.

If your company fits this mold, then joint ventures may be the best possibility for selling, distributing, or financing long-term export orders. Although using joint ventures for marketing and distribution is relatively straightforward, it may be helpful to briefly review the more prominent financing options.

FINANCING JOINT VENTURE INVENTORY

The biggest hurdle facing U.S. partners of foreign joint ventures seems to be arranging suitable financing for the joint venture's purchase of inventory exported from the United States.

When exporting materials, parts, or components to a joint venture, you are in essence exporting to yourself. Traditional sources of trade finance recognize this anomaly and are usually cool about providing funds. This means that barring unusual circumstances, the most likely financing will come from or through your joint venture partner. This may take the form of:

1. Loans or equity contributions from partners
   - Who are foreign subsidiaries of U.S. parents, or,
   - Who are domiciled in Western Europe, Japan, Taiwan, or other industrialized country
   - Who are domiciled in a third country that is party to a free trade agreement with your host country
2. Host-country government export credit facilities (in those cases where your partner is a host-country national)
3. U.S. bank trade finance secured by guarantees from host-country banks or government agencies
4. Lines of credit from U.S. branch banks in the host country.

Contributions from Local Partners

Getting working capital from a local partner is clearly the best way to go. Not only does this relieve the joint venture of costly bank debt, it also enables U.S. partners to completely bypass what can be a bureaucratic nightmare of U.S. government aid programs. However, if your joint venture is in a soft-currency country, it could make sense to provide for the conversion of local currency to U.S. dollars, other hard currency, or usable products or services, as in countertrade transactions.

Host-Country Export Credit

Most industrialized countries and several Latin American and East Asian nations maintain government-sponsored export credit facilities to finance exports from the host country and, not infrequently, imports for local joint ventures. Many foreign export credit programs are far more comprehensive than those provided by Eximbank and have specific financing facilities to assist local companies to import products deemed to be desirable for improving the local economy. Products and services for infrastructure development, environmental cleanup and protection, telecommunications, and waste management are a few examples of "desirable" imports in many Third World countries, especially Latin America.

U.S. Banks and Host-Country Guarantees

If your company has good relations with a major U.S. bank and your joint venture partner has the same with a host-country bank, it should be possible to arrange for your partner's bank to guarantee trade finance from your bank. This doesn't always work, however, if you work with a smaller U.S. bank. Lacking an understanding of international trade, these banks continue to shy away from financing any form of foreign trade or direct investment—regardless of guarantees. Nevertheless, your U.S. bank is certainly worth a try.

Foreign Branch Banks

Obtaining trade finance from a local branch of a U.S. multinational bank is usually a much easier and cheaper way to go. Most countries in Latin America, for example, have branch offices of Citibank, Chase Manhattan, Bank of America, or Chemical Bank. As long as you establish a working relationship with the U.S. offices of these banks, obtaining credit from the foreign branch is usually relatively straightforward. Such multinational U.S. banks also have branch offices in many western European countries.

When forming a joint venture in countries other than Latin America, Western Europe, or Canada, however, it's usually necessary to work through non-U.S. banks. Barclays, Hong Kong and Shanghai Bank, many Japanese banks, Midland, Deutschebank, and several other European banks maintain branch offices throughout the world. Once again, the first step is to establish a relationship with the bank's home office or its U.S. branch. Then trade credit from a foreign branch should be easily arranged.

Countertrade Joint Ventures

Small companies find it extremely difficult to negotiate and administer complex countertrade contracts. Countertrade deals of nearly any type or size require at least three and usually four high-caliber managers dedicated to the task. Since hiring so many specialists is too difficult and costly for many smaller companies, the only feasible way to tap countertrade benefits is with a partner that has the skills that your company may lack. Although intermediaries can assist in the negotiation and management of countertrade transactions, turning this responsibility over to a foreign partner, either from the host country or a third country, is rapidly becoming a popular alternative. With local knowledge and political connections, a qualified joint venture partner usually provides better results in the long run.

Of course if countertrade transactions involve parallel trade or buybacks with or from a host-country supplier, there isn't much choice. Some type of partnership arrangement with a local company is necessary to make the sale. A local countertrade partner should also have the appropriate connections to arrange for bank guarantees against trade credit.

LOCATING JOINT VENTURE PARTNERS

Large corporations have a relatively easy time locating suitable joint venture partners for practically any purpose. They drop their lines in the global pond and competitors, suppliers, and aggressive foreign traders scramble for the bait. Smaller companies, especially those relatively new to exporting, aren't as fortunate. In fact, the first time a company attempts to set up a foreign joint venture can be a nightmarish, costly experience.

The difficulty in finding a joint venture partner stems not from a dearth of sources, but from too many. A practically unlimited number of intermediaries, government bureaus, international publications, trade groups, and multinational agencies willingly provide leads and direct contacts to potential partners. In fact, the variety of sources is so staggering that it's easy to become mired in the process without achieving your end goal.

For simplicity, sources of joint venture partners can be conveniently grouped into major categories; pragmatically, however, many overlap and should be used simultaneously. The following represents one such grouping:

1. U.S. government agencies
2. U.S. government publications
3. American Chambers of Commerce
4. The World Bank
5. Development banks
6. Multinational accounting firms
7. Foreign consulates
8. Multinational investment banks
9. Foreign branches of U.S. banks.

U.S. Government Agencies

A wide variety of federal agencies stand ready to help U.S. companies locate nearly anything they need to enter foreign trade: financing, market/product statistics, foreign customer lists, foreign agent and distributor contacts, listings of intermediaries and consultants, and, perhaps most important, potential joint venture partners. Some are more effective than others, depending on location of the market, company size, and industry. The following summarizes the major agencies that currently offer the most help in locating joint venture partners for small businesses. (See Chapter 4 for additional details.)

1. *U.S. and Foreign Commercial Service (US&FCS)*. The US&FCS and its [sister organization in the Department of Commerce, the International Trade Administration (ITA), offer a surfeit of information covering every aspect of international trade. These organizations maintain a worldwide network of 126 offices and more than 500 nationals who gather trade data from every corner of the globe. This data is then assimi-

lated in a monstrous computer database called CIMS (Commercial Information Management System).

For a nominal charge, or none, a company can obtain reports, periodicals, computer data banks, and other material. One segment of the database lists potential foreign joint venture partners, together with the products/services they are interested in representing or producing. The ITA's custom research service creates special, on-request reports (for a small fee) about marketing and joint venture leads in several European, Latin American, and East Asian countries. These reports also include data concerning competition, trade barriers, sales potential, and so on.

Further information can be obtained from your local US&FCS office or directly from

> U.S. Department of Commerce
> Room H2106
> International Trade Administration
> U.S. and Foreign Commercial Service
> Washington, DC 20230

2. *U.S. Trade and Development Program (TDP).* The TDP is an independent government agency within the International Development Cooperation Agency. TDP has an exclusive mandate to promote U.S. exports for major development projects in middle-income and developing countries. Its Washington staff of twenty-two works directly with foreign agencies to sort out viable projects and product needs.

Since the agency's aim is to help U.S. exporters, one of the requirements for technical or financial assistance is that a U.S. company be involved in the project. To accomplish this, the agency helps U.S. firms locate appropriate foreign joint venture partners. Contact the agency at

> U.S. Trade and Development Program
> SA-16 Rm. 309
> Washington, DC 20523-1602
> Telephone: (703) 875-4357

3. *Overseas Private Investment Corporation (OPIC).* In addition to providing political risk insurance and financing for foreign direct investments, OPIC field officers maintain active listings of potential joint venture partners in the 100-plus countries that qualify for OPIC assistance. Contact OPIC at

> Overseas Private Investment Corporation
> 1615 M St. N.W.
> Suite 400
> Washington, DC 20527
> Telephone: (800) 424-6742 or (202) 457-7010

4. *Department of State, Foreign Service.* Foreign Service representatives stationed around the world direct the administrative programs of the Department of Commerce in more than eighty-two countries where Department of Commerce people are not stationed. U.S. firms looking for joint venture partners in these countries should contact either the appropriate State Department desk officer or

> Office of Commercial, Legislative and Public Affairs
> Bureau of Economic and Business Affairs
> U.S. Department of State
> Room 6822
> Washington, DC 20520
> Telephone: (202) 647-1942

5. *U.S. Agency for International Development (USAID).* USAID administers most of the foreign economic assistance programs for the U.S government. In addition to evaluating and funding foreign government and foreign private sector development projects, the agency provides excellent leads to joint venture partners in those countries that benefit from its development aid services. Contact Agency for International Development (AID/USDBU)

> Department of State Building
> 320 21st St., N.W.
> Washington, DC 20523
> OR
> Technical Assistance Service
> Telephone: (703) 875-1551

6. *Latin American/Caribbean Business Development Center.* This organization is part of the ITA and operates in conjunction with USAID in publishing a monthly bulletin about regional business news in the Caribbean, Central America, South America, and Mexico. One feature of the *LA/C Business Bulletin* is a "bulletin board"-type synopsis of American firms looking for regional joint venture partners and regional firms looking for American partners.

World Bank

The United Nations' World Bank is a multilateral lending agency that comprises four closely associated institutions:

- *The Bank for Reconstruction and Development (IBRD)*, which lends funds directly to governments of creditworthy developing countries with relatively high per capita income
- *The International Development Association (IDA)*, which provides assistance on concessional terms to the poorest developing countries that are not sufficiently creditworthy for IBRD funding

- *The International Finance Corporation (IFC),* which promotes growth in developing countries through support of the private sector
- *The Multilateral Investment Guarantee Agency (MIGA),* whose purpose is to encourage foreign investment in developing countries by providing guarantees to foreign investors against losses resulting from noncommercial risks.

Although the IBRD and the IDA are of interest to consultants who wish to bid for foreign government sponsored projects, they do not offer assistance to companies trying to locate joint venture partners. The IFC and the MIGA, however, are very much in the forefront of this endeavor.

Through loans and equity contributions, the IFC collaborates closely with project sponsors (nearly always foreign companies). When the sponsoring company is a joint venture with a host-country firm, the IFC can be a valuable financing source. IFC officials can be contacted at Business Development Department, International Finance Corporation, 1818 H Street, N.W., Washington, DC 20433, (202) 473-1950.

MIGA does more than insure against political risk. It also provides advisory services to developing member countries on means to improve the local economic environment to attract foreign investors. Part of this service is to identify and qualify local joint venture partners for foreign firms. Further information can be obtained from Multilateral Investment Guarantee Agency, 1818 H Street N.W., Washington, DC 20433, (202) 473-0179.

American Chambers of Commerce

American Chamber of Commerce offices around the world keep track of local business, economic, and political developments that affect U.S. business interests. One of its activities is staying abreast of local firms looking for American joint venture partners. ACC offices throughout Latin America are especially helpful in this regard.

Multinational Accounting Firms

Multinational accounting firms also provide direct leads to joint venture partners. All have qualified international departments in their U.S. home offices and staff international consulting departments in London, Tokyo, and other major cities. In addition to consulting activities, personnel from offices around the world serve as intermediaries for sourcing joint venture partners and negotiating joint venture contracts.

Foreign Consulates

Many foreign consulate offices keep track of economic and business activities in their home countries in addition to serving as liaison centers. Not infrequently, they have the wherewithal to offer suggestions about sources of home-country business information pertaining to financing programs, market statistics, and potential joint venture partners.

The response from consulates of poorer, less-developed countries is often quite meaningless; however, some provide excellent leads. Consulate offices of

Western European and many East Asian countries, on the other hand, all maintain extensive literature and contacts in the commercial area. This information is available for the asking and often includes helpful leads to companies looking for joint venture partners, for trade either in their home country or in third countries. U.S. country desk officers have the names of commercial attaches and the current addresses and telephone numbers of consulate offices.

INTERMEDIARIES AND JOINT VENTURES

First-time U.S. exporters frequently find it impossible to conduct any significant business in foreign lands (especially setting up joint ventures) without the assistance of an intermediary. Although direct solicitation and one-on-one contract negotiations are commonplace in the United States, the rest of the world relies on intermediaries to bring two parties together. International investment banks and international consultants serve as the most visible, and the most legitimate, sources of intermediary assistance.

In some underdeveloped areas (e.g., most of sub-Sahara Africa, India, and nearly all Islamic countries), local intermediation can best be accomplished through either local trading firms that specialize in consulting to foreign companies, government bureaucrats in commercial agencies, such as the central bank, or ministries of finance and trade. These emissaries obviously do not advertise their talents. They often conduct business surreptitiously and informally. Yet their services are usually essential for sourcing and setting up joint ventures.

Local American Chamber of Commerce offices, branch offices of major foreign banks, and local offices of multinational corporations should all be able to provide leads to the type of intermediary you need.

Professional international consultants provide a much easier and faster way to obtain advisory assistance. Locating an international consultant in the United States, Europe, and the more developed nations of East Asia seldom causes a problem. Professional societies have membership rosters. Trade publications carry advertisements or announcements. Phone directories frequently carry listings under "Consultants." Universities and colleges generally can help locate affiliated consultants.

In less-developed countries, however, the search for a qualified consultant can be a long, arduous task, often ending in failure. In some countries they just don't exist. In this case, local correspondents of multinational accounting firms often take consulting assignments as intermediaries.

Foreign affiliates of U.S. international laws firms take on intermediary assignments related to joint ventures in Latin American and some Southeast Asian countries. If local circumstances indicate a need to cut through bureaucratic red tape for clearance to set up a joint venture, local attorneys generally have more connections than consultants. Any international law firm (Baker & MacKenzie is the largest and best known) maintains directories of foreign correspondent firms capable of handling such engagements.

Occasionally, foreign service officers in U.S. embassy offices can be helpful in providing leads to capable intermediaries. They seldom do the work themselves, but they usually maintain a plethora of commercial and political connections, just for emergencies.

Foreign branches of U.S. or British banks generally know who's who in the local business community. If qualified consultants are around, these bank managers know how and where to contact them. This can be a excellent source of information in parts of the Middle East and Africa. Intermediaries may be able to keep a low profile in the general business community, but it's hard to remain invisible from local bankers. In poorer countries, local bankers rank right up there with political bureaucrats as sources of intelligence.

Once you have located apparently qualified intermediaries, it's necessary to screen out those that you obviously cannot work with. Language barriers, pressure from government officials or aid agencies to team up with a certain consultant, and different work standards are but a few of the obstacles to be overcome. In the face of such pressures, it's crucial to remember that the intermediary you choose will, in essence, act as your agent for sourcing joint venture partners and negotiating venture agreements; therefore, he must be trustworthy and able to communicate with your home office.

Chapter 18

Acquiring a Foreign Company

Many businesses find that once a foreign market has been successfully opened through exporting, they can achieve further growth objectives by establishing a production, distribution, or retail facility on foreign soil. While this can be a logical next step for companies with a solid background in exporting, it can lead to catastrophe for those that are new to exporting. The possibilities for acquiring a foreign business, as discussed in this chapter, relate only to those companies that have progressed sufficiently in foreign trade to have the resources and savvy to undertake such a strategic move.

U.S. companies have three options for establishing a foreign presence:

- Form a joint venture (see Chapter 17)
- Start a facility/business from scratch
- Acquire a going business.

Although the difficulty of starting a new business from scratch varies somewhat from country to country, no one should mistakenly believe that offshore business start-ups are as easy or fast as beginning a new business in the United States. Every country has more stringent laws, tax structures, labor requirements, and nationality barriers than the United States. No country in the world encourages new business start-ups like the United States. And nowhere except in the United States do markets accept new companies, new marketing techniques, and new products with such enthusiasm.

With the exception of Canada in certain instances, starting a business from scratch in any foreign country is far more difficult and costly and runs a higher risk of failure than forming a joint venture or acquiring a going business. One word of caution, however: If your company has not been involved in business acquisitions in the United States, it should probably not attempt one overseas. A strange cultural environment is not the place to learn the ropes of this complex process.

Nevertheless, buying a going business has several attractive features:

- *Market presence.* A going business has already made the investment in time, people, and facilities to establish itself in the marketplace. Its products may be different from but still complement those of a buyer, so that a marriage enhances the sales of both companies.

- *Established networks.* Going businesses already have distribution channels, sales networks, customer bases, and supplier agreements. In addition, many foreign companies (large and small) have marketing and distribution networks, as well as supplier contacts, in third countries to handle export marketing and materials sourcing.

- *Trained personnel.* Management personnel in each functional activity are probably already in place, alleviating the need to immediately recruit new talent (as is the case in a business start-up). Trained labor will also likely be in place, reducing the cost and time of recruiting and then training new workers.

- *Facility and equipment.* Since factory, warehouse, office, or store, as well as production and office equipment, is already in place, the leasing of new facilities or the importing of new equipment (both of which can be time-consuming and costly) is unnecessary. Moreover, many countries continue to enforce restrictions against importing production assets. Furthermore, it may be that functioning production lines can be more easily merged with those of the buying company than new machinery and equipment would be.

- *Negotiated contracts.* A number of contracts must be executed when starting up a new business. Union contracts, sales representative agreements, supplier contracts, negotiated pricing structures, leases, tax permits and licenses, pension arrangements, employment contracts, and a variety of other legally binding arrangements are always required to operate a business. Buying a going business with these contracts already in place enables a company to get its own products up and running in the new market much faster than starting from scratch.

UNIQUE ASPECTS OF FOREIGN ACQUISITIONS

In contrast to American business acquisitions, very seldom does 100 percent of the ownership of foreign companies change hands. Majority control, yes—provided it does not violate local laws—but not 100 percent. In cases where foreign majority ownership is forbidden, it may be that minority positions afford sufficient management control to make the deal viable. Even when 100 percent foreign ownership is allowed, it may make more sense to acquire a lesser share, not only to keep the acquisition price down, but to reap the same benefits from remaining shareholder(s) as from a joint venture partner.

In addition to ownership percentages, foreign acquisitions differ markedly from domestic ones in respect to

1. Structuring the buying entity
2. Complying with special tax laws and other regulations
3. Sourcing targets and financing the deal
4. Valuing the business.

Buying Entity

It is usually prudent to make a foreign acquisition through a separate corporation—independent, but owned by a U.S. parent. This corporation should be registered in the acquisition candidate's country of origin. In many Western European countries, preregistered corporate shells can be readily purchased through a local law firm. In less-developed countries, a joint venture entity owned in part by the U.S. acquiring company and in part by a local company or the remaining minority shareholders of the acquisition candidate is often the best choice.

Compliance with Tax Laws and Regulation

U.S. tax laws that apply to foreign acquisitions and the operation of foreign subsidiaries are very complex and subject to frequent changes. Topics that involve provisions substantially different from those applied to U.S. acquisitions and operations include

- Allocation of acquisition purchase price
- Capital structure of acquiring entity and target candidate before and after acquisition
- Licensing of intangible property (if applicable)
- Management and technical service fees paid between foreign subsidiary and U.S. parent
- "Base companies" as intermediaries
- Intercompany pricing arrangements.

U.S. legal counsel should be a key member of your acquisition team. Such counsel should be experienced in all U.S. tax laws related to foreign acquisitions. A knowledge of tax laws in the target candidate's home country is also desirable; however, for smaller acquisitions, a correspondent tax attorney in the host country should suffice.

In addition to tax laws, it's important to check out other host-country and U.S. regulations that may affect either the form or the substance of the acquisition. Interpretations of host-country contract and labor laws, as well as trade regulations, must come from foreign legal counsel. As for U.S. regulations, any or all of the following may apply:

- The Justice Department's Antitrust Guidelines for International Operations
- The Foreign Corrupt Practices Act, which stipulates the types of records that must be kept by U.S. firms and all offshore subsidiaries, as well as provisions prohibiting kickbacks, bribes, and so on to foreign parties
- The Anti-Boycott Regulations of the Export Administration Act
- The Trading with the Enemy Act
- The International Investment and Trade in Service Survey Act.

Most business managers would agree that esoteric tax matters belong in the domain of professional advisers. And rightly so. Planning and operating a business is challenge enough; taxes belong in someone else's bailiwick, especially the complex set of rules affecting foreign-source income. Therefore, the following discussions should be tempered by ongoing advice from your tax counsel.

Tax Planning and Controlling-Interest Investments

A number of matters enter into effective tax planning when buying a controlling interest in a foreign company, both before the actual sale closes and after the acquisition. Basic questions focus on ways to minimize foreign taxes in the host country and to maximize foreign tax credits against U.S. taxes.

Financing a foreign acquisition with bank loans or other debt issues also must be weighed against potential tax effects. In many cases, it makes sense to set up an intermediary foreign holding company to hold the acquisition debt. This gives the holding company a deduction for interest expense in the holding company's host country.

Under certain circumstances, however, the IRS could invalidate the deduction for U.S. tax purposes by recharacterizing interest payments into a different basket for foreign tax credit limitations. (See Chap. 3 for discussions related to "basket" provisions and other tax matters.) Financing a foreign acquisition presents a whole series of interesting and complex tax questions that must be recognized prior to structuring investment vehicles. Not only do creative tax strategies play a crucial role in the type of financing used for the acquisition, they also affect the management and capital structures of the acquired company, intercompany pricing policies, and the potential future disposal of the company. This is definitely not a subject to tackle without tax counsel.

The laws in many countries, especially in Latin America, the Caribbean, Eastern Europe, and Southeast Asia, offer foreign companies significant tax incentives in exchange for equity investments in local businesses. In most cases, local partners, either individual or companies, must participate in the ownership of the business. At times, resident nationals must also have a hand in managing the business.

In an effort to support the economic development of these Third World nations, the U.S. government provides special tax breaks for American investors—some by legislative order, others on a case-by-case basis. Without question, Puerto Rico continues to be one of the most attractive locations for American companies.

As a U.S. commonwealth, Puerto Rico falls under the U.S. court system, tax system, postal service, and military. Puerto Rican citizens are also U.S. citizens. As part of the joint Puerto Rican-U.S. effort to develop the commonwealth's business base, tax exemptions of up to 90 percent for periods of from ten to twenty five years are available to U.S. companies that set up or purchase a business in Puerto Rico. Additional tax savings as well as financing incentives may be realized under the Internal Revenue Code's Section 936. (See Chapter 11 for details of this program.)

Furthermore, private placements of bonds by the government of Puerto Rico and commonwealth financial institutions have increased the amount of the 936 funds available for investment in Puerto Rico or other Caribbean islands.

Strategic Considerations

Two primary questions come into play when evaluating an offshore acquisition:

1. How strong is the country's economy, and what are the future prospects of economic growth?
2. How competitive is the acquisition candidate in its current markets?

Country surveys as described in Chaps. 5 and 6 should be the first step in evaluating a country's economic status and future potential. During the surveys, gather as much macroeconomic data as possible from U.S. government sources and host-country agencies. In addition, it's a good idea to check out the country's credit rating. Government bond credit ratings assigned by international credit agencies (e.g., Standard & Poor's and Moody's) tend to be a fairly good barometer of international confidence in a country's economy.

The evaluation of a company's profit-making potential is usually more complex and subjective. One of the difficulties encountered with offshore businesses is that the standards of efficiency, productivity, and asset maintenance are very different from those in the United States. Buying businesses through a privatization program can be especially treacherous: Many governments follow a policy of selling these businesses and properties in an "as is" condition. Since very few, if any, have been run efficiently or profitably by government bureaucrats, this may mean that they are in at least as bad shape as distressed U.S. businesses.

Much of the equipment and machinery in manufacturing companies may be obsolete or in need of repair. Factory buildings may not have been maintained. Labor productivity is usually far below American standards. Companies very often have redundant personnel. Managers tend to regard lifetime job security as their right.

Add to these hurdles the normal confusion of inadequate financial reporting standards; strange corporate, labor, and tax laws; peculiar quality standards; less-than-efficient transportation and communications modes; failing power systems; and often-corrupt distribution systems, and one must ask, why bother?

As with any good investment, the answer leaps out: because the potential for substantial returns from new markets, natural resources, and low-cost or technically proficient labor may be excellent. Also, competition may force an overseas presence, and despite these difficulties, it's still easier, faster, and cheaper to acquire a going business than to start one from scratch.

Moreover, smaller businesses or those in less developed countries can usually be acquired at prices substantially below market value. The next question, then, is: How does one determine market value?

Valuing Foreign Acquisitions

Typical business valuations begin with a company's financial statements. In the United States, clearly defined regulations from the Securities and Exchange Commission underlie financial statements from public companies. Less clear, but equally universal, the Financial Accounting Standards Board's generally accepted accounting principles are the foundation of private company financial reporting. Even very small companies must, as a minimum, comply with IRS bookkeeping requirements. Together, these regulatory requirements enable a high degree of comparability among the financial statements of all companies and provide a sound basis for performing a business valuation.

The same cannot be said of financial reporting standards in other countries. Many less-developed countries have very lax standards—or none at all. Each country in Western Europe and East Asia maintains its own accounting standards. Such a hodgepodge makes comparative analyses of the financial performance of companies resident in different countries virtually impossible.

For example, the immediate write-off of inventory and equipment purchases in one country and the charging of purchased goodwill directly to stockholders' equity in another makes comparative book values irrelevant. Financial statements that are prepared in accordance with local tax laws might permit equipment and/or inventory to be written off as purchased (as in several European countries). Balance-sheet assets may be carried at replacement cost values (as in Japan and other East Asian nations). Germany permits unreported reserves to be carried off the balance sheet. The United States permits last-in, first-out (LIFO) inventory valuations. Many less-developed nations do not require any specific format or content for financial statements. Others do not require periodic financial statements at all.

Although the International Accounting Standards Committee (IASC) is attempting to establish worldwide uniform reporting standards, little progress has been made in implementing its suggestions. One of the main obstacles is that the IASC insists, among other matters, that accounting methods used for tax purposes must conform to those used in financial statements—contrary to virtually all existing national accounting practices, including those followed in the United States.

Gradually, financial reporting standards around the world are becoming more uniform, but not fast enough to treat foreign business valuations with the same degree of confidence as in the United States.

Without worldwide financial reporting standards, it is very difficult to analyze a target company's historical performance. Consequently, business valuations must be made with incomplete and/or inaccurate internal financial data and rely more heavily on nonfinancial analyses. Also, when using formal discounted cash flow analyses, be sure to attach a high enough capitalization rate to compensate for the uncertainty of future performance.

In the end, traditional valuation techniques won't work here. A different approach must be used, often based to a large extent on personal judgment.

Although each case in every country requires a slightly different strategy, here are the rather broad rules followed by U.S. companies that claim to have paid reasonable prices for viable foreign businesses.

1. *Industry and competition.* Go after businesses that complement your U.S. business or that are in industries with which you have extensive experience. The risk is high enough without adding unfamiliar products or processes. Try to locate a company that makes products for export, pref-

erably products that can be used or distributed in U.S. markets. Alternatively, select companies that produce goods or services for local markets without major competition—a very likely condition with privatized companies, since state-owned businesses generally do not compete in the same markets as private enterprises.

2. *Size.* Stay with smaller businesses. The big ones—companies in telecommunications, transportation, energy, and so on—are usually priced too high and the competition from large multinationals is too intense to make them worthwhile. Smaller businesses may take more effort to rejuvenate, but the chances of success are far greater. Ideally, the target business should be no larger than its U.S. parent, and preferably smaller.

3. *Management.* Select only those businesses that have, as a minimum, one or two trainable key managers who are willing to work for an American owner. Many will not, even though they say they will in the beginning. It's important to ferret out those with anti-American feelings. That isn't very difficult and should be intuitively sensed during a first meeting. Also, insist on visiting the facility and meeting key managers before offering a bid. Buying a pig in a poke in a foreign land can be much worse than doing so at home.

4. *Financing.* Keep your equity investment to a bare minimum. Many businesses can be purchased with debt/equity swaps—either government or private debt. If that isn't possible, the purchase of nearly all smaller businesses can be financed through local capital markets or with OPIC assistance. Local development banks are also a possibility. For Latin America, the Inter-American Development Bank can furnish information about local development banks and other sources of assistance. As a general rule, try to keep equity contributions to no more than 25 percent of the purchase price.

5. *Infrastructure.* Investors not accustomed to the Third World often become frustrated trying to conduct business when the electricity fades in and out or goes out completely; when the telephone won't work or when a call won't go through; when water supplies dry up; or when the transportation system breaks down—all common occurrences. Part of the due diligence process should be a survey of other businesses in the locale owned or managed by foreigners—preferably Americans. How do they cope with infrastructure failures? What is the frequency of such failures? How does the government respond? Negative reactions generally indicate problems to come and probably are an excellent reason to back off.

ACQUISITION THROUGH PRIVATIZATION PROGRAMS

As the Iron Curtain fell, country after country saw the possibilities of rebuilding its economic base by switching from a state-controlled to a market economy. Governments in Eastern Europe, the erstwhile Soviet republics, and Latin America surmised that the Western European-American models that fostered free-market competition would in all likelihood be the fastest way to regain economic, social, and hence political stability. The focal point of such conversions was the privatization of state-owned businesses.

Swept by a wave of democratization, one government after another has initiated privatization programs to sell part or all of the ownership of government businesses to private-sector companies. Although full ownership may be out of the question, for foreigners to acquire majority interests are usually permitted.

As an acquisition strategy, buying privatized businesses might make a lot of sense. In many cases they can be purchased with far less cash than standard acquisitions, mainly through debt/equity swaps. Debt/equity swaps involve the buying of discounted government debt in the secondary market and then swapping it for equity interests in local operating companies.

Other than starting a new business from scratch—which in a foreign environment can carry a higher risk than many smaller companies are willing to take—companies can make a foreign direct investment by purchasing an equity interest from either a private seller or a foreign government. The latter method is often the most expeditious because less-developed-country government bonds sell in the secondary market at prices below par. In severely distressed countries, substantial discounts are possible. For example, during 1992, Peru's obligations went for fourteen cents on the dollar. At the other end of the spectrum, Chilean obligations exceeded ninety cents on the dollar.

In Latin America and the Caribbean, and to a lesser extent in Eastern Europe and the Commonwealth of Independent States (CIS), the onslaught of government privatization programs financed with debt/equity swaps has opened a whole new market for foreign acquisitions.

DEBT/EQUITY SWAPS

Beginning with the 1980s Latin American debt crisis, a new twist was added to the traditional financing ploy used by debt-poor companies (swapping unmanageable debt obligations for equity shares): applying it to government debt. Latin governments defaulted on billions of dollars of foreign bank loans, and to save their skin, U.S. banks had to come up with creative means of recouping whatever they could. The result was an attempt to swap partial debt obligations for equity interests in state-owned Latin businesses and financial institutions. The strategy was sound, but its implementation failed: The banks wanted only solid investments, and of course there weren't many of those around. Consequently, few swaps were consummated.

However, the effort did open secondary markets, and the swap process inherited a life of its own. New buyers and sellers came forward from countries throughout the world, and in short order, debt/equity swaps hit the private sector. Today, in public as well as private markets, companies of all sizes, financial institutions, and government-owned businesses are trading notes, bonds, and other debt instruments for equity shares.

Here is one way government debt/equity swaps can work. A company first purchases a debt instrument in the secondary market at a substantial discount from its face value—for example, fifty cents on the dollar. The company then offers to exchange this obligation with the debtor government for local currency. The rate of exchange might be, for example, equivalent to 75 percent of the debt. Soft currency is then used to build or purchase a plant or other facility in the host country for half the cost of an investment with U.S. dollars. Of course, companies must use their own funds to acquire the debt instrument in the first place, but most consider that a small price to pay for a bargain-basement investment.

Debt/equity swaps may be used to finance the acquisition of private-sector companies as well as government privatizations. However, don't expect corporate bonds to be selling at the substantial discounts common with Third World government obligations. For example, assume that a Spanish company, Porsada, had $5 million in bonds outstanding. A U.S. company, AmeriCo, purchases $3 million of the bonds at market prices. AmeriCo then offers to make a swap with Porsada, trading the bonds for a controlling equity interest.

Now go one step further. Assume that Porsada's bonds traded in the market at a discount of 25 percent from par. AmeriCo could buy the bonds, engineer a swap, and exchange par value bonds for an equal-value equity share, in effect paying less than market value for a controlling interest.

The debt/equity swap process has begun to feed on itself, expanding to such an extent that it now encompasses every conceivable type of swap arrangement. Nevertheless, the widest application continues to be in emerging countries, swapping discounted debt for privatized businesses.

Acquisitions of Eastern European Privatized Companies

During the early 1990s, the privatization of East German industry started one of the hottest business acquisition markets in the world. Privatization programs in Poland, Hungary, the Czech Republic, and Slovakia are also in full swing. And programs in Russia and a few other former Soviet republics are beginning to roll. Literally thousands of companies either are already on the block or will be in the near future.

An increasing number of midsize U.S. companies view the acquisition of a controlling interest in an Eastern European company as an entree to the European Union (formerly called the European Community). Be aware, however, that privatized businesses in East Germany or other East European countries, carry far greater risk to U.S. companies than similar investments in Latin America.

Converting a business run by ineffective bureaucrats, as in Latin America, is far easier and less costly than changing the habits of workers and managers indoctrinated with seventy years of communist welfare-state traditions. Furthermore, the physical condition of factories and production machinery in Eastern Europe is deplorable. Furthermore, the region's environmental degradation is nearly insurmountable, distribution channels are decrepit, and infrastructures are in a state of collapse.

On the plus side, European workers are generally well trained and highly skilled. Consumer markets are relatively sophisticated. And at least in East Germany, Poland, and Hungary, state divestment procedures are in place and working.

To inquire about opportunities for buying a European business through one of the privatization programs, many of which can be effected with various versions of debt/equity swaps, check out the British publication *Privatisation International*, 91 Grove Park, London SE5 8LE.

ACQUISITIONS OF LATIN AMERICAN PRIVATIZED COMPANIES

Opportunities for acquiring privatized businesses in Latin America and the Caribbean are far greater than in Europe, and most carry significantly less risk for small and midsize U.S. companies. This sell-off of state-owned businesses has become an integral part of economic reform programs being implemented in virtually every country in the region.

Privatization programs that have been in progress for several years in Mexico, Chile, Jamaica, and a few other countries are now winding down. However, the Argentine privatization program is still in high gear. And Brazil, Venezuela, and Colombia have barely started. Other Latin American countries remain in various stages of testing privatization administration procedures and expect to sell off hundreds of businesses over the next eight to ten years.

Contrary to much of the media coverage about massive utilities, airlines, and conglomerates being sold, the greatest number of privatized companies are small businesses that carry very low price tags. They can be found in virtually every industrial segment—manufacturing, distribution, retail, and services. Larger state-owned privatizations are generally in telecommunications companies, toll roads, airlines, and steel mills. Selling prices also vary all over the lot, from very small (under $2,000 for a small Peruvian communications company) to very large (a few going for more than a billion dollars).

TARGETING FOREIGN ACQUISITIONS FOR DEBT/EQUITY SWAPS

As previously described, many governments will swap discounted debt for equity in a privatized business. In most countries, this is the least risk, highest potential way to go. As a start, look at privatization programs in those countries with government debt selling at substantial discounts.

Before buying the discounted debt, check out the government's willingness to make a swap and whether or not an available business meets your needs. As a general rule, foreign investors should not agree to less than a 50 percent discount of the difference between the debt's market price and par value.

For example, assume the market price of government bonds was thirty cents on the dollar (or 30 percent of par value). Normally a debt/equity swap must let the government show a gain—for political reasons if nothing else. In this case, the seventy-cent spread could be halved, so that the exchange value would be 30 plus 35, or 65 percent of par. The swap transaction gives the government a gain of thirty five cents on the dollar, and the foreign company gets the business for a cash outlay of only thirty cents on the dollar. The trick, of course, is to establish a realistic value for the business.

Once the selling price has been agreed upon and the amount of government bonds required to meet this price has been negotiated, the bonds can be purchased on the open market and the swap concluded.

A slight variation might occur when the target business is privately owned. Follow the same negotiating procedures, but now when the government buys its bonds back at 65 percent of par, take payment in local currency to pay the private seller. To make this scenario work, the host-country government must play a prominent role in negotiating the business selling price. In the United States that would never happen; but in Latin America political favors change hands more openly, making government intervention a way of life.

PROFESSIONAL ASSISTANCE FOR FOREIGN ACQUISITIONS

When making foreign acquisitions either through privatization programs or by buying private companies directly, professional assistance is a must. Locating appropriate consultants, attorneys, and public accountants can be a nightmarish experience without some place to start.

U.S. companies run into the same regulatory, language, and local custom problems when trying to make a foreign acquisition as they do when looking for appropriate joint venture partners. The secret to success in both pursuits is to sign up with an experienced professional adviser who can arrange all the necessary local details without requiring an inordinate amount of guidance.

Companies interested in exploring the privatization route in Latin America will find that they can get the best professional help from U.S. banks with Latin American interests (Citibank, Chemical Bank, Bank of America, Chase Manhattan, and Bankers Trust), international consultants that specialize in Latin America; and multinational accounting firms. These players are experienced in sourcing privatization opportunities, clearing the path with local bureaucrats, negotiating acquisition deals, and arranging appropriate debt/equity swaps.

If there is a possibility of tapping local capital markets or other local sources for fresh debt or equity capital, either to make the acquisition or to fund it once acquired, it might make more sense to use a well-known American, British, or Swiss investment bank as adviser. However, although they do handle deals in Latin America, most specialize in Europe and in the Asia/Pacific region.

Another reason for using an intermediary (generally a consulting firm) is that privatization work can often be grueling, frustrating, and fraught with political overtones. Civil servants usually want to be led through each step of the process, all the while expecting the buyer (or intermediary) to engage in bureaucratic hand-holding, and of course entertaining. Mountains of documents must be completed and then managed. Comfort letters sent out to every conceivable interested party. Memorandums circulated by the truckload. All the typical bureaucratic bunk one expects from securely positioned civil servants.

To further complicate matters, most companies being privatized are in a horrible mess internally: incomplete recordkeeping, poor employee morale, outdated and poorly maintained production equipment and facilities, and employees fearful of working in a privately owned company. No one wants to buy a pig in a poke, and qualified intermediaries can make sure this doesn't happen.

With diverse backgrounds and a self-serving interest in global expansion, acquisition intermediaries also provide a valuable service in evaluating a country's economic future, business base, and competitive conditions vital to expansion or new investment decisions. And finally, by keeping tabs on worldwide political and economic developments, these global advisers develop a broad view of international opportunities.

In addition to sourcing potential acquisition candidates and putting together the best financing package, professional advisers can assist in negotiating the best purchase terms and coordinating prospective merger or joint venture arrangements. As an added incentive, many professional advisers will accept equity shares in the project as partial payment of their fees. This can be of enormous help during the transition period, providing a U.S. parent company with cultural insights and host-country contacts that could cost an arm and a leg, as it were, if obtained from independent advisers.

If you are seriously considering a foreign acquisition as an integral part of strategic growth strategies, another book in this series, *Entrepreneurial Growth Strategies,* includes a chapter about foreign acquisitions that has additional material and suggestions.

Selected Bibliography

Ian Guild & Rhodro Harris, *Forfaiting*. New York: Universe Books, 1986.

A.B. Manring, *Exporting from the U.S.A.*. Vancouver, BC, Canada: International Self-Counsel Press, Inc., 1986.

J. Oxelheim and C. Wihlborg, *Macroeconomic Uncertainty: International Risks and Opportunities for the Corporation*. New York: Wiley & Sons, 1987.

Matt Schaffer, *Winning the Countertrade War*. New York: Wiley & Sons, 1989.

Lawrence W. Tuller, *Doing Business in Latin America and the Caribbean.* New York: AMACOM, 1993.

——, *Going Global: New Opportunities for Growing Companies to Compete in World Markets*. Homewood, IL: BusinessOne Irwin, 1991.

——, *High-Risk, High-Return Investing*. New York: Wiley & Sons, 1994.

——, *McGraw-Hill Handbook of Global Trade and Investment Financing*. New York: McGraw Hill, 1992.

——, *World Markets Desk Book*. New York: McGraw Hill, 1993.

A Basic Guide to Exporting. Washington, DC: U.S. Department of Commerce, 1992

Exporting Trading Company Guidebook. Washington, DC: U.S. Department of Commerce, 1987.

Index

transaction, timing of, 41-42
Transactions, 151
transactions
   finance, 152
   offset, 163
      structure of, 163
Transimport, 207
transport, 105
transportation
   cars, personal, 111
   international
      mechanics, 235
      principles, 235
   local carrier arrangements, 235
travel, tips, 122-124
Travel Assistance International, 93
tree-trade areas, 38
Triangular Processing, 279
trucking, 105
typhoid shots, 116

U
UltraSafe, Inc., 277-278
UNDP
   see United Nations Development
      Program
unions, 104-105
Unique aspects of Foreign
   Acquisitions, 299
United National financial
   organizations, 45
United Nations Agencies, 182-186
   International Finance Corporation,
      182, 183
   Multilateral Investment Guarantee
      Agency, 183
   United Nations Development
      Program: Investment Feasibility
      Study Facility, 185
United Nations Development Business,
   78
United Nations Development Program:
   Investment Feasibility Study
   Facility, address of, 185
United States and Foreign Service
   Corporation, 28
unitizing
   advantages of, 238
   description of, 238
Unitizing, Palletizing and
   Containerization, 238-239
UPS, 247
Uruguay Round or General Agreement
   on Tariffs and Trade, on intellectual
   property rights, 250
U.S. Agency for International
   Development, 74, 178, 179
   address for, 294
   as government to government
      program, 179
   private businees aid, 179
   source for joint venture partners, 294
U.S. Agency for International
   Development Consultant Registry
   Information System, 75
U.S. Agency for International
   Development Small Business Loan
   Portfolio Guarantee program, 181

U.S. and Foreign Commercial Service,
   65
   address of, 293
   purpose of, 68
   source for joint venture partners, 292
U.S. Council for International
   Business, 94
U.S. Customs
   antidumping regulations, 274
   drawbacks, 272
   duty-free items, 271
   entry documents, 269-270
      baggage declaration and entry,
         270
      bill of lading, 270
      commercial invoice, 270
      consumption entry, 269
      immediate exportation entry, 270
      immediate transportation entry,
         269
      warehouse entry, 269
      warehouse withdrwal for
         consumption entry, 270
   formal entry process for imports,
      269
   import duties, 270
   removal of goods from, 270
U.S. Customs Service, 57, 75
U.S. Department of Agriculture,
   156-157
U.S. Department of Commerce, 64
U.S. Department of State, Office of
   Commercial, Legislative, and Public
   Affairs of, 74
U.S. Export Trading Companies,
   204-205
U.S. Foreign Corrupt Practices, 82
U.S. Foreign Corrupt Practices Act, 114
U.S. Import, quotas of specific goods,
   273-274
U.S. Import Restrictions and Quotas,
   272-276
U.S. Importing, foreign-trade zones,
   276
U.S. Postal Service, 75
U.S. Trade and Development Program
   address of, 293
   source for joint venture partners, 293
U.S. Travel and Tourism
   Administration, 71
U.S. Treasury, 50
USAID
   see U.S. Agency for International
      Development
US.Customs, officials of, role in
   importing, 268
US&FCS
   see U.S. and Foreign Commercial
      Service, 292
   see U.S. and Foreign Commercial
      Services
U.S.Import, trade barriers, 272-273
Using Leasing to Finance Expansion,
   252
Using Leasing to Finance Exports, 252
Using Tax-Haven Countries with Other
   Foreign Subsidiaries, example of,
   261-262

USTTA
   see U.S. Travela and Tourism
      Adminstration
utilities, 106

V
vaccinations, 92
Valseon Corp., 211
Valuing Foreign Acquisitions, 302-304
Veneauela, complications of sellling in,
   209
venture capital
   International Finance Corporation,
      183
   see Caribbean Basin Partners for
      Progress, 181
VER
   see voluntary export restraint
VF Corp, on copyrights, 251
VF Corporation, 201
videotapes, 68
Visa card, 93
voluntary export restraint, 35-36

W
Wall Street Journal, 11
Walter Heller Overseas Corp., 149
warehouse, Customs-bonded, 269
warehousing, foreign, 20
Washclor Systems Corp., as foreign
   joint venture, 282
Washington Post, 11
Weltight Sasha and Door Co., 25
What Tax Havens Do, 253-254
When is an Agent an Agent, 209
Why Advertising Campaigns Fail,
   235-236
wire transfers, 47, 109
withholding taxes, international, 57-58
Working Capital Guarantee program,
   157
Working for Estimating Incremental
   Export Costs From a Non-U.S.
   Location, 216-218
Worksheet for Estimating Incremental
   Export Costs, 214-216
World Bank, 45, 48, 182
   source for joint venture partners, 294
World Fact Book, The, 64
World Leasing Yearbook, 150, 252
*World Markets Desk Book: A
   Region-by-Region Survey of Global
   Trade Opportunities, The*, 12
World Trace Finance, Inc., 151
World Trade, 77, 234
World Trader Data Reports, 65-66
World Trader Data Reports, 142
Wraxall Group of Britian, 208
WTDR
   see World Trader Data Reports, 66

Z
Zantac, 213
ZE-RITE, 269